More praise for *The Art of Parenting Twins*

"Patricia Malmstrom and Janet Poland write on an important subject from a completely unique perspective. Few have had Pat's experience working with twins, their families, and the numerous individuals who help them adjust to living on a day-to-day basis. A parent with little or no prior experience will come away with the impression that a true guidebook has been found."

— Louis G. Keith, M.D.
Northwestern University Medical School

"I wholeheartedly recommend *The Art of Parenting Twins* to parents and expectant parents, childbirth educators, physicians, nurses, social workers, and teachers. The authors' expertise makes this a richly rewarding guide to the multiple birth experience."

— Elizabeth Noble, PT
Author of *Having Twins: A Parent's Guide to Pregnancy, Birth, and Early Childhood*

"What comes through on every page of this book is experience and lifelong commitment to multiples—both as a parent of twins and one who works with families, campaigning for greater recognition of their needs. Those of us who work with multiples often dwell upon what can go wrong. I am pleased that the last chapter, 'Celebrating Twinship,' does end by stressing that it can be 'good fortune' to be a twin. It is also 'good fortune' to have a book such as this one."

— Professor David A. Hay
School of Psychology,
Curtin University, WA, Australia,
Director LaTrobe Twin Study,
and National Patron, Australian Multiple Birth Association

"This wonderful book encompasses the two authors' lifetimes of experience. We can all benefit from the information—it is so thorough, accurate, and useful!"

— Marshall and Phyllis Klaus
Neonatologist and Psychotherapist
Authors of *Bonding, Mothering the Mother,*
and *Your Amazing Newborn*

"This book equips parents to anticipate the particular aspects of twin pregnancy and child care that might not be immediately obvious. In the end, it is the quality of knowledge of the parents, as well as their professional care providers, that will improve the lives of twins and their parents. I warmly recommend this book to expectant twin parents (and their parents), as well as to twin clubs and all professionals whose work involves the care and nurture of twins."

— Geoffrey A. Machin, M.D., Ph.D.
Twin Researcher and Carer

"Written with clarity, intelligence, and accuracy, this handy book is a 'must have' for parents of twins and other multiples, multiples themselves, and professionals or organizations concerned with guidance and counseling. One could not ask for a more resourceful book."
—Adam P. Methany, Jr., Ph.D.
Director, Louisville Twin Study
Professor of Pediatrics
Department of Pediatrics, University of Louisville

"Each chapter is filled with thoughtful insights, practical tips, and information on where to get help. The authors describe the growth and development and needs unique to multiples as they go from embryos to adulthood. Patricia Malmstrom speaks from the heart and mind of one who has not only studied multiples, but raised them as well."
—David A. Lee, M.D.
Neonatologist
California Pacific Medical Center

"Authors Malmstrom and Poland package words of wisdom with reality-based advice that will give parents the guidance they need to raise their multiples with confidence and joy."
—Jane Greer, Ph.D.
Consultant to Twins and author of
Adult Sibling Rivalry and
How Could You Do This to Me?:
Learning to Trust After Betrayal

"Ms. Malmstrom's book is down to earth and yet probably the most comprehensive one on this topic. An excellent book both for parents and for professionals who are in the field of parenting education."
—Helen Reid, LCSW
Director, Early Childhood Center
Cedars-Sinai Medical Center

"Malmstrom and Poland offer strategies to help families enjoy the many benefits of twinship all the way through the school and teen years. Caring for twins is at least a two-person job. *The Art of Parenting Twins* will prepare you well for the challenges and fun ahead."
—Calvin J. Hobel, M.D.
Miriam Jacobs Chair and
Director of Maternal Fetal Medicine
Cedars-Sinai Medical Center
Professor of Obstetrics, Gynecology and Pediatrics
UCLA School of Medicine

THE
ART OF
PARENTING
TWINS

THE UNIQUE JOYS
AND CHALLENGES OF
RAISING TWINS AND
OTHER MULTIPLES

PATRICIA MAXWELL MALMSTROM

AND

JANET POLAND

A SKYLIGHT PRESS BOOK
BALLANTINE BOOKS · NEW YORK

A Ballantine Book
Published by The Ballantine Publishing Group

Copyright © 1999 by Patricia Maxwell Malmstrom and Skylight Press

www.randomhouse.com/BB/

LIBRARY OF CONGRESS CATALOGING-IN-PUBLICATION DATA
Malmstrom, Patricia Maxwell.
The art of parenting twins : the unique joys and challenges of raising twins and
other multiples / Patricia Maxwell Malmstrom and Janet Poland.—1st ed.
p. cm.
ISBN 0-345-42267-8 (TR : alk. paper)
1. Twins. 2. Multiple birth. 3. Child rearing. 4. Parenting.
I. Poland, Janet. II. Title.
HQ777.35.M35 1999
649'.144—dc21
99-28672
CIP

Text design by Holly Johnson

Cover design by Min Choi
Cover photo courtesy of Superstock
Back cover photos (clockwise): © D. E. Cox/Tony Stone Images;
© DiMaggio/Kalish/The Stock Market; © Rob Lewine/The Stock Market;
© Ken Korsh/FPG International; © Index Stock

Manufactured in the United States of America

First Edition: June 1999

10 9 8 7 6 5 4 3

to the memory of my mother and best friend, Jean Maxwell,
&
to the memory of Sheryl McInnes, longtime director of the
Parents of Multiple Births Association of Canada, and my
generous mentor,
&
to my family, Carolyn, Diana, Krista, Kelda, Ed, Craig, Dave,
Robb, and Erik for their constant support and encouragement,
&
to Kris Matarrese, Chair of the Board of Twin Services, Inc.,
since 1990, for her steadfast leadership.
Patricia Maxwell Malmstrom

to my husband, Gary Blackburn, for his patience and support . . .
& to my sons, James and Jordan, who keep me on my toes . . .
and who remind me every day that raising a family is an art,
not a science.
Janet Poland

CONTENTS

CONTENTS

ACKNOWLEDGMENTS

I owe deep appreciation to the thousands of parents of twins and triplets who, by sharing their health risks and parenting challenges with me and my staff at Twin Services, Inc., during the past twenty years, have taught me the breadth and depth of their special needs. From them I have also learned much about the day-to-day heroism of parents who keep putting one foot in front of the other to care well for their multiples in the face of sometimes staggering difficulties.

We both extend a very special thanks to the multiples and the parents whom we interviewed who generously contributed their thoughts and experiences, which have greatly enriched the manuscript.

There's never enough space to thank everyone who contributed, but I would like to mention groups of major importance. Much credit is due the alumnae of our TWINLINE® counseling and referral staff, who during its many years of operation, helped to elucidate twin issues and develop supportive coping strategies for parents: Rachael Biale, Jean Crooks, Elinor Davis, Teresa Ebel, Julie Ferris, Nancy Flaxman, Maureen Frainey, Catherine Girardeau, Celina Hernandez-Ramirez, Jean-Marie Knudsen, Jean Kotcher, Christine Leiverman, Karen Riebel, Karen Rouse, Sue Rulli, Jeanette Staley Caro del

Castillo, Dianne Thomas, Yolanda Thompson, Valerie Veza, Jennifer Wachter, Paula Wagner, Marilyn Wedge, Patt Young ... and to our bookkeeper, Michele Simon, and our office managers Michele Mowry and Sue Rulli, who kept the whole system working, mail lists, computers, and all—while fielding phone calls from distressed parents.

The ideas, help, and encouragement of members of Twin Services' advisory board and our California Twin Service Networks have all contributed to the development of Twin Services' information base, its programs, and its publications: Myles Abbott, Marcia Alessi, Susan Alt, Laura Baker, Tom Bates, Rose Bemis Hayes, Lilian Black, Janet Bleyl, Wendy Block, Gail Brohner, Albert Brooks, Beverly Brutzkus, Surry Bunnell, Cerise Cameron, Daychin Campbell, Sean Casey, Kay Cassill, Piera Cirillo, Beverly Clark, Betty Cohen, Barbara Cohn, Bari Cornet, Betty Crews, Robert Derom, Susanna Distefano, Muriel Dulberg, Pat Erickson, Bill Evans, Susan Evans, Diana Friedman, Lois Gallmeyer, Claudette Garner, Jane Greer, Clarence Grim, Elmer Grossman, Marianna Grossman-Keller, Lila Gruzen, Erica Gunderson, Debra Habor, Helen Harrison, Ruth Hass, Karen Henry, Calvin Hobel, Katie Hoekstra, Francie Hornstein, Debbie Isumizaki, Don Johnson, Patsy Jones, Ellie Journey, Hatsue Katsura, Michael Katz, Don Keith, Louis Keith, Marshall Klaus, Phyllis Klaus, Lisa Kleppel, Jean Kollantai, Kathy Kneer, Jean Knote, Donna Launslager, David Lee, Neil Levy, Susan Lockwood, Stuart Lovett, Mary Lynch, Geoffrey Machin, JoAnn Madigan, Adam Matheny, Sheryl McInnes, Mona Mena, Marion Meyer, Susan Millar, Nancy Miller, Bridget Moran, Helen Mortensen, Marjorie Moser, Susan Munoz, Barbara Murphy, Charlotte Newhart, Elizabeth Noble, Roberta O'Grady, Amy Osterholm, Cecelia Ozaki, Ron Parker, Ruth Parker, Betsy Partridge, Isabel Perez-Yanez, Sharon Pollack, Bruce Raskin, Helen Reid, William Rhea, Susie Robertson, Judith Rosenberg, Dan Safran, Nancy Segal, Robin Sewitz, Susan Ford Shaw, Marilyn Silva, Julie Strauss, Dani Taylor, Diana Taylor, Ellen Tempkins, Mildred

Thompson, Gloria Thornton, Stacey Trujillo, Barbara Unell, Neils Waller, Ann Watkins, Elaine Westendorf, Lori Williams, Steve Wolan, Bob Zimmerman, Caroline Zlotnik, Pat Zook.

Many foundations and individual donors have played a vital role in making Twin Services' programs available for parents and providers. I am deeply grateful for their support. Special thanks are due the two organizations which helped launch our programs: BANANAS Childcare Information and Referral, our initial fiscal sponsor; and the Morris Stulsaft Foundation for its donation of a start-up grant. The Bay Area Chapter of the March of Dimes, the California Wellness Foundation, the Goldman Foundation, the James Irvine Foundation, and the San Francisco Foundation have provided critically needed support over many years. The California Department of Health, Maternal and Child Health Branch, supported our TWIN-LINE service for twelve years. The U.S. Department of Health and Human Services, Maternal, Infant, Child, and Adolescent Health Bureau, supported the development of our training services. Our programs have benefited much from their generosity and the good counsel of their staffs. In addition I have always been able to count on the advice, information, and support of the National Organization of Mothers of Twins Clubs (U.S.), the Parents of Multiple Births Organization (Canada), and the many multiple-birth organizations participating in the international Council of Multiple Births Organizations.

None of this would have been possible without the dedication of a long line of twins, parents of multiples, health-care providers, and supportive members of the business community who have served on the Twin Services, Inc., Board of Directors: Terry Pink Alexander, Arnold Blustein, Lori Breunig, Albert Brooks, Margaret Burdge, Robin Calo, Dick Daum, Yvonne Dotson, Barbara Dunlap, Pam Gill, Gigi Greenhouse, Denise Harter, Nancy Hilton, Alan Houser, Cheryl Jacques, Ellen Keeshan, Stella Ling, Carolyn Lund, Phil McGough, Sally McGough, Clinton Monroe, Maggie Owens, Eileen Pearlman, Laura Perloff,

Stephanie Rivera, Cornelia St. John, Frances Sturgess, Tom Waite, Mary Wieland, Diane Wyatt, and Priscilla Wrubel. Special thanks are also due our current Board of Directors—Chair Kris Matarrese, Pam Gill, Laura Perloff, and Frances Sturges—for encouraging me to take a study leave to write this book and for their permission to incorporate data and quotations from Twin Services' records.

We are especially grateful to Meg Schneider and Lynn Sonberg of Skylight Press who were instrumental in developing this project. Not only did they bring the two of us together to form a productive and mutually supportive team, but they also provided their valuable insights and eagle-eyed editing throughout the endeavor. And we are also grateful to Elisa Wares, our editor at Ballantine, who provided essential finishing touches.

Patricia Maxwell Malmstrom

INTRODUCTION

Six years ago, two of our daughters were pregnant. Early in Cam's pregnancy she had a uterine ultrasound examination. She called us from the radiologist's office: "We're having twins!" she said, her voice shaking. "Come over tonight; we need to talk!" A few hours later my wife and I arrived at Cam and Steve's house. They were sitting side by side on the sofa, in utter silence, looking pale and dazed. As Pat Malmstrom and Janet Poland would say, they were suffering from twinshock, a condition completely familiar to every reader of this book who has been pregnant with twins.

Several weeks later, our other pregnant daughter had an ultrasound. "Oh," said the technician, "there are two!"

"No," said Marianna, "it's my sister who is having twins." Malmstrom and Poland would probably say that she had twinshock as well, a fine example of the "this can't be happening to me" variety.

Well, the ultrasound studies were correct. Both Cam and Marianna were carrying twins, and when they came to term, within two days of each other, our daughters each delivered identical twin girls. When our three-year-old granddaughter Leia heard the news, she remarked, "Some people only have one baby at a time."

It is handy for a family to have a pediatrician grandfather, and I soon began to hear questions about the babies. After nearly four decades of practicing and teaching pediatrics, I expected myself to be able to understand pretty much any medical or developmental problem that came along. But despite having had twins under my care in practice, there were a great many practical things I had not managed to learn. We would all have been happier if we had had copies of this book to consult.

The Art of Parenting Twins is the product of Pat Malmstrom's more than two decades' immersion in the world of twins and other multiple-birth babies and their families. Her academic training in early childhood education and her own experiences as a mother of four children, including twin girls, led to her work at the wonderful Berkeley institution called BANANAS. This is a parent-run child care information and referral center that serves as a rallying point for local people concerned with nearly every aspect of family life. At BANANAS, Pat Malmstrom founded the TWINLINE, a service designed to bring accurate information and much-needed support to families struggling with the multiple problems of multiple births.

The TWINLINE has grown into an independent organization called Twin Services, Inc., which has pioneered the development of multiple birth support services and resources. Twin Services, Inc., currently provides a host of parent education materials dealing with twin issues and offers training in the care of multiples and their families for professionals.

Over the years literally thousands of parents of twins and other multiple-birth babies have consulted with Pat Malmstrom and her staff at Twin Services. This experience led to her continuing studies of twin development, which have been published in both academic and popular journals. And they led her to become a leader in the International Society for Twin Studies, a consultant to national and regional Mothers of Twins Clubs worldwide, and a sought-after lecturer and teacher.

While Pat Malmstrom has focused on multiples, her co-author, Janet Poland, has had a career as a journalist, writer, and editor, while raising two teenage boys. Ms. Poland has long been interested in issues of child health and child development. She has written five books and numerous magazine and newspaper articles for parents.

The Art of Parenting Twins represents a fusion of their skills and experience. Malmstrom and Poland introduce us to the big issues of twin parenting, the overarching questions that parents of twins contemplate, such as the complexities of the twin-to-twin relationship, the problems of school placement (one classroom or separate classrooms?), the relationships of twins to their friends, and managing the stresses of family life with twins. In this clearly focused book they show us dozens of details about taking care of twins (and triplets and other multiple-birth babies) in ways that differ from the care of single-birth children. They wisely limit their subject to the special issues of multiple-birth children and their families. You will still need a general baby book about illnesses, allergies, accidents, nutrition, immunizations, and the other aspects of raising kids that all parents face. But this book is an indispensable guide to the problems and possibilities of twin parenting, and an introduction to the complicated world of multiple-birth family life.

It seems to me that this book has several special virtues. First, it is based firmly on an accurate understanding of the scientific study of child growth and development, as well as the medical aspects of multiple birth. The particular developmental patterns of multiple-birth children are carefully explained, the discussions of multiple-birth pregnancy and childbirth are clear and precise, and the potential problems of the newborn are delineated precisely in real English rather than medical jargon. Janet Poland's writing experience has helped shape this into an unusually accessible book.

Second, the book is intensely practical because it is based on such a depth of everyday experience with the lives of so many twins and triplets and other multiples. It represents the distilled wisdom of Pat Malmstrom and her staff of TWIN-LINE counselors and of parents themselves who have struggled with the problems, recognized the possibilities, and delighted in the solutions.

Third, the book alerts parents to the pitfalls of twin parenting, including especially the powerful and misleading mythology surrounding multiple births. As soon as your twin pregnancy is announced, you will become the recipient of barrels of unasked-for, useless, and mistaken advice. Nearly everyone you meet will know many things about twins that are not true, and they will graciously unload this nonsense all over you. Reading *The Art of Parenting Twins* will help you to protect yourself. It is an excellent place to find reliable answers.

Six years have passed since the ultrasound examinations that catapulted our family into the world of twins. Our daughters were each very big with child when they came to term. By that time the mothers, fathers, and grandparents had all passed through the stages of twinshock and were anticipating the four babies with enormous excitement. The two sets arrived, all in great shape, and we were engulfed by the wonderful reality, the endless effort, the blizzards of diapers, the countless nursings, the twinkle of flash cameras (how did people manage to have babies before the invention of photography?), and the parade of friends and neighbors bearing the casseroles that kept the parents from starving. Watching these little girls grow has been a truly amazing experience. The rapid appearance of clear temperamental differences as each child expressed her own individuality, the complexities of twin-twin relationships, and the variations in physical and intellectual development—these are just a few of the aspects that command our attention. Make no mistake, twins are hard work, but they also bring so much joy.

If you are reading this book while pregnant with twins, know that this is a grand adventure on which you and your family are embarking. If you already have twins, your journey is underway, complete with its pleasures, concerns, exhaustion, and excitement. To all of you present and potential parents of twins, triplets, and even larger families of multiple-birth children, congratulations, and Bon Voyage!

Elmer R. Grossman, M.D.
Clinical Professor of Pediatrics, Emeritus
School of Medicine, University of California San Francisco
Author of *Everyday Pediatrics for Parents*

PART ONE

———

IN THE BEGINNING

CHAPTER ONE

THE MIRACLE OF MULTIPLES

WHAT YOU NEED TO KNOW ABOUT TWINNING

Week eight: Kelda noticed Krista in their crib. She turned her head toward her, and her eyes widened in amazement. She smiled, and Krista smiled back with delight.

I found these lines scribbled in an old notebook I'd used as a journal when my daughters were babies. They remind me of my delight in witnessing the signs of connection between my newborn twins. Sleep-deprived though I was, and overwhelmed as I sometimes felt, there was always an undercurrent of wonder sustaining me in my daily routines. There can be no better job, nor greater challenge, than raising twins, triplets, or more.

It's more difficult than raising "one-at-a-time" children. But it's different, too. It's not just twice as much work (or three or more times). Raising multiples means that parents need a whole new way of looking at their children, their family dynamics, and themselves. They need to know what's good, what's difficult, what to expect, and how to make the best of this most exciting adventure.

I know. I'm the mother of four daughters, two of whom are twins. For more than twenty years, as founder and director of a nonprofit counseling and advocacy organization called Twin Services, Inc.®, I've counseled parents of twins, done research into twin development, and prepared material for parents on

3

everything from signs of premature labor to the social lives of fifteen-year-olds.

Time and again over the years, desperate mothers would call me and say, "Nobody told me it would be like this." They'd say those words with a mixture of joy and panic, exhilaration and exhaustion, fascination and bewilderment. I've heard them from the mouths of parents of twins, triplets, and quadruplets, parents who are struggling through all the stages of the experience—from before the actual births to well into their multiples' adult years.

Now, more than ever, there's a real need for this information, because multiple births have risen dramatically over the last twenty years. The double strollers at the mall, the pictures in the newspapers of tiny quadruplets cuddled by dazed parents, the worldwide fascination with the birth of septuplets in Iowa and octuplets in Texas—all are part of a dramatic trend. Since 1975 the number of twin births has increased by about 50 percent. The increase in higher-order multiples is even more dramatic. In one year, 1996, the number of triplets and higher-order multiples increased 19 percent. That year more than 100,000 babies were born as twins, 5,298 as triplets, 560 as quadruplets, and 81 as quintuplets or more.

The causes of this increase are related to delayed childbearing. Women in their thirties are more likely to conceive dizygotic ("fraternal") twins naturally than women in their twenties. And older women are more likely to have problems with conception and seek infertility treatments, which also increase the likelihood of multiples.

According to one U.S. study, the rise in the number of twin births paralleled that of single babies from 1960 to 1973, and the number of triplet births remained fairly constant. After 1973, assisted reproductive technology—including ovulation-stimulating drugs—became available, and more women were starting their families at a later age. Between that year and 1990, the number of single births rose 32 percent, twin births rose 65 percent, and triplet and higher-order births increased by more than 220 percent.

It is interesting to consider that for all the twins who are born, research suggests that many more are conceived. Sometimes a multiple conception results in the spontaneous loss of one or more embryos and the survival of a single baby; the lost embryo is referred to as a "vanishing twin."

Geneticist Charles Boklage believes that most human pregnancies are lost before they are diagnosed. It is not surprising, then, that the majority of twin conceptions produce the birth of one baby. He calculates that for every live-born pair of twins, there are eleven single babies who are the survivors of a twin conception.

Whatever the cause of the increasing numbers, more and more parents are finding themselves embarking on the most challenging adventure of their lives: having, raising, and loving their multiple babies. And they need information that's specifically about multiples. As one mother told me, "Talking to people with singletons doesn't answer my questions. I want contact with twin people."

Parenting twins and other multiples is a combination of hard work and devotion that draws on the deepest resources of love, inspiration, knowledge, and sheer energy. But too often parents begin this adventure unprepared. They may lack accurate information about how to cope with the logistical or emotional challenges. Or they may be burdened with myths and romanticized images that cloud the real issues of twinship and the real needs of their children. As one mother told me, "I expected my twins to be a matched set, like two little bookends. It's so wonderful to discover the differences between them."

Through my work I've seen over and over again how important it is for parents of multiples to have as much practical, psychological, and intellectual information as possible. Information, I am convinced, is the only way for parents to cope with their inevitable anxieties and misconceptions and prepare for the adventure of twin parenthood.

The worries and concerns begin with the anticipation of birth and continue through infancy, the preschool period, school age, the teen years—and beyond. They move me with their poignancy and urgency:

- If I breastfeed my triplets, can I be sure they will each have enough?
- How can I possibly bond with so many babies?
- Can I safely watch all my children during a walk in the park?
- How can I help one triplet who is so painfully shy when the others are so bold?
- How can we afford a family vacation?
- Will I ever have a worry-free romantic dinner with my husband again?

Many of the families who contacted Twin Services made their initial contact when they first learned they were having twins, and continued that contact as their children grew—during those difficult infant days, as their children entered school, became teenagers, and went off to college. As I look back over the stories of these families, I see that the most successful parents, those whose children thrive, have several qualities in common.

Let me share with you what I think you'll need as you embark on your journey.

- *A solid foundation of information.* You'll want to know what is unique—both troublesome and joyous—about being the parent of twins. You'll need accurate, up-to-date information on which you can base the most important decisions of your and your children's lives. You need to know what causes twinning, and what kind of multiples you have—

monozygotic, dizygotic, or perhaps (in higher-order multiples) a combination.

You'll need to know what the implications of multiple births are for the prospects of breastfeeding. You'll need to know that most twins develop normally, and that when developmental delays do occur, they usually are attributable to prematurity rather than to twinship. You'll need the most recent research about twins and multiples of all ages, medical advice about how to have a healthy pregnancy and how to care for premature infants, and information about the emotional and social development of twins and other multiples.

• *Understanding and reassurance.* You'll need to give yourself permission to savor the full experience of raising and loving your multiple children, and acknowledge your full range of emotions—everything from despair to elation.

The families who thrive reach out to others, listen to others, share what they've learned with others. When the going gets tough, they know they're not alone. Maybe you're so tired you realize you've bathed the same baby twice—or you're so exhausted you dream about running away. Whatever your stresses, you'll take comfort in knowing that many others have had these experiences and lived through them.

Often parents who have just brought their newborn twins home from the hospital ask, "What are we doing wrong? Why is this so awful?" When I explain that everyone with four-day-old twins feels like this, they breathe a big sigh of relief.

• *Advocacy skills.* Raising twins is not just a matter of dealing with sleep deprivation and coping with too many mouths to feed. You will also find yourself fighting for what your children need in a world that does not always understand what is best for them.

Your birthing team may be enlightened about twin-specific prenatal care and preterm-birth prevention, or it may not.

Hospital staff may be sensitive about the relationship between your newborns, or they may not.

You may be encouraged to breastfeed, or you may have to convince your doctor that you can successfully nurse your triplets.

Your children's friends may be sensitive to the needs of preschool twins to be included together in social invitations, or they may not.

And so it will go, right on through your school's policy about placing twins together or apart in kindergarten. At these times, you will find yourself drawing upon all of your knowledge, resources, and creativity to make the case for the best care for your children.

PARENTS NEED UNIQUE STRATEGIES AS TWINS GROW

The twin parenting experience is not static—the issues and challenges change from year to year. Each stage, from infancy to adolescence, calls for different strategies.

INFANCY

This is the most difficult stage for parents of twins because of the sheer logistics of managing more than one baby—and doing so after a pregnancy that often leaves mothers exhausted. Among the practical concerns are telling "identical" babies apart, breastfeeding two or more babies, coping with premature babies, developing strategies for managing the household, and finding the best equipment and supplies. At this stage parents need survival skills—and an occasional pep talk to help them visualize an easier road ahead.

One mother of triplets, for example, was shy about asking for help. She kept putting off the friends and neighbors who asked to come and visit the babies because she didn't feel up to entertaining. Finally it dawned on her: "Invite people over at bath time! They get to see the babies, and I get extra hands to help my slippery little ones with their baths."

TODDLERHOOD

At this stage twins begin to come to terms with their "couple" status and build the foundation of a lifelong relationship. In Chapter Ten, I'll discuss how twins help each other understand the world, how to keep an eye on two or more toddlers, how to encourage language development, and why it's crucial to avoid labeling twins ("the shy one, the bossy one").

THE PRESCHOOL YEARS

During the busy days of three- and four-year-olds, the twin relationship begins to stabilize and the children begin to master relationships beyond their immediate family. As the twins—both as individuals and as part of a multiple group— get to know other children and adults, they will strengthen the skills they will draw upon during their school years. Chapter Eleven will help you along as you coach your twins' early social development and prepare the children for success in school.

SCHOOL AGE

During these years, your children will make great strides in their academic and social development. They'll learn new skills, make new friends, and—inevitably—be compared with one another. You'll be making decisions about whether to place twins in the same class (and what to do when the school does not support your wishes), how to help the children cope with academic and social pressures, how to manage competition between the children, and how to help your twins navigate the newer terrain of peer relationships.

ADOLESCENCE

For all children, adolescence is a period during which the individual separates from parents. Twins and multiples have an additional task: separating, to some extent, from one another. You'll need to look at the process of adolescence in new ways as you help your children deal with issues of independence, privileges, limits, and sexuality.

HOW PARENTING MULTIPLES IS DIFFERENT

When parents have twins, they must deal with a panoply of attitudes, expectations, and romantic images that can interfere with the job.

PARENTAL EXPECTATIONS MAY BE OFF BASE

Since most parents of twins are not twins themselves, the news that their children will be multiples can be unsettling. Some optimists think the experience will be perfectly manageable, but many parents are quite frankly terrified. You may find that the experience brings profound and sometimes troubling thoughts to the surface—thoughts about identity, individuality, intimacy. What makes us different from one another? What makes us unique? How much the same are we? How separate should people be, how attached?

The dream of one-to-one closeness between mother and child may seem elbowed aside by the active one-on-one bonding between twins, to the exclusion of the mother.

Or another ideal of the perfect threesome at bedtime has to adjust to reality. One mother was so wedded to the image of two toddlers cuddling on her lap for stories that she kept trying to arrange bedtime that way, even though her dizygotic twins had distinctly different ideas about what the routine should be. One boy would cuddle up for the story, while the other insisted on roaming.

"I finally woke up and realized I was creating a problem where there wasn't one," she said. "Now my husband takes one of the children while I read to the other."

All kinds of expectations, big and small, can be thrown out of whack. One mother who had planned to take her new baby to her law office when she went back to work was stunned at the news she would have twins. "But two babies won't fit under my desk!" she exclaimed.

PARENTS HAVE TROUBLE RECONCILING MYTHS WITH REALITY

I feel strongly that society shortchanges twins when it romanticizes or mythologizes the idea of twins and other multiples. We use twins symbolically, for our own purposes. In doing so, we depersonalize them. For example, one mother told Twin Services, "Television makes having twins out to be a fairy tale. The reality is so different. The first three months, we didn't know if it was day or night—whenever they slept, we slept. They don't show that on TV."

As you and your multiples grow and thrive, you'll "unlearn" lots of these myths. You'll learn that twins may play together well, or they may compete intensely. You'll learn that the conventional wisdom about "developing" their individuality is often simplistic.

But it's better to be prepared for society's expectations about twins, and your own. In Chapter Three of this book, we'll go into greater detail about the assumptions others may have about your children, assumptions you yourself may have, and how reality will serve your family better than myth.

PARENTS GET TOO MUCH ADVICE FROM TOO MANY PEOPLE

Having twins and multiples will thrust you and your family into the glare of celebrity, whether that's something you want or not. Part of the preparation for the twin experience is knowing what to expect from friends, family, and total strangers.

Perfect strangers may stop you on the street and ask you how you conceived your children (a question that parents of single babies are not customarily asked). Neighbors will spotlight the twins and constantly compare them to one another: "Which one is the good one? Which one is smarter?" Friends will offer advice: "You'd better put them on different soccer teams or there'll be trouble" (or "You'd better put them on the *same* soccer team").

You'll need strategies to fend off unwanted comments and questions. When one mother who wheeled her twins to the market in a baby carriage felt too tired to handle endless questions and comments, she propped empty grocery bags at the foot of the carriage so that the babies wouldn't be visible to prying eyes.

As their children grow older, parents need to be careful to respond in a way that teaches the twins good things about themselves. When a stranger says, "Wow! Twins! Better you than me!" the children need to hear a positive response: "I'm glad it's me, too."

One mother of triplets is often asked by acquaintances, "How do you *do* it?"

"I do it with joy," she replies.

THE BIOLOGY OF TWINNING

It's important to take a moment to discuss the kinds of twins, the terms we use to describe them, and the biology of twinning.

There are two basic categories of twins: monozygotic, which are commonly but inaccurately called "identical," and dizygotic, which are commonly but inaccurately called "fraternal." Triplets and higher-order multiples may be polyzygotic (each developing from a separate fertilized egg), monozygotic, or a combination.

Monozygotic twins result from the division of one fertilized egg, or zygote. Because of that, they have the same genetic heritage, but they are not "identical" in the strict sense of the word.

About one-third of twins are monozygotic. They are always the same sex and are usually very similar in appearance, although there may be slight differences in their hair color and the shapes of their faces, and they may have different birthmarks. However, if there is a large discrepancy in their birth weights, monozygotic twins may be very different in appearance at birth. In addition, one may have a serious health problem and the other not. Unless the differences in birth weight and health are great, however, these twins will grow up to resemble each other closely.

How is it possible for monozygotic twins, who share the same genetic heritage, to have such differences? The fertilized egg from which they result divides within fourteen days of ovulation. If the division occurs within five days after fertilization, each fetus will have its own placenta and chorionic membrane, and its own amniotic sac, or inner membrane. This is true for about one-third of monozygotic twins.

The majority, those for whom the division occurs between days five and seven, will share one placenta and will have separate amniotic sacs. In 2 percent of monozygotic twins the division occurs after day eight, in which case they will share one placenta, one chorionic membrane, and one amniotic sac. These embryos, who develop side by side in one amniotic sac, are at grave risk, having a fifty-fifty chance of survival.

About 25 percent of monozygotic twins are "mirror" twins, with similar but opposite physical characteristics. They may have hair whorls that turn in opposite directions. One may be left-handed and one right-handed. Sometimes even inner organs such as the appendix are on opposite sides. Such differences are associated with the late division of the zygote.

Those monozygotic twins (about 66 percent) who share one placenta may not get equal access to the nutrition their placenta provides. One twin may be attached to the placenta in a favorable position near the middle, while the other may be off at one end. It is also possible that their circulatory systems interconnect to some degree. When the interconnection involves major veins and arteries, they are at risk for such life threatening problems as twin-twin transfusion syndrome and growth retardation.

Dizygotic twins are thought to occur when the mother produces two eggs during the same ovulatory cycle, which are then fertilized by two different sperm. Two-thirds of twins are dizygotic. It is not accurate to call them "fraternal," because only one quarter are both boys, or brothers. Another quarter are both girls. Half are a boy and a girl.

Because they always have their own placentas, dizygotic twins are more likely to have similar birth weights than monozygotic pairs. However, after birth, dizygotic twins' weights rapidly diverge, while monozygotic twins' weights quickly become more similar. Monozygotic twins with separate placentas are more likely to have similar birth weights than monozygotic twins who share one placenta and may have unequal access to the nutrition it provides.

Might there be a third kind of twin that's half identical? One theory holds that after the first cell division of an egg, both the egg and its polar body (the smaller offshoot that still contains the appropriate number of chromosomes) may be fertilized by two different sperm, so that the mother's genetic contribution is identical, but not the father's. This possibility is proposed as an explanation for differences in monozygotic twins. So far this theory remains unprovable in practice. However, common differences in monozygotic twins can much more easily be explained by differences in their attachment to the placenta and prenatal experiences in the womb.

There is another theory to explain these differences. Charles Boklage, the geneticist, questions the common assumption that dizygotic twins are no different from single-born children. He suggests that perhaps they are the result of an egg that divides before fertilization and is then fertilized by two sperm.

Besides genetics and the placenta, there are other aspects of the prenatal environment that affect the growth and development of multiples. Position in the womb, amount of freedom of movement, birth order, and birth experiences are all environmental factors that contribute to appearance, health, and personalities.

Although the terms *monozygotic* and *dizygotic* may be a bit daunting at first, I believe they are important. They are precise, and they keep us focused on what is true about twins, rather than what is commonly assumed. Monozygotic twins are not identical in the sense of being duplicates of one another. They are entirely separate individuals who share a powerful bond and have much in common. But the term *identical* can lead to misunderstandings. One mother of monozygotic twins once told me, "My daughters aren't identical twins—I can tell them apart easily!"

What Causes Twinning?

There is still a great deal we do not yet know about the biology of twinning. What causes a fertilized egg to divide into monozygotic twins is still something of a mystery.

We do know a bit more about dizygotic twinning, however. Maternal age is a factor. A woman's chance of having dizygotic twins increases between the ages of thirty-five and thirty-nine; twin births for women in that age group occur at three times the rate for women under thirty-five.

If the mother is herself a dizygotic twin, her chances of having twins are almost twice that of the general population.

Mothers of dizygotic twins tend to be taller, heavier, and older than women who conceive single babies or monozygotic twins.

Ethnic origin seems to be a factor in the rate of twinning as well. The highest rate of twinning in the American population is among black women, with 25.8 multiples per 1,000 live births; the lowest rate is 11.2, among mothers of Chinese descent. In between are Alaskan natives, with 24.9; whites, with 19.6; American Indians, with 18.8; Japanese, with 17; Hawaiians, with 15.3; and Filipinos, with 13.2.

Women who bear dizygotic twins have higher levels of follicle-stimulating hormone (FSH), which stimulates the production of eggs. Levels of this hormone rise with maternal age, and are also found at elevated levels in obese women. This may explain why twinning rises with maternal age and occurs more often in heavy women.

Although the causes of twinning are fascinating, and it's helpful to know all you can about your children's origins, the biology is only the beginning.

THE HARDEST JOB IN THE WORLD—AND THE BEST

Over the years I have come to view the experience of raising twins as similar to preparing an expedition to climb Mount Everest. You wouldn't expect to set off on such a grueling adventure without a complete and first-rate support system, including expert guides, functional equipment, and lots of information. And yet, as exhausting and difficult as the process is, the adventure is unparalleled and worth the sacrifice.

I am convinced that with the proper preparation, information, and support, parents of twins can cope as well as mountain climbers.

A WORD ABOUT TERMINOLOGY

This book is for all parents who anticipate or have had multiple births. That includes everything from twins up to octuplets (so far). Technically, of course, twins are two babies, and triplets and beyond are referred to as "higher-order multiples." But it's awkward to refer to "twins and higher-order multiples" throughout the book, so we'll use the term *twins* to refer to all multiples. Much of what applies to raising twins applies to triplets, quadruplets, and so on. When it's appropriate to focus on the special circumstances of higher-order multiples, we'll do so.

Throughout this book, I refer to experts and researchers who have contributed to our understanding of twin development. When I refer to lay people—children or parents—I have changed the names. The only exceptions to this are my own daughters, Krista and Kelda.

This book is the outgrowth of what I've learned from my own research and from the thousands of parents who have sought counseling from, or shared their experiences with, Twin Services. I'm writing it along with Janet Poland, the author of numerous books about child development and child care, who brings her own perspective to the task. When I write in the first person, I'm referring to myself, Patricia Malmstrom.

I believe the twin relationship is a birthright we all can envy. It is not characterized by a submersion of independence, or by a crippling dependency on another person. Rather, it is a relationship that can provide children with a unique resource. With this book as your guide, you'll be able to help your multiples thrive as individuals and remain a source of support and intimacy for one another over a lifetime. And you'll be able to travel on that journey with them, helping them through the occasional rough patch, but delighting in all the fun that lies ahead.

CHAPTER TWO

GET READY, GET SET

PREPARING FOR A WHOLE NEW WORLD

When my daughter Krista was born, she weighed five pounds, eleven ounces. Considering that I'd gained forty pounds, my doctor was surprised at how tiny she was. "She's too little to be there alone," he said. "Quick, let's get the other one out."

Sure enough, nine minutes later Kelda was born—quite a surprise to my doctor, but not to me and my family. I'd gained weight rapidly and felt movements that I knew couldn't have come from just one baby, so I'd been prepared for this.

Diagnosing multiple pregnancies was an inexact science before the advent of ultrasound imaging. In 1973, when my twins were born, barely half of all twin births were confirmed ahead of time.

Today, assuming the mother has received good prenatal care, delivery room surprises like mine are rare. Nowadays families have time to prepare for the birth of their multiples. They have a precious opportunity to make the pregnancy as healthy as it can be. They have time to arrange their households and careers ahead of time. They have time to read about raising twins and learn everything that's possible to learn ahead of time. Once those babies arrive, there won't be time for planning. Life will shift into the present tense—getting through one day, or one hour, at a time.

However, this gift of time is not without its cost. Knowing in advance about twins or triplets can also mean months of anxious worrying: "How will I cope? Will this traumatize my older child? How will we pay the bills?"

A ONE-TWO PUNCH

Every pregnancy is life-changing. You worry, you plan, you dream. You visualize what it will be like and anticipate what it will involve. With twin pregnancies, you don't just get two babies—you get two separate life-changing pieces of news. First there's the news that you're pregnant. And just when you're starting to get used to that idea, you learn that you're having more than one. So in addition to all the plans you have to change and preparations you have to make, you now have to give up the dreams and fantasies you had about you and your single baby.

Take the experience of one couple I know who tried for some time to conceive. When they became pregnant, they were ecstatic. They hadn't used fertility drugs and had no reason to suspect a multiple birth.

"Then, the day after we started telling everyone about my pregnancy, I had a miscarriage," Ellen recounts. "I was in bed all week, crying."

Soon after, her doctor ordered an ultrasound to determine what had gone wrong. She lay sorrowfully on the examining table, her husband at her side, as the technicians examined her uterus. Ellen recalls, "Suddenly they said, 'Wait—what's this? It's a baby!'

"I couldn't believe I was still pregnant! I was trying to get used to that, and then my husband pointed to the screen and said, 'What's that?'

"The technician checked, and said, 'That's *another* baby!'"

Ellen had conceived triplets and lost one to miscarriage. She had gone from wanting a baby, to getting one, to losing a baby, to getting a baby, and finally to getting two babies. Small wonder that parents of multiples feel their heads spin.

Over the years Twin Services has heard from thousands of parents who are expecting twins or higher-order multiples. I've often heard from panicked mothers who have just learned that theirs is a multiple pregnancy. Sometimes they call us before telling their family and friends.

Often they're like the mother who called to say, "I've just learned I'm expecting twins! I'm so excited!" There was a pause. And in a small voice, the woman added, "And I'm so *scared*! What do I need to know? How do people manage?"

This mother's reaction is typical. One study reported that when couples first learn of a pregnancy, 88 percent describe themselves as happy. But when they first learn of a multiple pregnancy, that figure drops to a 54 percent. Surprise, shock, and uncertainty are the most common reactions to the news that this miracle is even more miraculous than they expected.

This mother was frightened, too. And why not? She knew twins are hard work. She knew the pregnancy might be more difficult, the babies more fragile.

Yet she was a wise woman indeed. She knew she needed to prepare. She wanted to know what she needed to learn, and how other people manage.

Her response to the news of her impending multiple birth was healthy. She was honest about her feelings, both positive and negative. She was eager to buckle down and do her homework. She was hungry for news of other twin families, how they managed, and what she might learn from them.

A MAP OF THE EMOTIONAL TERRAIN

In my years of talking to the parents of twins and other multiples, I've observed a pattern of emotional reaction to the news of their multiple pregnancy. Many pregnancies are planned, but no one really *plans* to have twins. When couples learn that they are pregnant with more than one, the surprise of the news is compounded by the surprising intensity of their emotional reactions. Here's how it often, but not always, proceeds.

DISBELIEF OR DENIAL

"I remember suddenly seeing a frozen look on the face of the technician performing my ultrasound," recalls one mother. "She said, 'I'd better get the doctor,' and left me lying there not knowing what terrible thing she'd seen. Later, when we saw the three babies, my husband refused to believe it."

That sense of denial—"This cannot be happening!"—is a typical and entirely normal response. The realization that we are pregnant, that wonderful things are happening unseen within us, is often just about all the amazement we can handle. One baby is hard enough to believe—two or more are impossible!

"It was a complete shock," recalls the father of monozygotic girls. "My mind ranged from two cribs to two college educations in two seconds. It was amazing I stayed on my feet."

Sometimes, however, disbelief can become denial. Instead of accepting the news, parents may simply refuse to face it at all. While parents may not deny the twin pregnancy itself, they may be unable to face the fact that it will make a difference in their lives. That's unfortunate, because it's important to use those brief months of pregnancy to prepare for the challenges ahead; refusing to face them takes precious time away from that preparation.

ELATION AND AWE

"I was overjoyed! After all those years of trying, to find out I would have *two* babies—it was just too much!"

"It's a miracle! My prayers have been answered—and then some."

"How can I be so lucky? I feel blessed."

How can we not be delighted when we realize we're producing something so miraculous? You may think, "I've never won a raffle, never been singled out for any special glory—and now this!"

Elation is a common and most enjoyable reaction. It doesn't always last long, however; soon it may be replaced by a less positive emotion.

PANIC AND DREAD

The highs are often followed by lows. In the still of the night, dread takes over. "I was thirty-nine when I became pregnant for the first time. My girls were conceived through in vitro fertilization, and I'd never quite believed I'd ever really have children. Then when I learned I was expecting twins, I panicked. I was almost forty, I knew nothing about babies. How would we cope?"

Sudden worries may intrude on your thoughts: "We just got our last child into her own bedroom, and now this—two more babies!" Or "How will I keep my job? What if I need to be on bed rest?"

OVERCONFIDENCE

"I can do this. Lots of people have two children."

"My mother raised five kids. How hard can three be?"

Often our emotions rebound from fear or panic to confidence—sometimes overconfidence. We focus on the positive side of things, which is all to the good. Yet we often try to cope emotionally by brushing aside the very real concerns and problems that having twins or more will bring.

The problem here is that overconfidence can cause us to waste precious preparation time, especially if we conclude that we won't need any particular support after the babies arrive.

"I'm just not comfortable asking for help" is a common response—and a potentially disastrous one—among mothers expecting multiples. "We'll manage on our own. If we run into trouble, we'll worry about it then."

DEPRESSION

Often, after the initial excitement has worn off, sober second thoughts kick in. As the pregnancy wears on (and wear it does), mothers may become more and more fatigued and uncomfortable. In this state, the downside looks bleaker than it would if the mother were rested and full of energy.

As a twin pregnancy progresses, the mother's abdomen grows much larger much faster. It's common to be the size of a term pregnancy at six months. The skin stretches. It's difficult to move or to sleep. You may think, "I can handle this." Then you look at the calendar and realize you have three months to go!

The pregnant mother in one couple I counseled recently was the picture of depression—her posture and her pinched features all indicated that she had given up, had no zest left for the challenges that lay ahead. Fortunately, her husband was supporting her by gathering information and making plans for their future.

BALANCE

It's perfectly normal to feel *all* of these emotions, in no particular order, and to go back and forth between them. That does not mean you are manic-depressive. It doesn't mean you are abnormal or a bad parent. It simply means you are emotionally open to the amazing and challenging adventure you are embarking upon.

Ideally, mood swings taper off as you adjust, as you become more prepared and educated about the twin experience. As you organize your household, sit down with your employer to discuss leave and benefits, interview child care or support people, and learn all you can about multiple pregnancy and parenting, your emotions will become more stable and more positive. You will face your adventure honestly, without illusions, but full of optimism.

HOW YOU FEEL DEPENDS ON WHO YOU ARE

MOTHERS

Mothers are the ones who carry the babies, bear the discomforts of pregnancy, give birth, and must face the early days in a state of physical exhaustion. It's understandable that along with their excitement about the babies comes worry about their own ability to be a capable and loving parent when the twins arrive.

Sometimes the mother is the only person who feels these worries, especially if everyone around her is focusing only on the exciting and fun aspects of the experience.

"My parents were just floating when I told them we were expecting twins," recalls one mother. "But I cried for a week."

Mothers still are the ones who face the greatest burden and bear most of the responsibility for the care and well-being of their children. The highs and lows of their emotional reaction reflect this.

FATHERS

Fathers, like mothers, react with a range of emotions, from pride and joy to fear and anxiety. Some fathers get stuck in the overconfidence stage, brushing off their wives' concerns about how the family will manage. These fathers may not consider how important their own role will be in the care of the babies, especially if they were not much involved when their older children were tiny.

More often, however, fathers do share the mothers' concerns. Often they focus their worries on finances. "How will we feed all these kids? What about clothes, braces, college? Can we afford a bigger apartment?"

The father may realize that he'll have to divide his energies between helping with the babies and earning a living—maybe as the sole provider for the first time in the couple's life together. If this is the first pregnancy, a wife who was employed may have to rethink her career plans after twins or triplets enter the picture, and that will place greater financial responsibility on the father.

The need to rearrange career plans may apply to both parents. Fathers, too, may think, "Will I be able to take a promotion that requires me to travel and to work weekends? Can I afford not to, with this growing family?" He may feel some resentment at the need to adjust his goals.

Having twins can force couples to redefine their relationship, especially in terms of household and parenting responsibilities. Not all fathers think this through during the pregnancy, but it hits home with a vengeance when the babies are born.

Sometimes the announcement that his wife is expecting twins brings on considerable attention and praise. A father expecting twins or more may find himself the subject of admiring jokes about his manhood—attention that he may or may not appreciate.

SIBLINGS

"What will become of my son when I bring the twins home? We were planning to start him in preschool when they're born, but will that add up to too much change all at once?"

25

The birth of a younger sibling is always a major event in a child's life. When that birth brings two or more little ones into the family, older children can suffer. The child's home and routine are turned upside down, and parents suddenly devote all their time and attention to the babies.

The reactions of siblings—and the best course of action—depend on many factors, but the most essential one is the age of the older child. We'll discuss tips on helping brothers and sisters adjust in Chapter Seven. For now, consider how to prepare your older children for the changes that lie ahead.

For children under age three, talk about the upcoming birth, but don't expect a great deal of understanding. Get books from the library about new babies arriving in the family; explain that in your family there will be two babies. Buy two baby dolls for them to play with, to make the experience more tangible.

Preschoolers understand more, although that understanding is limited. They may know other children who have or will have baby siblings. You can say, "John's mommy is going to have a baby also. Your mommy is going to have *two* babies." Never miss a chance to say, "Mommy and I will still have plenty of love for you."

A wonderful way to involve children this age in the birth is to help them make something for the babies. A simple activity would be to make a picture book about the family. Young children can dictate the words to you and add their own drawings.

Routines are appealing and comforting to children of this age. If your young child will move to a different bedroom to make room for the twins, or change caregivers, or begin nursery school, make an effort to make major changes before the babies arrive, so as to give your older child a chance to feel more settled.

Older children may ask many questions and express hostility as well as enthusiasm. Talk with your school-age child about the ways in which things will change, and the ways in which they will stay the same. Above all, reassure your child that no matter how tired and distracted you may be while the babies are small, you will still love him or her the same as ever.

It's helpful when children can actually do something as they sort out their feelings. They might make a photographic scrapbook about the family, and even take the photos themselves.

A more complex project, but a long-lasting one, is baby quilts. Such a project could involve children of any age, and could be directed by a mother on bed rest. Very young children can choose the cloth and the colors. Children old enough to draw can draw pictures on cloth with a waterproof pen. The designs can be used as is, or the outlines can be filled in with fabric pieces. Children who can handle scissors can cut out pieces and arrange them into a picture using contact glue. And older children who have mastered the sewing machine can do the sewing.

School-age children may hear upsetting stories about twins from their friends or in the media. While I was expecting my twins, my second daughter, who was seven, came to me and said in a small, worried voice, "Mommy? If the babies are stuck together, I hope it's just at the toe, because we could snip them apart with the nail scissors."

It's important to keep the discussion going with your children so that they can air their concerns and gain some reassurance. The best way to do this is for the adults to model it by talking openly about their own feelings.

HOW YOU FEEL DEPENDS ON YOUR LIFE SITUATION

Your emotional response to learning about your multiple pregnancy will vary from day to day and from week to week. But your life situation and the unique history of your pregnancy will also affect your mood and your response.

FIRST-TIME PARENTS VERSUS
SEASONED VETERANS

If the twin pregnancy is your first, your sense of awe and amazement may be particularly strong. Yet the idea of having two or more tiny babies thrust into your inexperienced arms may add to your anxiety about the future.

Experienced parents may have similar responses, but from a somewhat different standpoint: They *know* how wonderful babies are. And they *know*—all too well—how much work is involved.

And seasoned parents have the additional concern of the older children's well-being.

"When I found out I was expecting twins, I cried. I was so sad, because I realized I was about to lose the special time I had with my two-year-old daughter. I was prepared to have another baby, but *two* more babies! How would I have enough time to be as close to them as I was to my daughter?"

PRIOR INFERTILITY

When parents have taken fertility drugs or made use of in vitro fertilization, they are probably prepared for the possibility of bearing two or more babies. Yet their reaction may be intensified by feelings of gratitude and awe. After all, a few short months ago they were childless, and sad about it. Now they're about to be parents—of triplets!

It's so miraculous, you can hardly believe it's happening. And yet sometimes you worry so much that you find yourself wishing it weren't happening. And then you feel guilty that you're feeling resentful rather than grateful.

Parents who have undergone lengthy fertility treatments may be more sophisticated about obstetrics than other parents, and may use this sophistication in positive ways or negative ways. They may use their knowledge to make sure the pregnancy is as healthy as possible and be ready to act at the first sign of any problems. Or they may just worry themselves sick about everything that could possibly go wrong.

STRESSES WITHIN THE MARRIAGE

Any pregnancy can aggravate tensions within a marriage, but when the pregnancy involves twins or triplets, the aggravation is greater. We tend to sweep problems under the rug and, for a time, ignore the lumps. Having multiples strips away the rug.

This is especially true when one of the couple's disagreements was about the number of children to have, or whether to have children at all. You may have arrived at a resolution to this disagreement through negotiation—but the negotiations were based on one baby. Now you learn that two babies are on the way, and you may feel betrayed.

The couples who do best are those wise enough to expect some tensions in their relationship. They understand how essential it is that the family stay together and the relationship remain strong. If your relationship has some weak points, or if you have trouble communicating with your partner, now is the time to begin working on those areas. If you can articulate what's bothering you, state your needs, and listen attentively to your partner's concerns and needs, you'll be more able to weather the inevitable stresses of twin parenting.

MONEY WORRIES

It is perfectly reasonable to have money worries. Twins and higher-order multiples can turn any family's financial situation upside down. Even with insurance, the copayments for extended hospitalization can make a major impact.

If the family is on shaky financial ground to begin with, the impact of the babies on the household can be devastating. We've long observed that most families find their financial picture worsens with twins. Their capacity to generate income goes down, while expenses go up.

When money is an issue, it's more difficult to feel joyous about the prospect of twins—yet it's even more important than ever to plan, prepare, and build a supportive network.

LOSS OF ONE OR MORE BABIES
BEFORE BIRTH

Fetal loss is a risk of multiple pregnancy. When the pregnancy continues with one or more surviving babies, parents must deal with almost unbearably strong emotions, both intense grief and intense love for the remaining infants.

As if that weren't enough, parents may have to cope with the complex feelings that surround fetal reduction—when one or more embryos in a multiple pregnancy is aborted in order to provide the remaining babies with a better chance of survival. In such cases, all the varied and swirling emotions described in this chapter are intensified by feelings of guilt and grief over the lost child: "I was so happy about these babies—I'm grateful for the three I have left, but all I can think about right now is the one I had to lose."

Allow yourself to grieve for your loss. Recognize that this process takes time, often a very long time. Don't feel that you must be finished with the grieving process by the time your healthy babies arrive. You don't "owe it to them" to block out your sadness over their lost sibling. Rather, as time goes by, your sorrow will ease at its own pace.

We'll discuss the issues of loss further in Chapter Fifteen.

FEELING WHAT YOU FEEL,
NOT WHAT YOU *SHOULD* FEEL

"Everyone around us thinks it's great that we're expecting twins," says one mother. "But they're not the ones who are going to have them. We're worried about how we're going to manage. We're in shock."

Most people respond positively when they hear you're expecting more than one baby. It's natural for friends and family to be excited and thrilled. But their jollity can be hard to take if you're feeling anxious or depressed. It's essential to sort out your own feelings from other people's, and to remember that your feelings are the important ones.

LAY CLAIM TO YOUR EMOTIONS

"I know I should be happy, but I feel awful."

Others may tell you what you "should" feel, but your emotions belong to you alone. You may feel bad about negative feelings, but you need not apologize for them.

ACCEPT THE FULL RANGE OF YOUR EMOTIONS

If you find yourself riding the emotional roller coaster I described above, it's helpful to keep in mind that it's normal, and your down periods will soon become ups. Those feelings are all rational in their own way. When you're feeling up, enjoy it. When you're feeling terror and dread, take pride in your own honesty about the challenges you face.

Remember also that negative feelings about an impending multiple birth do not mean you don't love your babies now or that you won't love them fiercely when they arrive.

TALK ABOUT YOUR FEELINGS

It's helpful if you can share your hopes and fears honestly with someone. If that someone is your husband or wife, or a parent or best friend, so much the better. But if you are severely anxious or depressed, you should find a sympathetic professional or support group.

Allow Yourself to Release, with Some Sadness, the Dream of a Single Baby

It's natural to feel sad and disappointed when your plans and expectations are upset. When you first became pregnant, you may have imagined yourself bonding with one child, and pictured that child's welcome into the family. When one child becomes two or more, you have to shift gears. And to make that shift successfully, you have to say goodbye to the old images to make room for the new.

Ease Your Mind by Planning and Preparing

The more tasks you accomplish before the babies are born, the better off you'll be later. But equally important is the *emotional* benefit of planning. The more of the following preparations you can make ahead of time, the calmer, more optimistic, and more realistically confident you will be.

PREPARATION TIME— MAKING THE MOST OF A GOOD SITUATION

Home and Household

Where, oh where, will you put all those babies? What about cribs, diapers, child care, getting to and from work? Practical matters can weigh heavily during your pregnancy, so the more you can resolve, the calmer you'll be. As one expectant mother wrote to me, "Questions as simple as whether we will need two cribs right away might seem silly, but so far no one has had the answer. Whether or not to breastfeed and what type of diapers to use could make a large difference in our planning ahead."

Indeed, now is the time to organize your thoughts, your questions, your household. Once you have settled some of these questions, you will find yourself feeling more capable and more upbeat.

Are you moving into a bigger house or apartment? Will your older child have to move to a different bedroom? Will you need to make room for a relative or nanny? Now is the time to plan, organize, and begin to delegate.

Yet it can be hard to plan, hard to know where to begin. Two factors complicate this planning stage.

First, parents may await the birth of their multiples with apprehension. They worry that something might be wrong with the babies, and fear making too many preparations. The sheer act of selecting names or shopping for layette items seems to tempt fate.

Second, the size of the task is daunting. "Where will we fit everyone?" "What if breastfeeding just doesn't work out? Should we buy bottles just in case?"

"We have a two-year-old, and I just found out we're expecting triplets," said one mother. "Where do I start? Where can we find a stroller for four?"

This is the time to be realistic and practical. You won't jinx your pregnancy by planning—rather, you'll be giving your babies a better beginning. You don't need to buy every item of the layette in the early stages, but you do need to address the most essential matters.

The most important preparations—other than those related to your health—relate to your support system. A network of helpers is much more important than a beautifully decorated nursery. Once you have them in place, they can help you cope with other matters.

Make basic decisions about sleeping arrangements for babies, older siblings, adult caregivers.

You may not get all your shopping done before the births, but you can do research about what to buy and where to buy it.

You can also locate sources of inexpensive or used baby equipment and clothing in advance. That way, for example, if your babies are born prematurely, you'll know where you can find small-size baby clothes. View your role as that of planner, organizer, and decision maker. Specific details (such as stocking the bureau drawers or shopping for clothes) can be delegated if necessary. Thus, when you give the green light, your designated baby clothes shopper can head for your designated baby clothes source to pick up what you need.

Focus on thinking through scenarios. Who will watch the older children if I have to be in the hospital for a long stay? How will we organize the morning rush? What will we do if I have a cesarean delivery?

After the babies arrive, you'll know what quantities and sizes of clothing your children will need. However, it's wise to have a modest supply of essentials laid in ahead of time. We discuss layette items and other practical details in Chapter Six.

THE ALL-IMPORTANT SUPPORT SYSTEM

If you've just learned that you're expecting twins, you may wonder how people manage two newborns without help. The answer is that most people *don't* manage very well without help. You're almost certain to need some assistance, whether it's a neighbor helping out during bath time or a full-time nanny.

I've heard parents of older twins brush off the need for support. "It was the best time of our lives," they say, "and we didn't have any help." On closer examination, however, it becomes clear that what they mean is they didn't have any *hired* help. Their aunt and uncle moved in and helped round the clock. Or an elderly neighbor came by every day to pitch in. Or there were three other families with twins on the same block, and the families shared child care duties every day.

I'm convinced that there are no "supermoms"—just good storytellers. So you'll be better off if you accept the idea that the job you'll be doing is too big for one or two people, and you'll need some extra hands.

Questions to consider about help: Are you comfortable having someone live in? Do you have room for another adult? Can you afford to pay? Can you afford *not* to pay? Are you the kind of person who can handle neighbors dropping in on your home at odd hours, or will you be happier with a schedule? Do you like having lots of company, or would you benefit more from helpers who run errands or drop by with groceries?

Now's the time to start investigating your options. And remember: Don't wait for people to volunteer. Discuss your needs with them. Tell people what you need, and work with what people can offer.

When people say, "Can I do anything to help?" don't be shy—be ready. Say, "How nice of you to offer! Let's see . . . could I call you to pick up dry cleaning or do a quick grocery run for me? Could you watch Andrew occasionally when I take the twins to the pediatrician?"

Sources of support include:

- Family members. Grandparents, brothers and sisters, in-laws, nieces or nephews—anyone whom you trust and who volunteers to help out can be invaluable. Whether it's a major commitment, such as your mother agreeing to watch the babies while you're at work, or your brother and sister-in-law offering to take care of them once a week while the two of you go out for dinner, now is the time to talk to your family about what you might need.
- Friends and neighbors who can be lined up for help with bathing, errand running, delivery of meals, or entertaining an older sibling for a few hours.
- Volunteers from your church, synagogue, or parents-of-multiples organization.

- Neighborhood teenagers who are available for baby-sitting.
- A housekeeper, nanny, or au pair.

Consider bringing in your support people before the babies are born. In my own case, I was on bed rest and unable to shop. I hired my helper ahead of time to help organize the household and the babies' things. This was helpful in two ways: She took care of the tasks I could not handle, and she knew where everything was and how I wanted things organized ahead of time.

EXPAND YOUR KNOWLEDGE BASE

You're not going to have much time to relax with a good book when your twins are small. Your pregnancy is a good time to learn everything you can about multiples, as you're doing now. Refer to the bibliography for recommended reading on twins and multiples.

I've found that couples often differ as to how much they want to know. That terrified mother I mentioned earlier has a husband with his sleeves rolled up and who's reading everything he can get his hands on. His wife will probably become more confident over time, but at least one member of the team is energized and motivated to learn all he can right now.

I grant that there are aspects of multiple pregnancy and its risks that can be quite frightening. But I'm convinced that ignorance is not bliss. The more you know about this remarkable adventure, the more you can enjoy the good parts and cope with any difficulties.

Now is also a good time to locate support groups and organizations that you may find invaluable later on. Ask other parents of twins what groups they have found useful. Check your library for books and pamphlets. Locate local resource organizations and groups before you need them. There are organizations and newsletters and support groups for almost every possible aspect of the multiple experience.

Finally, take advantage of this planning period to educate yourself about child safety and baby-proofing techniques. There are excellent books available that will tell you in detail how to make your home safe and how to keep your children safe. We've listed some in the Resources.

Twins are at greater risk of accidents and injury than are single children, as we outline in Chapter Ten. The best safety policy is to be ready before the need arises. You may not have to put covers on your electrical outlets when your twins are newborns, but you need to be ready to take such precautions when the time comes. Now, before you are involved in caring for your twins, is the time to read about safety and plan your safety strategy.

THINK AHEAD ABOUT NAMING YOUR BABIES

We discuss the implications of names for your twins in Chapter Eight. Give some thought to your selections now, while you can reflect calmly. Once you get to the hospital, you may find it hard to think clearly. And you'll grow tired of hearing your babies referred to as "Baby A" and "Baby B" by the hospital staff.

FACING THE FUTURE WITH JOY—AND CONFIDENCE

Time after time, parents of multiples report back to me that they are doing beautifully—because they were prepared. Like the mother who admitted her fears earlier in this chapter, they were excited one moment, scared the next. They wanted to know everything they could about how to manage when their babies were born.

Like that mother, the strength of their hopes and fears pulled them toward the sources of support and information they needed. They knew they had to have a plan and a support system. As a result, they had the confidence and optimism to be able to savor the pregnancy and fully appreciate what is a once-in-a-lifetime experience.

CHAPTER THREE

DEBUNKING MYTHS ABOUT TWINS

THE TRUTH BEHIND THE FICTION

"*I thought my twins would just be sitting there looking cute,*" one mother recalls. "*After they were born, reality hit. There I was, up to my elbows in poop, and nobody was looking cute!*"

A romanticized image of having twins is just one of the many unrealistic assumptions parents may acquire. Twins lend themselves to romance—not only are they charming as infants, but they have figured in legends and myths throughout history, symbolizing both good (prosperity and good fortune) and evil (conflict and economic hardship). There's the good-twin-versus-evil-twin scenario, played out in the story of Romulus and Remus; the devoted twins who could not live without each other, in the Castor and Pollux myth; and the bitter rivalry of Jacob and Esau.

Everyone stands ready to contribute to the mythology. Literature, television commercials, friends, relatives, and even strangers in the supermarket all have something to say. Twins and supertwins attract more attention than single children, and it sometimes seems that everyone has an opinion or story about how difficult it is to raise twins, and the troubles the children may face as they grow.

Even the positive remarks exert a subtle influence on parents' perceptions. "If this is supposed to be so wonderful, and I am so lucky," an overwhelmed parent may think, "why don't I feel that way? There must be something wrong with me."

The birth of twins has always been considered a notable event. Historically, most societies viewed twin births as supernatural events. When their arrival coincided with a good harvest, twins were associated with good fortune. When twins arrived in hard times, they became evil omens.

The amount of resources available for their care was, and still is, the main influence on a society's view of twins. When enough food, water, and shelter are available, twins are welcome. When supplies are scant, twins are an unwelcome burden.

Apparently this has been the case throughout the history of North America. A study of attitudes about twins in 172 northwest American Indian tribes found that large tribes that had high competition for available resources disapproved of twins. Women of these tribes, like the Kawaiisu, avoided eating eggs with double yokes and fruits with two pits in an effort to reduce their risk of twinning. Smaller tribes were ambivalent about twins. While the arrival of twins added welcome numbers to the tribe, the scarcity of adults made their care difficult. Midsize tribes where resources and group support were in balance valued twins and their parents. For example, the Kwakiutl celebrated the supernatural powers of twins by giving their parents a year of rest while other members of the tribe cared for the babies.

Today few parents of multiples get a complete rest, nor would they want to be separated from their babies. However, the friends, relatives, and volunteers from parents-of-twins clubs who help parents are part of this venerable tradition.

It isn't surprising that myths about twins reflect tremendous interest in the unique characteristics of twinship—the biology of twinning, the possibility of "special powers," and a relationship that begins in the womb. Nor is it surprising that attitudes toward twins are affected by their impact on their families and society.

What is surprising is that today, in spite of the fact that we no longer consider twin birth supernatural and we have a greater understanding about the twin relationship, we parents and our multiples are susceptible to advice and professional opinions that are rooted in myth.

Even more surprising, given statistics that demonstrate an elevated risk of child abuse in families with multiples (from two and a half to nine times the risk for families with only single children), is how little we do to ensure that families with multiples have the resources they need to cope with their special challenges.

Our popular culture celebrates twins. They are the subject of situation comedies and movies. But when it comes to the nitty-gritty of raising them, we leave parents pretty much on their own.

Learning the facts about twins will help you recognize the myths, so you won't be swayed by fictions. You will have the tools and the confidence you need to help your multiples successfully navigate their difficulties and to enjoy the many benefits of their special situation.

Myth: Every pregnant woman thinks she's having twins.
Fact: Pregnant women can identify the presence of more than one fetus.
Impact: My first personal experience with the negative impact of twin mythology was during my pregnancy. My obstetrician dismissed my suspicions of twins with a glib "Every pregnant woman thinks she's having twins."

But as long ago as that was, I still remember how difficult it was for me to override my upbringing, which told me that the doctor always knows best. I had to learn to listen to the evidence I was experiencing daily—the constant, separate movement in different places at the same time, which could only be accounted for by twins.
What you can do: Be aware of how your body is feeling. Pay

attention to all your symptoms. If you have any suspicions that you may be carrying twins or more, be sure to speak up to your physician and insist on an ultrasound scan for an accurate diagnosis.

In my study of 336 mothers of recently born multiples, 71 percent reported suspicions of twin pregnancy before it was confirmed medically. Many of the 239 women who reported the specific symptoms they associated with multiples said that they experienced a constellation of symptoms. The physical symptoms most frequently reported were: elevated size or weight gain (72 percent); greater fetal movement (42 percent); and separate fetal movement (24 percent).

Myth: A twin pregnancy is no different from a single pregnancy.
Fact: Pregnancy involving more than one fetus is very different from a single pregnancy. The mother's body is providing all of the nourishment for twice (at least) the number of growing embryos. The embryos share the womb. Because of this, twins are at risk for the problems associated with a shared placenta and a shared amniotic sac. Twins also have an elevated risk of preterm birth and low birth weight.

Research indicates that to reduce the risk of preterm labor and improve outcomes, the mother needs enriched nutrition to ensure the optimal growth of the babies, and to make it possible for her body to support the additional physical demands of the pregnancy.

She must also have adequate rest and relief from stress to reduce the risk of preterm labor. The growth of the fetuses and their attachment to the placenta (or placentas) must be monitored for possible problems.
Impact: Obstetricians and parents may not be aware of measures that can contribute to the birth of healthy, full-term twins.

For example, it is not uncommon for a mother expecting twins or triplets to be given a handout on nutrition designed for a single pregnancy. One such expectant mother of triplets asked, "Should I multiply by three?"

When a mother I know found out that she was expecting twins, she was commuting an hour each way to a full-time job she loved. No one had mentioned to her that the physical demands of her work schedule might affect the pregnancy.

She became more and more tired as the pregnancy progressed. The only other pregnant women she knew were carrying single babies and coping very well at work. Influenced by their example and her doctor's silence on the subject, she overrode her fatigue and carried on at work.

Not until after her twins were born two months early and required two months of hospital care did she learn that rest is an important part of managing a twin pregnancy. She says that had she known then what she knows now, she would have left work weeks early to improve her chances of carrying the babies to term.

What you can do: Learn about twin pregnancy and do all you can to take good care of yourself. Don't try to be a hero. And do make sure your obstetrician is knowledgeable about multiple-birth issues.

Myth: When there is one placenta the twins are monozygotic; two placentas mean they are dizygotic.
Fact: About one-third of monozygotic twins have separate placentas. It is also possible for the two separate placentas of dizygotic twins to fuse, so that there appears to be only one. It is not possible to accurately determine whether twins are dizygotic or monozygotic by simply counting their placentas.

There are important psychological and health reasons for twins and their parents to know their true zygosity. The development of monozygotic twins can be expected to be parallel. When one is developmentally behind the other, it is a signal to the parents that something may be wrong.

Because monozygotic twins have similar biology, their health may depend upon each other. If one is diagnosed with a serious illness, the other can be monitored for early symptoms. If one should ever need an organ or bone marrow transplant, the other is a perfect donor match.

Impact: Many monozygotic twins have grown up thinking they are dizygotic and vice versa, because their doctor used the number of their placentas to determine their zygosity. Such misdiagnosis deprives them of their birthright—their right to know and celebrate their biological origins and their identity as twins. It also deprives monozygotic twins of important health benefits.

Fetal pathologist Geoffrey Machin, who advocates accurate prenatal diagnosis of zygosity, tells of a pair of twins whose experience illustrates how serious misdiagnosis can be. One brother was an organ donor for the other. As it happens, the twins were monozygotic. But because their doctors believed them to be dizygotic, despite their similar appearance, they prescribed medication for the recipient to prevent organ rejection. For eleven years this man suffered the debilitating side effects of a drug he did not need.

What you can do: As we discussed earlier, do learn your children's zygosity.

Myth: You're lucky—you get both your kids at once!
Fact: Well, yes. We are. And we do. And it isn't easy.
Impact: Over and over we parents hear, "Oh, twins! I know what it's like. I had my kids close together, too." Such remarks, though empathic and well meant, dismiss the unique challenges of twin care.

I've talked with many parents who are actually successfully mastering the nightmarish, sleep-deprived fog of the early days but are thoroughly demoralized because it is so hard that they think they must be doing something "wrong." What's worse is that because they were unaware that it would be hard, they hadn't prepared a support system ahead of time. And because they are feeling guilty, they are reluctant to ask for help now.
What you can do: Prepare. Prepare. Prepare.

Myth: **Twinning skips a generation.**
Fact: Oh, no, it doesn't! Dizygotic twinning is hereditary. Women may inherit the tendency to produce more than one egg during a cycle from either their mother or their father. It has long been believed that monozygotic twinning is not hereditary, but research has not yet been able to account for the fact that many families have multiple sets of monozygotic twins.

Recent data are demonstrating that there is an increased incidence of monozygotic twins among twins conceived with the assistance of ovulation-stimulating drugs or in vitro fertilization. Much further study is needed in order for us to understand all of the factors that contribute to twinning.

Impact: This myth has misled many women who have twin siblings into believing they are "immune" to the risk of twinning. And when they become pregnant they may disregard symptoms of twins.

What you can do: Respect your symptoms. Whether or not twins "run in your family," speak to your obstetrician if you have any suspicion that yours is a twin pregnancy.

Myth: **You can't breastfeed your twins because you'll never have enough milk.**
Fact: Milk supply increases to meet demand. Women who breastfeed twins produce more than twice as much milk as women nursing one baby. Mothers breastfeeding triplets or more produce the amount needed.

Impact: Women are told that they can't breastfeed twins, depriving their babies of the benefits of breast milk, which is the optimal nutrition for newborns and an important source of immunities.

What you can do: Plan to breastfeed. Share the facts about the importance of breastfeeding with your loved ones and enlist their help with related practical matters. (You will need it.) See Chapter Six for more on breastfeeding multiples.

Myth: **It's so much easier with twins. Everyone helps you, and you get lots of discounts.**

"Did you see in the paper about that woman who had sep-tuplets? What a deal—they're getting a new house, and a van, and all the formula and diapers they need for a year!"

Fact: Actually, volunteers who can give parents relief from round-the-clock care of multiples babies may be in short supply when the relatives live far away from the family, and friends are busy working. As I explained in Chapter Two, developing a support system before the birth is the key to healthy family survival.

Furthermore, the arrival of multiples is seldom anyone's ticket to prosperity. Even when the birth creates an extraordi-nary response, this is not a financial "easy street."

Although limited discounts are available from some manu-facturers of baby products, most of the cost of medical care, equipment, clothing, diapers, and food are double for twins and increase with the number of infants.

Impact: Expectant parents of multiples, lulled by unrealistic expectations of financial benefits and volunteer help, may not be prepared to cope with the financial impact and physical stress of caring for their newborns. Unfortunately, a tragic out-come of these heightened stresses is the elevated incidence of child abuse among families with multiples.

What you can do: Prepare a support network ahead of time. Do whatever it takes to insure all family members get adequate sleep. Never leave the babies alone with inexperienced care givers. And to ease the financial squeeze, search out sources of discounted and recycled baby products and supplies.

Myth: **Twins always look alike and act the same.**

"Oh, they can't be twins. They sure don't look alike!" This passerby's complaint on hearing that my babies were twins reflects one of the common myths about twins. I recall with embarrassment how indignant I was that my fifth-grade class-mates Carol and Joan called themselves twins. Carol was a tall blonde, and Joan, who was much shorter, was a brunette. "How dare they pass themselves off as twins!" I thought. "Twins are supposed to look just alike."

Fact: Dizygotic twins such as Carol and Joan may or may not look alike. But twins they are. There may even be observable physical differences in monozygotic twin pairs. Such differences are usually more subtle than the differences between dizygotic twins. One may have a mole where the other doesn't, for example. The shapes of their faces may differ. They may be different heights and weights. Their hair color may be slightly different.

As far as behavior is concerned, monozygotic twins have the same biological heritage and are much more likely than the rest of us to have similar mannerisms. That's not to say, however, that dizygotic twins and other pairs of people, such as married couples, don't sometimes act alike.

Impact: This myth sometimes has the positive effect of protecting twins who do not look alike from unwelcome public scrutiny. They can "pass" as single-born children. However, such "invisible" twins may suffer from lack of respect for their special relationship.

And, on the down side, it may be that monozygotic pairs become constrained by loved ones and others who expect and promote their sameness.

What you can do: Treat your children as the individuals they are. Give them what they need when they need it, whether their needs are the same or different.

Myth: They'll always be competing with each other.

Fact: Yes, siblings compete. And of course, it is natural for twins to compete—but not all the time.

Impact: When their grown-ups believe that competition is part and parcel of twin life, and consequently fail to set limits on their struggles, twins may take each day as a battlefield. The Smith twins, now in their forties, are still one-upping each other at every opportunity even though they live on opposite sides of the country.

Their parents now realize that their misunderstanding about what is healthy competition misled them into urging their daughters to battle in every arena. Consequently, their relationship growing up was characterized by extremes. One minute they were embracing and supporting each other, and the next they were going for each other's throats.

What you can do: Set clear limits. Help the children channel their competitive energy into sports and other productive pursuits.

Myth: They'll be slow to develop compared with single kids.
Fact: Twins as a group are not slow to develop. Premature and low-birth-weight babies, however, are at greater risk of developmental delays, and twins are often born early or small.
Impact: Whatever the cause, slowness in a multiple may be written off as "normal" for twins, postponing or eliminating the chances for timely corrective care.
What you can do: If your babies were premature, they should be monitored for symptoms of developmental problems. If one or more of your babies is lagging in development in any area, be sure to follow up with your doctor so that proper evaluation can be made and, if necessary, preventive treatment can begin.

Myth: Twins are two halves of a whole and share everything.
Fact: Twins do share their parents and their siblings. But they are first of all individuals who deserve their own toys and clothes and presents.
Impact: This myth conveys the completely erroneous notion that twins are content to be treated as if they were one person. Witness the Hallmark birthday card that reads, "For the Twins: Two Special Birthday Wishes." I remember how much each of my daughters treasured her birthday cards, carrying them around until they were dog-eared and falling apart. It is hard to imagine what they would have done with one card to share between them. Adult twins have often told me about

their pain as children when they were expected to share a card or a present on their birthday.

What you can do: A word to the wise ahead of time may help friends and relatives avoid becoming the cause of painful memories. An inexpensive card or present for each child is indeed better than one costly gift to be shared.

Myth: Twins always can be counted upon to play well together.

Fact: Twins are siblings. Playing together is a skill that comes more easily for some brothers and sisters than for others. Temperament and compatibility strongly influence how well twin siblings get along with each other. When they are getting along well, their play is a marvel of cooperation and fun. When they aren't, they can be fierce adversaries.

Impact: The idea that twins are automatically good companions may mislead parents into assuming that there is something wrong with their twins when they don't get along. And when they do get along, parents may be lulled into thinking that their twins do not need contact with other children.

What you can do: Set age-appropriate limits on aggressive behavior. Be a good coach and referee. Make opportunities for each child to play separately, and with other children.

Myth: Which one is the good one? Which one is the bad one?

Fact: Twins are not born into predetermined roles any more than single-born children are. Each newborn infant has a unique temperament and style, which may make the baby's care more or less difficult. This in no way indicates a predisposition to be "good" or "bad." In our eagerness to tell our babies apart, it's natural for us to search for differences, and to use those differences to describe them.

Impact: I was astonished the first time someone asked me which one of my babies was "good" and which "bad." Unfortunately, it wasn't a sometime thing. And sometimes it's the parents themselves who define their babies this way. I have heard many times since on our telephone counseling services from mothers who believed that all twins are like Esau and Jacob, one "bad" and one "good."

The call that has lingered longest in my memory was from a young mother who told me that she had figured out which of her four-day-old boys was the "bad" one. When I asked her why she thought that was true, she said, "The nurse says he's my fussy one."

This call demonstrates the myth's insidious power. Here is a nurse who succumbs to the myth by using negative behavior to differentiate between the babies. In doing so she unwittingly hands the mom the clue she has needed to label her babies.

What you can do: Think of your children's differences in positive terms, lest negative labels become deterministic. Only use good or neutral qualities or characteristics to describe them: "He's the chatty one; she's a watcher."

Myth: One will always be the leader and one the follower.

Fact: What is true is that the balance of leadership between the children in any pair of twins or set of higher-order multiples is an interplay of temperament, ability, and inclination. In the early years twins "try on" many different kinds of balancing acts, and usually settle into a dynamic pattern of alternating leading and following in all or some of their activities.

Impact: This myth assumes that only one of a twin pair can flourish. My first personal encounter with it came when a professor of linguistics reviewed the crib conversations I had recorded between my two daughters as part of a master's thesis when they were learning to talk. I expected that she would be as interested as I was in the subject matter of their conversations. But what impressed her most was the fact that each baby took turns introducing topics into their conversations. The professor had assumed that one would be the leader and always set the agenda.

The danger of this myth is its potential to lock one twin

into the position of "leader" and the other into the position of "follower." Children pay attention to the words we choose to describe them. If we choose words that limit them, we short-circuit their exploration of different roles—and that exploration is a normal and necessary path in twin development.

What you can do: Avoid labels such as these. Support their experimentation with different roles. Think of their strengths in relation to other children their age and in relation to their interests. For example, if one of your three-year-olds is physically adept and seems to dominate their play, you might describe him as a very social little guy. Your other child may be quiet, tolerant, and responsive to music, so you might describe him as musical and good-natured. This will leave room in your mind and theirs for each to develop both leader and follower skills.

Myth: They'll have trouble learning to talk.

Fact: There is nothing in the nature of twins that makes them less able to talk than single-born children. (In fact, some twins actually learn to talk sooner—there is evidence that dizygotic girls often master language ahead of other twins and ahead of single babies as well.)

But the twin situation does make the early language-learning process quite different in multiples. They will certainly develop a sophisticated nonverbal communication system; having been companions since before birth, they will be able to convey their feelings and observations quite well with gestures and sounds before they become good talkers. And often their busy parents may not be able to talk with them as much as is necessary for the timely development of language.

That said, it is true that because twins suffer a disproportionately high rate of low birth weight and prematurity, they are at elevated risk for physiological problems, such as hearing loss, that affect language learning. Wise parents always check when they're not sure.

Impact: The danger of this myth is that parents and caregivers may assume that difficulties with language are normal and miss the opportunity to get help for what may actually be a correctable problem.

What you can do: If you find yourself worrying that your children's language is not developing at an age-appropriate rate, have their hearing checked. If no hearing problems are found, check with your pediatrician or ask your school district for a referral to a specialist who can make an evaluation.

Myth: They'll have a secret language and you won't know what they're saying.

Fact: It may be true that you have a hard time understanding the baby talk of your toddlers, but research has found that true secret language in twins is extremely rare and is the result of extreme deprivation or isolation.

Twins are quite likely to develop complex "baby talk," a combination of poorly pronounced and made-up words that can baffle strangers and busy, preoccupied parents. Sometimes the older children in the family become the interpreters for their parents. Sometimes no interpretation is needed.

I remember my two communicating quite clearly that they wanted more milk by banging on the refrigerator door with their empty bottles while shouting, "Bore, bilk, baba!"

Impact: Here is an example of how this myth can distort professional perception of twins. A psychologist from a large pediatric hospital once called me with excitement to consult regarding a pair of toddler twins who she was sure had developed their own language. When I observed them, they were not using standard pronunciation, but they were using standard English words that I could easily understand.

When I inquired about hearing disorders, the psychologist confirmed that the toddlers had hearing loss. In her enthusiasm for diagnosing a "secret language," she overrode the obvious effect of hearing loss on their speech.

What you can do: Talk with your twins while you are feeding and changing them and working around the house. Make a special time to read or play with each one for a few minutes every day, and pay attention to their language. Encourage them to use words when they want something. Help them learn new words by pronouncing them slowly and clearly.

Myth: Twins should be separated in school for their own good.
Fact: Twin pairs vary in their need to be in separate or the same classrooms from year to year. There is no one formula that fits all twins all of the time. In general, twins benefit from placement together when they are starting preschool and elementary school. There is no research supporting the idea that separation is necessary for the growth of individuality at this stage. In fact, the evidence suggests that twins who are separated inappropriately are liable to regress and cling more tightly to their relationship.
Impact: In an effort to do "what's right" for twins, parents and school personnel may separate young twins before they are ready. Ironically, this practice can create the opposite of its intended effect. Often young twins worry about their twin when they're apart, especially in new situations. Together, they can relax and focus on the experience at hand.
What you can do: Each year assess your children's needs for placement together or apart and ask the school for what you think your children need. We'll discuss this in more detail in Chapter Twelve.

Myth: They'll never make friends with other children.
Fact: Twins have a head start when it comes to learning social skills. Most twins are very good company for each other during their early years but, given the opportunity, will enjoy playing with other children. When they were little, my daughters would sometimes come together to complain to me, "We doesn't got nobody to play with."
Impact: This myth may prompt anxious parents to go overboard scheduling a ceaseless round of play dates, leaving the children little if any quiet time. On the other hand, a parent

who thinks it's hopeless to expect twins to socialize outside their twosome may not make the effort at all.

What you can do: Gradually, as your energy and time permit, give your children opportunities to play with other kids. Encourage their friendship with others. Remember, too, that each child may have his or her own timetable for social development. Don't expect them to be equally enthusiastic at the same time.

Myth: The rate of homosexuality is higher in twins than in single-born children.

Fact: Homosexuality is no more frequent in twins than in others.

Impact: This myth is based upon the belief that homosexuality is caused by association and that, therefore, same-sex twins will be inclined toward homosexuality because of their close relationship. What is true is that homosexuality is more likely to appear in both members of a monozygotic pair who share the same biological heritage than in a dizygotic pair. This is strong evidence of a genetic origin of homosexuality.

What you can do: When friends and relatives bring up this myth, explain the facts. When and if your children bring it up, explain it to them as well.

Myth: The divorce rate for twins is higher than the divorce rate for single-born children.

Fact: Research indicates that divorce rates of twins and single-born adults are the same.

Impact: This myth adds to the negative picture of twinship and may cause unnecessary worry among twins and their families. We discuss issues of courtship, marriage, and divorce in later chapters.

What you can do: Help stop the spread of this myth by giving the correct information when the topic comes up in conversation. If your children ask you about this myth, reassure them that it is not true.

Myth: Twins have ESP and can read each other's minds.

Fact: Research so far discounts the notion that twins have extrasensory perception and can reliably read each other's minds.

However, anecdotal evidence suggests that many twins, much like some husbands and wives or other close siblings, are so "in tune" with each other that they can complete each other's sentences and anticipate each other's intentions. In my family, for example, no one will ever play Pictionary against our twin daughters. When they team up, they are unbeatable. All one of them has to do is make a straight line on a page and the other knows immediately what she is about to draw.

Impact: This myth thrives on fascination with the occult and belief in the magic of twins. Everyone I meet has at least one story to tell to illustrate the psychic powers of twins. Twins themselves often tell such stories about their own experiences. On the other hand, several have asked me if there is something "wrong" with them because they haven't felt each other's pain, sensed each other's thoughts, or known when something bad has happened to their twin.

What you can do: Treat your twins' relationship matter-of-factly. When and if they do experience "mind-reading" experiences, enjoy the fun. But avoid showcasing what is a normal artifact of their close relationship, lest they feel pressured.

CHAPTER FOUR

YOUR MULTIPLE PREGNANCY

GIVING YOUR BABIES A HEALTHY START

Pregnancy is an anxious time for all mothers, but this is especially so for women expecting twins or more. Indeed, there is more to worry about: "Will the babies be healthy? Will they be born too soon?" The mother's health and well-being are a cause for concern as well: "How big will I get? How will this pregnancy be different from my previous one? Will I stay healthy? What about labor and delivery?"

If you have already experienced a single pregnancy, you probably will find that your multiple pregnancy is different. First, you will indeed get bigger—and you will get larger earlier in your pregnancy than would be the case with one baby, because multiples grow rapidly during the second trimester. Second, you are likely to feel more discomforts associated with pregnancy, including heartburn, hemorrhoids, varicose veins, fatigue, and nausea. And third, you are also at greater risk of premature delivery.

YOUR MEDICAL TEAM

You must be confident that your medical support personnel, whether obstetrician, midwife, or physician's assistant, understand multiple pregnancies and can guide you through what may be a high-risk pregnancy. You have a right to the best care for yourself and your babies during your pregnancy and after. This is a time to take charge of your medical care, and to choose a team that understands your needs.

This is not the time to stick with a doctor who thinks twins are "no big deal," who tries to limit your weight gain because that's what he or she was taught decades ago, or who refuses to pay attention when you explain why you think you might be carrying twins.

CHOOSING AN OBSTETRICIAN

Here are some questions to ask when interviewing a prospective obstetrician:

- How many sets of multiples do you deliver a year? (About five per year should be enough.) What is the average length of the twin and triplet pregnancies that you have cared for in recent years?
- Do you encourage more frequent prenatal office visits for multiple pregnancy than for singles?
- How do you reduce the likelihood of preterm labor in multiple pregnancies?
- How and when will you diagnose the number of placentas and chorionic membranes? Will you use detailed ultrasound? Will you be sure that after the delivery the placentas go right to pathology for a complete examination to verify diagnosis and confirm zygosity?
- Can you explain how the number of placentas and chorionic membranes affects the level of risk? How do you handle these risks?
- Will you give us nutritional advice specific to supporting multiple pregnancy?
- Do you have relevant literature for us to read?

- Can you put us in touch with a parent support group right away?
- What symptoms might indicate complications with this pregnancy? (An acceptable answer would include all or most of the following: early labor pains, backache, fever, shortness of breath.)
- Will we have at least one prenatal appointment with a high-risk perinatologist? (A perinatologist has the skill to determine the number of placentas and membranes and to screen for risks.)
- Do you use multiple-birth-specific growth charts to evaluate the prenatal growth of twins or more? (Multiple-birth-specific growth charts both for ultrasound and for fundal height measurements are available in the literature.)
- Will a perinatologist be present or on call during our delivery? (If one isn't on call, serious consideration should be given to delivering in a larger medical center with a perinatologist on call.

If you are not satisfied with any of the responses to these questions, you may want to find another obstetrician. If your location or your health insurance limits your choice of physicians, you should be prepared to make at least one trip to a large medical center for a screening by a perinatologist. If the perinatologist identifies special risks, he or she will then be available to consult on or manage the case.

CHOOSING A PEDIATRICIAN

While you're selecting and assessing your obstetrical caregivers, this is a good time to consider your selection of a pediatrician or family practitioner. If you have other children, you may already be happy with their pediatrician. But whether you stay with your current pediatrician or select a new one for your multiples, you will want to give this matter some thought. The pediatrician will be your partner in your children's health and development for years to come, and your own peace of mind will depend on the rapport and trust you have with this professional.

Here are some questions to ask as you decide:

- Do your friends and acquaintances with twins have a recommendation? Ask them the reasons for their choice.
- Does your local parents-of-twins organization know of doctors in your community whom parents recommend?
- Ask the doctors you are considering how many patients in the practice are families with multiples.
- Does this doctor share your views about breastfeeding multiples? Will he or she support your efforts?
- Do you sense that this doctor will be sensitive to the feelings of your multiples as they grow? Will he or she be able to tell them apart, remember their names, and be sensitive when commenting on differences in their growth and development?
- Ask the doctor and staff whether they can do anything to make your visits easier. Perhaps they are willing to schedule appointments during slow hours, or send someone out to the parking lot to help you bring your triplets into the office.

Remember also that while professional reputation and credentials are important, they aren't enough. A positive chemistry between you and the doctor is important whether your children are single-born or multiples. And that good relationship should develop between the doctor and your babies as well.

I spoke with one mother of newborn twins who arranged a consultation with a pediatrician who had been referred to her by her perinatologist. His manner immediately put her off. "He was so arrogant," she recalls. "The phone rang while we were talking. It was a mother, upset about her child's illness. I could tell she was crying. The doctor yelled at the nurse for putting her through to him, and then yelled at the mother and hung up. Then he put on a sweet voice to get back to me. I walked out and found someone else for my babies."

While you are consulting with the pediatrician, be sure to ask for a schedule of immunizations, because you will need to plan ahead to make arrangements for visits to the pediatrician's office—no easy task when you have your arms full of babies.

YOUR HEALTHY PREGNANCY

Once you have settled on good obstetrical care, your major tasks during pregnancy are to obtain adequate nutrition, get enough rest, and be aware of signs of early labor.

The average gestation period for single pregnancies is forty weeks. For twins, thirty-seven weeks is considered a full-term pregnancy, but thirty-nine weeks is optimal. Multiples usually spend less time in utero than single babies, perhaps because there is a limit to how much the uterus can stretch before labor begins. So not only do twins have to share the available nutrients during gestation, they also have less time, on average, to develop.

Because true prematurity and low birth weight (below five and a half pounds) are considered such strong predictors of health problems, the key during a multiple pregnancy is to keep the babies from being born too early. Every additional day is precious, as is every additional ounce of weight.

DIET

"Before we found out I was having twins, my obstetrician kept scolding me for gaining so much weight," one mother told me. "I was ravenously hungry all the time and was eating constantly just to keep going. By the fifth month, I was getting so huge that he did an ultrasound test to determine the due date, thinking I must have gotten the conception date wrong. When he saw I was having twins, he decided I wasn't overeating after all."

This mother's babies were born at thirty-nine weeks, weighed over six pounds each, and were in excellent health. She gained nearly sixty pounds (and lost it naturally as she breastfed her twins). She heeded her body's signals to eat lots of good food.

Inadequate nutrition is believed to be a leading cause of premature birth and low birth weight in multiples. Until recently, physicians advised limits on prenatal weight gain, including twin pregnancy. Yet some studies have indicated that when women were encouraged to eat well and not limit weight gain, they—like this mother—have healthy, full-term babies in nearly every case.

One study found that when women were either underweight or of average weight before they became pregnant, the amount of weight they gained correlated clearly with the outcome; in other words, the more weight they gained, the bigger and closer to term the babies were. That relationship was less clear for women who were overweight before they conceived.

The latest guidelines, which were published in the newsletter of the American Dietetics Association, recommend that underweight women expecting twins gain forty to fifty pounds, women of average weight gain thirty-five to forty-five pounds, and overweight women gain twenty-five to thirty-five pounds.

Recommendations for triplets are fifty to sixty pounds for underweight women, forty-five to fifty-five pounds for women of average weight, and thirty-five to forty-five pounds for heavy women.

Weight gain is so important to successful multiple pregnancy that it can't wait—it has to occur early in a pregnancy that may not go to term. So it's important to eat well from the beginning, even if you find your appetite isn't very good.

Of course, that weight gain needs to be the result of a diet rich in essential nutrients. You can expect to double your intake of protein, to between 120 and 150 grams daily, and to increase your intake of carbohydrates and fats proportionately. The normal protein recommendation for a single pregnancy is 60 grams daily. A Canadian study recommends mothers increase daily protein intake by 50 grams per infant. A registered dietician can give you invaluable assistance in planning a personal menu to meet your particular needs, built around your food preferences.

As your pregnancy progresses, you may feel less able to shop for and cook complicated meals. At the same time, you'll find it harder to eat more than a small amount at a time. You can still fulfill your dietary needs with frequent small meals.

Soups, like vegetable, lentil, and split pea, are nutritious and convenient. You can make up a blender full of a high-protein milk shake and keep it in the refrigerator. You can snack throughout the day on foods prepared ahead of time: vegetables and fruits, nuts, hard-boiled eggs, cheese cubes, tofu, yogurt, and hummus.

When I was pregnant with my twins, my obstetrician's nurse told me I was gaining weight too fast and instructed me to stop drinking milk. When I told my husband about this advice, he handed me a quart of milk, which I drank then and there, straight from the carton. Clearly, my body knew better than the nurse what it needed.

Women who are expecting twins have an enormous need for nutrients. They are hungry, and for good reason.

REST AND BED REST

"I am five months pregnant with twins. My doctor says that in another month I should quit working and then be on total bed rest until delivery. How can I take care of my two-year-old and my house if I'm in bed for two or three months? Is this really necessary?"

The jury is still out on the benefits of ordering pregnant women to remain in bed for long periods. The reasoning is that activity, especially walking and lifting, puts downward pressure on the cervix and makes it more difficult for the multiple pregnancy to continue to term.

For women with strong risk factors for premature birth, bed rest can add weeks to the babies' gestation. However, it may not be necessary in *all* multiple births; recent research has produced conflicting conclusions.

Certainly reduced activity and plenty of real rest is essential, but being restricted to bed may not be. The woman quoted above needs a clear explanation for why her doctor ordered strict bed rest. Perhaps her medical history or the particulars of her pregnancy lead to this recommendation. If you are told bed rest is necessary for you, be sure to get a complete explanation of the justification and understand exactly what you can and cannot do.

The term *bed rest* really describes a range of limitations. The mildest form is what might be called "house arrest"—staying home, but with normal freedom of movement. More commonly, a pregnant woman is confined to her own bed. She may be able to sit up in bed, or she may have to remain flat on her back. She may be permitted to get up to use the bathroom, or she may need to use a bedpan. The most severe form is hospitalization, perhaps with an IV for continuous delivery of labor-suppressing medications.

Whatever the reasons, however, if bed rest is recommended and warranted, mothers face a logistical problem. The family will need to review the support plans they've made. It may be necessary to call in some of that volunteer help ahead of time, or use some of the budget to hire someone now.

Bed rest can be hard on the family, on the mother's general health if her body loses muscular tone, and on her emotional well-being. If you are forced into inactivity, you will feel like a human incubator, stuck in one place as your mind roams restlessly, thinking about all the things that need to be done. You may worry about using up your maternity leave before the babies even arrive.

Your partner, and other family and friends, may or may not be supportive. It's important for them to validate what you're doing and not imply that you're slacking off.

Here are some suggestions to make things easier:

- It will ease your mind if your supporters can handle some of the tasks that you know need doing.
- With your medical team's approval, do isometrics or mild exercises that can keep your muscles reasonably strong.
- Meditate. Think positive thoughts about what your quiet body is doing for your babies' well-being. Visualize them growing stronger every day.
- Make an effort to avoid topics that stimulate worries. Let your partner read about pregnancy risks and distill the information for you. This is not the time to dwell on Aunt Gertrude's stories about her neighbor's disabled twins.
- Find an activity that feels productive. Try some needlework, quilting, or sewing for the babies—anything you can do in bed. If you have older children, involve them—sharing an activity will boost everyone's spirits.
- Write in a journal. If you begin now, while you have time, you can add to the journal as your babies grow. After they arrive, you'll be busy, but you can grab a moment from time to time to capture a wonderful memory. You can also use the journal to record your bad days, too. Later you'll be able to put them into perspective.
- Catch up on your reading.
- Network with someone else on bed rest, by either telephone, mail, or e-mail (if you can fit in front of the computer).

Although it's hard to appreciate at the time, there is a benefit to home bed rest, especially if there are older siblings. This period gradually moves the mother off the center of the domestic stage, allowing the family to get accustomed to doing more without her. That softens the impact of her immersion in baby care when the babies arrive.

PRENATAL EXERCISE

Whether you are officially on bed rest or not, you will benefit from keeping your body as fit as possible during your pregnancy. As your pregnancy progresses, the strain on your abdominal muscles and on your pelvic floor will increase. You will be less able to move easily, so your large muscles will become less toned.

But the more fit you are during your pregnancy, the healthier you will be and the sooner you will regain your prepregnancy condition after the birth. If you were active before you became pregnant, you may be able to continue some form of exercise. But whatever you do, it's essential to consult with your medical team about what exercise program is appropriate for you during your pregnancy. Multiple pregnancy is not the time to strain your body with a grueling workout routine. You will feel tired, which means your body is telling you to rest.

Gentle exercises you can do while resting in bed can help. Kegel exercises can tone the pelvic floor. Two excellent sources of information on exercise for multiple pregnancy are Elizabeth Noble's *Having Twins* and *Essential Exercises for the Childbearing Year.*

Finally, remember to be mindful of your posture. The increasing weight of your abdomen will put a strain on your back. Stand with your neck straight and your chin in, so that your body lines up straight. Pull your shoulders back and contract your abdomen. Tuck your buttocks under, and tilt your pelvis back.

RECOGNIZING AND PREVENTING
EARLY LABOR

When you are pregnant with twins, your goal is to get as close as you can to full-term pregnancy. A full term for twins, however, is typically two or three weeks less than for single babies.

This means that every additional week your pregnancy continues brings an enormous advantage to your babies. It makes a difference not only in their likelihood of survival, but in their chances of being born healthy.

Even if bed rest is not recommended in your case, it is advisable to rest as much as you can and reduce strenuous activity, especially after twenty weeks. Resting at least three times a day for one hour on your left side is recommended (resting on the left side eases blood circulation). Drink plenty of water all day long. Don't let yourself get thirsty. Try to avoid long commutes, heavy work, or moving to another residence during this time.

It's obviously also important that you know the symptoms of early labor and be ready to seek medical attention immediately if you experience them. I've spoken with women who delivered premature twins after ignoring contractions that they considered "false labor." Why didn't they call their obstetrician? "Oh, I didn't think they were serious," they say. Or "I know what labor pains feel like, and these didn't feel like labor pains."

It's important to be aware that you can have major contractions without pain, and that you must call for medical advice if you experience any contractions. It's essential to have instructions in self-monitoring from your doctor, and to be sure you understand those instructions.

The following are warning signs that premature labor may be beginning. If you experience any of them, you should lie down and place your hand on your lower abdomen to feel for hardening of the uterus, which means that it is contracting. Then call your doctor.

- Dull, low backache
- Menstrual-like cramps
- Pelvic pressure
- Abdominal cramping, with or without diarrhea
- Possible contractions
- "Feeling bad"

The following symptoms are danger signs indicating premature labor. You should go to the hospital emergency or admitting room immediately if you experience them.

- Water leaking or gushing from the vagina
- Bleeding from the vagina
- Contractions that come every ten minutes or less for one hour.

When your medical team diagnoses signs of early labor, they may admit you to the hospital or treat you as an outpatient. Following are techniques for monitoring or treating preterm labor.

- External monitoring, using a device you can wear at home, allows you to collect data on your contractions and call them in to your physician.
- Intravenous or oral medications, such as ritodrine or terbutaline, help suppress labor.
- Subcutaneous pump therapy administers those drugs more effectively and can be used at home.

ABOUT CHILDBIRTH CLASSES

Because of the likelihood of bed rest or early delivery, it's a good idea to sign up for childbirth preparation classes early.

Try to attend the classes during the fourth to sixth month (rather than the seventh, as would be typical in a single pregnancy). Ask for a class that's specifically for multiple births. If none is offered locally, ask if the closest teaching hospital has one. But even a general birthing class is better than none.

Because you may well deliver early, be sure your class includes a visit to the neonatal intensive care nursery.

LEARNING YOUR MULTIPLES' ZYGOSITY

There are many reasons why it's beneficial to you and your multiples to know their zygosity—whether they are monozygotic, dizygotic, or (in higher-order multiples) some combination of the two. I believe that it is their right to know as much about themselves as they can, and we discuss that aspect in Chapter Eight. But there are health benefits as well.

Monozygotic twins are perfect organ and blood donors for each other. This information can be life-saving in a medical emergency. Also, parents who understand that their monozygotic twins are likely to have similar developmental patterns will be alerted to possible problems when one twin lags behind the other. And the appearance of a serious illness in a monozygotic twin may be an early warning, allowing preventive treatment for the other to reduce that child's risks.

DIAGNOSIS BEFORE BIRTH

Using ultrasound, it is possible to learn whether the twins have one or two placentas during the first few months of pregnancy. If there are two placentas, they may be monozygotic or dizygotic. If there is only one, they are monozygotic and should be monitored closely for the risks and difficulties we discussed in Chapter One. Unfortunately, this is not yet the standard of care for twin pregnancies. Make sure that your doctor is aware of the importance of screening for a shared placenta. Advances in medical management of twin pregnancy are reducing the risks of twin-to-twin transfusion syndrome and other risks. If you learn that your babies share a placenta, you can contact the Twin-to-Twin Transfusion Syndrome Foundation for more information about current treatments.

DIAGNOSIS AFTER BIRTH

You may not know your babies' zygosity before they are born. There are several methods that can be used to make this determination after birth:

- *Inspection of the placenta(s).* The old practice of simply counting the number of placentas after birth to determine zygosity has been discredited. However, careful inspection by a trained pathologist can determine the zygosity with a fair degree of accuracy for some but not all cases.
- *Visual.* When same-sex infants have a strong resemblance at birth, it is tempting to assume they are monozygotic. But appearances are not an accurate gauge at this stage. Dizygotic multiples are more likely to have similar birth weights than monozygotic multiples. Since differences in birth weight have a tremendous impact on the appearances of the newborns, it is possible for newborn dizygotic multiples to look more similar than they will in a few months and for monozygotic multiples to look less similar than they eventually will.
- *Blood typing.* With a degree of accuracy of about 97 percent, comparison of blood factors was the most accurate test of zygosity available until the development of DNA sampling.
- *DNA fingerprinting.* This is the most recently developed technique for determining zygosity. It compares DNA sequences—the genetic makeup of twins. It is 99 percent accurate when performed correctly, and as the technique is refined, scientists expect it to become 100

percent reliable. This method is less invasive and more affordable than blood typing; it relies on analysis of cell tissue swabbed from the inside of the cheek.

AFTER YOUR BABIES
ARE BORN

Whether you have had your babies vaginally or by cesarean section, you will be somewhat uncomfortable after the birth. Your physical discomfort will be similar to that experienced with a single birth—it is temporary and usually improves with each passing day.

On the positive side, you are going to feel much lighter after your multiples are born. If your babies are full-term, you are likely to be carrying at least eleven or twelve pounds of baby, plus the weight of their placentas. After delivery, the release in pressure on your organs and joints can be a great relief.

But you still have a body that has been strained under the demands of a multiple pregnancy. Often the muscles along the midline of the abdomen separate, or become "unzipped." Usually the separation can be corrected with postpartum exercise. However, unless your babies are very small, your abdomen has likely been stretched a great deal more than it would have been with one baby. This can be distressing for some women. "I felt like the Goodyear blimp deflating"—that was one mother's reaction after her twins were born. Some women who are unable to lose their "twin belly" may consider "tummy tuck" surgery.

Whether or not you regain your girlish figure, you will benefit from regaining fitness as soon as you can after the birth of your twins. Raising twins is hard work, and you need a strong, healthy body to manage.

CHAPTER FIVE

SMALL WONDERS

PREMATURE MULTIPLES

In Chapter Four, we talked about the steps you can take to reduce the chances that your twins will be born premature: good prenatal care, adequate nourishment and rest, and understanding of the signs of premature labor.

In this chapter, we'll take a closer look at *why* it's so important for your babies to be born as close to term as possible. The more fully developed babies are when they leave the womb, the better their chances for good health. Every additional day can make a difference.

An average gestation for a single is about forty weeks, and most weigh between six and eight pounds at birth. Babies born before thirty-seven weeks are considered preterm, or premature; those who weigh less than five and a half pounds are considered low birth weight (and are usually premature as well).

The picture changes with multiple birth. The rate of prematurity for all babies born in the United States is about 11 percent, and their rate of low birth weight is 7 percent. For twins, the rates of prematurity and low birth weight rise to about 50 percent. Thereafter, the likelihood of early birth and low birth weight increases with the number of babies. With triplets, both rates are 90 percent. And for quadruplets and higher, they are 100 percent.

This figure is really quite astounding—it means that at least half of twins and other multiples are born early, and that completely redefines what's "average" or "typical." Clearly, preparation for premature birth and an understanding of its implications are essential for parents expecting more than one baby. That's because preterm birth and low birth weight bring a significantly higher risk of health problems and disability.

If the bad news is the rate of prematurity and small size among multiples, then the good news is that being born somewhat small and somewhat early as a result of a multiple gestation is not as bad as being born premature for other reasons.

For example, a single baby may be premature because of poor maternal nutrition, toxemia, or other complications of pregnancy. While these factors can occur in twin pregnancies, too, it's more common for twins to be born small after a healthy prenatal period. They're small because they're crowded in the womb, and the uterus has reached its carrying capacity.

KEEPING YOUR SPIRITS UP

Let's look on the bright side. Suppose you've had an uneventful pregnancy carefully monitored by your medical team. You've been eating and resting well and gained plenty of weight. Suddenly, at thirty-seven weeks, you go into labor, and your babies are born weighing five pounds each. Technically, those babies are premature—but they've probably had a better start than a single baby born that size and that early.

In fact, recent research has shown that multiple babies have a survival advantage during the second trimester. During this period, they mature more quickly than single babies— a blessing, since they may miss the final month or months of gestation.

Prematurity is still a risk factor for your babies, but the

prognosis for small babies has improved incredibly over the past few decades. For example, respiratory distress syndrome used to be fatal for 70 percent of its victims. Now that rate is 15 percent or less.

If your babies are premature, they may not need any unusual treatment beyond observation in the well-baby nursery, where they will gain weight. However, it's important to be prepared for the challenge. Prematurity can be serious indeed, so we must devote this chapter to its causes and prevention, what it can mean for the babies' future, and what families experience when their babies arrive so small.

LOW BIRTH WEIGHT AND HEALTH OUTCOMES

In one study, the best outcomes for multiple babies (defined as survival beyond the first year of life) occurred when they were born between thirty-seven and thirty-nine weeks (black babies did best at thirty-seven to thirty-eight weeks, whites at thirty-nine).

All things being equal, the higher the weight, the better the prognosis. Preterm babies who weigh more than 1,500 grams (three pounds, five ounces) have about an 85 percent chance of survival, and 75 percent of those have no disability.

The very tiniest babies—those between about one and two pounds—have only a 50 percent chance of survival, with a 25 percent chance of a chronic medical problem or disability among those who survive. Survival rates rise with weight; more than 98 percent of babies weighing between two and a half and five and a half pounds survive.

These numbers are changing as a result of rapid progress in this field, so the prognosis for your tiny twins may be better. But it should be clear that the longer they remain in utero, the better.

WHAT PARENTS OF
PREMATURE MULTIPLES FEEL

Those tiny babies aren't the only ones who feel fragile and vulnerable at a time like this. Mothers, fathers, and the entire family can feel a sense of shock, fear, anxiety, and guilt. As we've discussed before in this book, these feelings are natural and are best acknowledged and prepared for.

Parents who have had premature babies, whether or not the babies are multiples, will tell you that the experience takes a huge emotional toll. You, as the mother, are recovering physically and hormonally from the stress of birth and from the long months of strain on your body. You may have been confined to bed and be even less fit as a result. The babies' father feels helpless and worried about the well-being of his infants and of his wife. You may leave the hospital empty-armed, or with only one of the babies.

Clearly, you need support at this time. And one of the best supports, as our parents of premature multiples have told us, is information, knowledge, and encouragement.

If at all possible, expectant parents of multiples should consider visiting the intensive care nursery to see what these tiny babies look like and learn something about the treatment and procedures and equipment. Your babies may never need to be there, but it is helpful to visit ahead of time in case they do. It's also helpful to see babies in the regular nursery who have been transferred there from the neonatal intensive care unit (NICU).

You also need to know what to expect as your premature multiples grow. You'll need specific information from the pediatrician and the nursing staff about the babies' prognoses, about the procedures that are recommended, and about what you can expect.

Often premature babies may need only a few more days or weeks in the temperature-controlled setting of the NICU so that the biological systems that regulate body temperature, regulate breathing, and allow a baby to learn to feed orally can develop a bit more. The prognosis for such babies may be very good indeed.

Here are some typical reactions of parents:

- *Guilt.* "I felt that I'd done this to them—that I'd brought it on. And that I was hurting them more by allowing all those procedures to be done."

  "I racked my brain for all the things I hadn't done, or should have done, during my pregnancy. I got out of bed too much during the last month. I fixed up my older daughter's room instead of resting."

  Parents may feel uncomfortable with their own ambivalent feelings about fragile babies. Sometimes there's no immediate feeling of bonding. Sometimes the babies seem so frail, and their prognosis is so uncertain, that parents wonder if it would be more merciful if they didn't live, and that uncomfortable thought is usually followed by deeper guilt.
- *Anger.* "I felt mad at myself, mad at the staff for hurting the babies, mad at God."
- *Numbness.* "I couldn't bond, couldn't let myself care about them—they didn't seem like my babies."
- *Sorrow.* About neglecting an older child, or neglecting the healthier multiple in favor of the more fragile baby.

WHAT TO DO ABOUT THOSE FEELINGS

Don't wait to name the babies. Some parents find it hard to "commit" to such sick infants, fearing the worst. But you'll become attached more easily, and the babies will do better, when you speak to them lovingly by name.

Know that this bundle of difficult emotions is natural. Your normal trajectory of new-parent emotions has been disrupted by an early birth, and the bonding process is going to be different from what you would have experienced with full-term babies. Your feelings will settle eventually. You will love and delight in your babies soon. If there are setbacks and difficulties, you will face those as they come, and you will survive them.

Find a supportive listener with whom you can share your hopes and fears. This may be your partner, but you may also want to vent outside the family as well. "With my prior delivery, I 'held' my anxiety and didn't acknowledge it and went into depression," said one mother of premature twins who has two older children. "This time I talked to my family about my anxious feelings. I felt that it was okay to have them. And that kept me from going into depression this time."

Try to support your partner. Often it seems that the mother is worried about the babies and the father is worried about the mother—but it's not that the father isn't worried about the babies, too. The father may ask the mother to "lighten up" because he's worried about her. But the mother thinks, "If I lighten up, then no one will worry about the babies—and my concern is the only thing keeping them alive."

It's best for whoever is feeling stronger—mother or father—to try to promote the mental health of the other. For example, a concerned father can say to his wife, "What do you need, and when do you need it?" She might say, "I need to spend a full, uninterrupted day with the babies at the hospital nursery." A husband might answer the same question this way: "I need to know that you're going to survive this, that you're going to be around and alive when these kids grow up. I need to see you eat something and get some rest."

Avoid, if possible, insensitive people who make you feel worse. "I told you that you should have quit smoking," a relative might say, or "If only you'd quit work sooner." Certainly you wouldn't seek out the company of people who say upsetting things. However, it may be your father or your sister who says such a thing, and you can't afford to turn away from them when you need them so much.

Therefore, it's best to put these comments in perspective and try not to take them personally. Often they arise from the pain or worry our loved ones are feeling; what they're really saying is, "I didn't want this to happen."

Do what makes you feel better. One mother despaired of trying to pump her breasts when she was so weak and it was so difficult to transport the milk to the hospital. For another mother, however, this was just what she needed. "Pumping breast milk was part of the coping I did, a way not to get anxious," she says. "I told myself they were getting what they needed."

If the babies are in the hospital and you are home, take some time to get away from it all—go out to dinner with your spouse, exercise, go to a museum, take a bubble bath, read a novel. Many parents feel guilty about doing anything pleasurable during this critical time, but in the long run it will help you care for your babies. For the next few years you will seldom have time for a quiet evening in a restaurant. Doing so now is a valid use of your time as you wait for the babies to grow.

LOGISTICAL PROBLEMS

Life becomes complicated when multiple babies are hospitalized. It may be necessary for them to be in two different hospitals. Consider what family life is like when the mother, who is herself recovering from the stress of pregnancy and birth, must travel to two hospitals daily to visit and perhaps deliver breast milk. She may also have other children who need her at home.

One mother went into early labor with her twins when her husband was already hospitalized, undergoing surgery. She was taken to a second hospital, and her babies were transferred to a third.

For mothers who had hoped to breastfeed, there is the

sudden crisis of how to develop and maintain a supply of milk for babies who may not yet be able to take it. Just a few decades ago, the idea of breast milk for premature multiples (not to mention breastfeeding for any multiples) was almost unheard of. Formula could be measured and sterilized, could be administered whether the mother was present or not, and was thought to help babies gain weight faster.

Yet today mother's milk is recognized as beneficial for premature babies for several reasons. Breast milk varies, both in quantity and in composition, according to the growth needs of the babies being fed. When your babies are born early, you do produce milk—but it is a particular kind of milk that's made to meet the needs of premature babies. And even if your babies can't suck, it's advisable to pump your breasts to maintain your supply for when the babies are older, and to build a supply of milk to give them as soon as they can take it. Even before they can suck, tiny babies can be fed mother's milk through gavage feeding—a small tube through the nose or mouth that transports milk directly to the baby's stomach.

What this means logistically, however, is that you have to make frequent trips to the hospital to deliver milk, and you'll need to pump your breasts to build and maintain a supply.

One mother described the experience this way: "I was pumping my breasts at home using an electric pump, and then taking the breast milk to the hospital. They would freeze it there and use it as they needed it. When the babies came home, I would have to nurse them, then pump my breasts and give them extra milk by bottle because they couldn't nurse well. I was nursing, pumping, and giving them bottles every three hours, around the clock."

How to Make Things Easier

Invoke your support system to keep things stable in your home situation. Your helpers may watch your other children, shop, or otherwise ease your logistical burdens. But because your emotions are quite fragile, you will need to surround yourself with helpers who understand and make you feel better. Later, when the babies are out of danger, you can happily accept any willing pair of hands.

Visit the babies as often as possible, but accept that there may be days when you are exhausted and it's okay to check in by phone.

Take advantage of take-out and delivery food services shamelessly. This is not the time to economize by cooking, unless it's your favorite means of stress reduction. If you don't have other children, you and your partner can eat together in the hospital cafeteria or in a nearby restaurant.

YOUR PREMATURE MULTIPLES IN THE HOSPITAL

When babies are born too soon, the hospital must try to re-create the environment of the womb in order to allow them to complete their development. That means they must be kept warm, their breathing must be either monitored or assisted in some way, and they must be nourished in a form their immature digestive systems can handle.

MEDICAL RISKS ASSOCIATED WITH PREMATURITY

It can be frightening to consider all the complications that may arise in your premature multiples. However, it's important to recognize that most of these conditions can be corrected or treated, and often require only a period of careful monitoring. And it's better to familiarize yourself with the more common conditions.

- Neonatal jaundice—associated with immature liver function.
- Apnea of prematurity—irregular breathing.

- RDS (respiratory distress syndrome)—formerly called hyaline membrane disease.
- Bronchopulmonary displasia (BPD)—a degeneration of lung tissue as a result of prolonged treatment with oxygen or a ventilator. It means the baby may take longer to be weaned from the respirator.
- Retinopathy of prematurity—a disease of the blood vessels to the retina that can cause blindness if not treated.
- Anemia.
- Necrotizing enterocolitis—air pockets in the wall of the bowel, which can cause perforation. Surgery may be needed to repair the damaged bowel.
- Intraventricular hemorrhage—bleeding in the ventricles of the brain. Blood clots can lead to excess buildup of spinal fluid, causing complications that may require medication or surgery. Often the problem corrects itself.
- Hernia.
- PDA (patent ductus arteriosus)—failure of the ductus arteriosus to close. The ductus arteriosus is an opening just outside the heart, between the pulmonary artery and the aorta, that redirects blood to bypass the lungs during gestation. Normally at birth, blood is directed to the lungs and the ductus closes, but sometimes this doesn't happen. The problem often corrects itself; it is correctable with surgery if it doesn't.

LEARNING THE LAY OF THE LAND— AND A NEW LANGUAGE

According to their condition, your babies may be admitted to a Level II or Level III NICU. The higher level, usually at a teaching hospital, has the most sophisticated technology for the treatment of the sickest babies.

Consider giving birth at a hospital with a higher-level NICU if you know you will give birth early, or if there is some indication the babies will need an unusual level of care. Otherwise, if the babies are moved, you will not be able to be near them until you are released from the hospital.

When multiples are born premature, their conditions are usually not identical. One baby may be big enough to go home with you in a few days, while the other must stay in the hospital longer. Two or more babies may be in the neonatal intensive care unit with different medical difficulties requiring different treatments. One or more babies may, because of their conditions, have to be at another hospital. So if parents of one premature baby need to take a crash course in neonatology, parents of multiple preemies need that crash course times two, or more.

As your babies improve, they may be moved from the intensive care unit to a regular nursery. Although this transition is the mark of progress, you will have to get to know the staff and the policies all over again.

WHAT'S WHAT IN THE NICU

When you first enter the NICU, you may think you're on board the space shuttle. You're surrounded by blinking lights, wires, knobs, and monitors beeping and buzzing.

The babies may be in isolettes (formerly known as incubators). Or they may be on warming beds. If they need help with breathing, they may have—depending on the severity of their problem—an oxygen hood, a breathing tube, or a ventilator.

They may have leads, or wires, attached to machines that monitor heart rate, breathing, and blood pressure. The leads are affixed to the babies' skin with disks that look like round Band-Aids; these are stuck on with gel and don't hurt when they're removed.

The babies may be under "bili lights" for the treatment of jaundice. The light therapy breaks down accumulation of bilirubin in the bloodstream, which is sometimes necessary until the immature liver can do the job on its own. When babies are under lights, their eyes are usually covered for protection.

In the midst of all this technology, the baby often seems very small and frail. They lack subcutaneous fat, and their skin is delicate. Babies of all races may lack pigment. If they have breathing tubes or are on a ventilator, they may not be able to cry.

THE ROLE OF PARENTS IN THE NICU

How involved you can be in your babies' care may vary somewhat according to the hospital, but more and more facilities welcome and encourage parental involvement. That's an improvement from earlier days, when parents were often excluded entirely.

Probably you will be able to visit your babies and talk to them. You may be able to hold them, feed them, breastfeed them, and perhaps participate in their care (such as diapering). You can use this time to get to know them, so you'll be more comfortable when they come home. In some units you will be permitted to "kangaroo-carry" your babies—in a Snugli-type sling, with the baby's skin against yours.

For many parents, visiting the babies in the unit is painful at first. The newborns look so sick, so small, so unresponsive. Yet your visits are important on many levels. It does you good to spend time with them and to get to know them, even if you feel inadequate or even "unbonded" to some extent. And the babies need you. They've heard your voice during their time in utero, and they can respond to it now.

One mother who had serious complications during the birth of her monozygotic boys at thirty weeks wasn't able to see her babies for several days. The first time she was able to get to the nursery, her babies were in separate isolettes. "They seemed really scared," the mother recalls. "Then I spoke to them. When they heard my voice, Jared's eyes popped open."

That mother had given her babies something only she could give: her familiar voice. Your babies know their mother's voice and are soothed by it. When you visit and speak to your babies, they become more relaxed. Some parents bring audio tapes of themselves speaking, which can be played for the babies in their absence.

There is evidence that premature babies are comforted by maternal scent as well. In some hospitals you may be allowed to leave in your babies' cribs a cloth or nursing pad that has been close to your skin.

CO-BEDDING—A TWIN-SENSITIVE PRACTICE

Intensive care nurseries are, understandably, geared toward the care of individual babies—machinery, isolettes, and equipment are designed for the well-being of one tiny child. And that makes sense for a baby who has developed by itself. Yet it has also been standard practice for multiples.

We at Twin Services believe that practice should change—that premature or ill multiple newborns should be co-bedded where possible. Granted, in a small hospital there may not be sufficient staff to monitor more than one fragile baby in the same unit. But all things being equal, we favor co-bedding.

When you consider what these babies have already experienced—being thrust too early out of the soothing environment of the womb and into the noise, glare, and physical discomfort of life in the hospital—you wonder what added stress is caused by being separated for the first time from the comfort of the other baby.

There is considerable evidence that multiple infants who are co-bedded handle the stress of being hospitalized, and of all the procedures they must endure, better than those who are separated.

Hospitals vary in when, and if, they will place newborn multiples together. Some separate babies until they are free of tubes, then put them in the same open crib. Others are able to keep them together even while IVs and other equipment are attached. Some swaddle babies skin to skin in the same blanket. It's a wonderful sight to see tiny newborn twins stretching arms out and cuddling one another.

Preliminary research documents health benefits from co-bedding. It's worth asking if it can be done in your hospital.

MAKING THE MOST OF THE STAFF

You will be confronted with an array of doctors, nurses, and other staff at the hospital. Among them will be the neonatologist, the babies' attending physician, other doctors who monitor the babies when the attending physician isn't present, interns, residents, neonatal nurses, and assorted technicians and therapists.

The nurses in the unit are probably the ones you will see most, who will know your babies best, and with whom you may establish a close relationship. Neonatal nurses often love their charges with great passion. Parents sometimes feel jealous because the nurses love the babies so much and are so capable as well. It's best to view them with appreciation—they're doing their best for the babies, and will support you as well.

The nurses do vary, however, and you may find you prefer communicating with certain ones. "Some nurses were exceptionally helpful and some were not," one mother said. "Only one helped me nurse the babies at the same time. Some didn't want me to hold the babies when they were on the ventilators. When those nurses were on duty, I just put my hands on my babies and meditated."

Many parents, especially during the early fog of confusion and anxiety, find it difficult to follow the physician's explanations of their babies' condition and the recommended treatment. In order to give informed consent, you must be able to understand what the staff tells you. In any meeting, you should ask questions, take notes, write down terms, and ask the doctor to repeat anything you don't understand.

When meeting with your babies' doctors, ask if you can tape-record the discussion so you can play it back and digest the information later. If necessary, invite a friend or family member to attend the meeting and listen with you.

Finally, most hospitals have support staff who can help you with nonmedical problems. Seek help from social workers in finding financial or home help, support groups, help with lactation, or the rental of a breast pump.

YOUR PREMATURE MULTIPLES AT HOME

After the birth itself and your first view of your tiny babies, your most frightening prospect may be the idea of taking them home, where they will be your responsibility entirely. All the wires and tubes and machines that made you uneasy at first may now seem like old friends. How will your babies survive all on their own, with only you to recognize problems?

You should have a discharge plan for the babies, worked out with the staff. What monitoring will the babies need at home? What medications will they require? When should you call the doctor? What danger signs should you be on the lookout for? Will you be eligible for the services of a visiting nurse or public health nurse?

CARING FOR PREMATURE BABIES AT HOME

"We hadn't been sure if both our babies would be ready to go home at the same time. Then, all of a sudden, we found out they could both come home on the same day. They had been in the hospital for five weeks, and to have them back in my arms was just what I was waiting for, after all we'd been through."

Along with the joy of having them home is the "twin-shock" of caring for your babies on your own—and the stress is greater when they are premature.

A mother of premature boys who were born two months

early recalls, "Premature babies are not very responsive, so you give, give, give, give, and it's about four months before you get anything back. I think all the bonding that goes on with a new baby doesn't happen with a premature baby. It's probably delayed with twins anyway, so I think it's just that much harder work you're putting out for a little reward at first." This mother's experience is common. You need to have faith that the efforts are benefiting your babies, and that your relationship will blossom in good time.

But it's not easy. Newborn babies cry a great deal, and twins will of course cry twice as much. Also, premature babies have a different cry than full-term newborns. It has a higher pitch, and many parents find it more irritating. If you know this in advance, you can override your reactions and be able to tend to your twins lovingly. Their cries will mature in time.

The babies need to be fed very frequently. You may feel you are feeding almost constantly. You may have brought them home with apnea monitors that record their rate of respiration and sound an alarm if it is inadequate. Even when everyone is sleeping, you may be awakened—and upset—by warning buzzers.

It's important to get enough help at the beginning. As one father recalls, "Against better advice, we didn't get enough help. In retrospect, I would have done whatever I could to get help that wouldn't have cost a lot, to give us a break. And I wouldn't have been so reluctant to ask friends to help. The exhaustion of caring for preemie twins is cumulative. If you can stop it from happening, you'll feel better and everything will be better."

HELPING SIBLINGS ADJUST TO THE EARLY ARRIVALS

In Chapter Seven we will discuss your babies' homecoming and how your other children may respond. But when your babies are premature and cannot come home right away, their absence can be more difficult for your older children than the later adjustment when they settle in at home.

Part of the reason for the difficulty is that the parents are often not at home because they are visiting the babies. Older children may be able to go to the hospital, too, but they are more likely to be at home in the care of other family members, missing Mommy and Daddy.

And when the parents are at home, they may be too preoccupied, sad, or tired to relax with the other children.

Some suggestions for easing the sibling adjustment:

- For toddlers and preschool-age children, talk about the babies. Describe them and explain that they're too little to come home right now.
- If your children are able to visit the babies, do take them. Remember how disturbing the NICU and the sick babies looked to you the first time you saw them, and prepare your children. They may worry that the babies can't breathe in those "boxes," or that the wires and tubes hurt. They wonder if the disks sting like Band-Aids when they're removed. Try to explain the technology in a reassuring way, emphasizing what it does for the babies: "The isolettes keep them warm, and give them fresh air to breathe. The tubes give them milk, and the wires tell the nurses when they need something."
- Give young children teddy bears or dolls they can care for as though they were babies. You can talk about the equipment that the real babies are using in the hospital to get better—the isolette, the wires. You might even get them plastic boxes for the bears to sleep in.
- Older children may worry more about the well-being of the babies. Talk to them about what's going on. For some siblings, expressing their worries through drawings is helpful. You might encourage them to make a picture

for the babies. Or children can tape-record a song or story that can be played for them. These activities do more than keep the older children occupied. They underscore that you are still a family, everyone has a part to play, and everyone needs a chance to be heard and understood.

CHAPTER SIX

PRACTICAL MATTERS

SETTLING IN WITH YOUR TWINS

"We had no idea what tired was until the babies came home."

For all parents of multiples, there is that moment when the reality of a houseful of newborns hits home with astounding force—such force that we at Twin Services call it "twinshock."

In this chapter we'll discuss the practical aspects of that reality—what to expect; how to feed, bathe, clothe, and change so many babies; how to keep your home and baby supplies organized (somewhat); and how to get through the day and even get a little sleep during the night.

There is a wealth of excellent information about infant care available today (see Resources). And though most of that material is oriented to single babies, the essentials of bathing, diapering, and mixing formula are the same for all babies, whether they arrive one at a time or in groups.

How to apply the basics of infant care to a multiple situation is a different matter entirely. It's not just that everything takes twice as long (or three times, or four). Some things are humanly impossible if you apply all the standard rules and then double or triple them.

Why? Do the math!

If the new mother of a week-old infant nurses her baby ten times in twenty-four hours, and each feeding (along with diaper changes) takes up to one hour, she will spend nearly ten hours per day in feedings alone. If she has twins and simply doubles the time, that's twenty hours. Triplets becomes thirty hours—a mathematical impossibility!

Clearly, caring for multiple babies is different from caring for single babies, and different from caring for several children of different ages. As one mother of triplets, who herself was one of three children, recalls, "My parents had their hands full with the three of us, but not the way I have my hands full with my triplets. Because my brothers weren't the same age, we didn't all need the same things at the same time."

What you need is a system, and that's what this chapter is about.

This is the time to activate your support system—to bring in your troops of family, friends, neighbors, or hired people who will help you manage.

CRIBS, CRIBS EVERYWHERE: ORGANIZING YOUR HOME

Some of this, of course, you will have arranged before your babies arrive. You've probably mapped out the basic elements, such as who will sleep in what room and where you'll keep the babies' things.

You will have done some of your shopping for equipment and clothing. You will have borrowed what you can, if that is your preference, and you'll have scoped out suppliers for secondhand or low-priced clothing. And you will have decided how you'll handle diapers, balancing the costs and convenience of cloth diapers, disposables, or a diaper service. You may want to consider the environmental impact of disposables, and your capacity to handle the burden of laundering diapers as you make this decision.

Following are some suggestions for structuring your physical environment to make multiple care easier.

- For most families, having the twins sleep in the same room is easiest. At first you may want them in your room, so you can feed and comfort them easily during the night.

- Although each baby should eventually have a designated crib, twins often do well in the same crib when they are small. (That may not be possible for triplets and more.) They are used to being physically close, and they usually find it soothing to be able to touch each other.

- The crib is the site of the highest incidence of accidental infant death. Make sure your crib meets current federal guidelines for safety. For example, crib slats should be no farther apart than 2⅜ inches.

- If you do start out with one crib, it's a good idea to have a bassinet as well, for times when you want to separate the babies for some reason.

- If the babies have to share a room with an older sibling, make sure that the older child has a clearly defined part of the space. That's the easy part. It's the nightly sleep disruption that is much harder to cope with. At first our seven-year-old daughter felt privileged to have the babies in her room. But after a few wild nights she begged us for relief, and we moved their crib into our room. We all gained. The nightly kerfuffle was more contained; I could respond to their first whimpers for feeding, so it kept the noise level down; and because I didn't have to go very far to scoop them up to breastfeed, I could stay half asleep during the process.

- Consider more than one diaper-changing area. Have a basic changing table and supplies arranged in the babies' room, and another area set up in the living room, play area, or wherever you and the babies spend most of the daytime hours.

The amount of equipment and the number of changing stations you will need depend on the size and layout of your apartment or house. In a large home you may want to put a crib with changing supplies on each floor or at each end of the house for the first few months, so that you can keep the babies near you. In smaller quarters, you may find you can manage well by using a double stroller for daytime care inside while they are small. They can sleep in the stroller and be wheeled from room to room.

• Put the baby clothes and other necessities where they're most likely to be used. There's no point in running up and down the stairs to get a change of clothes if you spend most of your time with the babies in the family room downstairs. Keep everything you'll need accessible, even if your arrangement is not conventional. You may find that an assortment of plastic laundry baskets is more useful than expensive baby furniture.

• Designate "baby-safe" areas of the house. When they are tiny, your babies may spend time on the floor, propped against pillows, or playing in a pillow fort surrounded by soft barriers. Later, when they begin to crawl, you'll need baby gates. Get a book on baby-proofing and follow its advice carefully.

• As soon as the babies come home you should have a smoke alarm in the room or rooms where the babies sleep, and "tot-finder" decals on windows.

• Designate an adults-only area, if you have room. One mother of preschool quadruplets who is fortunate enough to live in a large house has one room (the family room) that is given over entirely to baby needs, with nothing breakable, a handy changing area, and thick carpeting. She has another room—the living room—that's designated as a "no-toy zone." It's a refuge—the one part of the house, and her life, that does not revolve around the children.

SO MANY BOOTIES, SO LITTLE TIME

Parents who are expecting twins often wonder how much clothing they'll need for multiple babies. The following is a basic layette for newborn multiples, in quantities needed per baby. Clothing size will depend on the babies' birth weights.

Remember also that your standards for dress and household tidiness may have to loosen up a bit during this difficult year. If your babies are warm and cozy and reasonably clean, you're doing fine. Don't waste your time folding laundry, for example. Once again, those plastic laundry baskets may be all the storage you need for clean baby clothes. The key in clothing is to do what works—don't make things harder by trying to overorganize the babies' clothes or supplies.

BASIC LAYETTE FOR EACH NEWBORN MULTIPLE

Clothing
Five or six T-shirts or "onesies" (snap-crotch T-shirts that cover the diaper and make the babies look more "dressed")
Three or four one-piece outfits or stretch suits
Two pairs of socks
One pair of booties
One sleeping bag with hood, or blanket sleeper, if your climate warrants
One sweater or jacket
Four to six pairs of waterproof pants, if using cloth diapers
Three or four receiving blankets

Bedding
Several crib sheets
A moisture-proof mattress pad
One crib blanket
A crib bumper

Bath and Grooming
You'll also need basic bath and cleaning supplies,
    including:
Mild soap
Petroleum jelly
A plastic bathtub (although many parents prefer the
    kitchen sink for baby baths)
Baby thermometer
Blunt scissors or clippers designed for safely trimming all
    those tiny nails
A dozen cloth diapers for general mopping and blotting
Disposable diapers as needed, or cloth diapers from a
    service (consult with diaper service for quantities)

SO MANY MOUTHS TO FEED!

Some of my fondest memories of the infancy of my twins are of
the nursing sessions we shared in the still house at four A.M.
Comatose though I was, as I held them close and listened to
the tiny, rhythmic swallowing noises they made, everything
seemed right. That's not to say it is always peaceful and easy,
but breastfeeding has so many benefits for all of you that it's
very much worth the effort to get going.

As we discussed in Chapter Three, one of the unfortunate
myths about multiples is that mothers can't breastfeed them. And
it's a myth that has persisted even in the medical community—as
though twins throughout history were fed on Similac.

One mother who'd had a difficult labor and delivered her
twins by C-section recalls a recovery room nurse telling her,
"It's too bad you won't be able to breastfeed."

"I just burst into tears," she recalls. "Nothing about this pregnancy and birth had gone as expected, and I was devastated to think I couldn't even nurse my babies."

Fortunately, this woman sought out support and information from Twin Services and was able to nurse her twins. But her story is not at all uncommon.

The idea that you must feed multiple babies formula is a misfortune, because they are often born small and are in particular need of a good head start. They need all the benefits they can get, and breast milk is by far the best food for newborns.

It's understandable, however, that people can be persuaded not to try. Just as twins themselves are most in need of the best nourishment possible, so the mothers of newborn multiples are in need of all the help and rest they can get. To some, breastfeeding seems like an impossible extra strain on an already stressed new mother. To some extent, this attitude is a consequence of myths about breastfeeding and ignorance about lactation. In particular, medical professionals and mothers alike are concerned that the mother cannot possibly make enough milk for more than one baby.

But your body can and will produce enough milk for your babies. In addition, breastfeeding is beneficial for you, the mother. It causes the uterus to contract, helping your body return to its prepregnancy condition more quickly. And the close physical contact involved in nursing promotes bonding between mother and babies.

There's a further benefit for the parents of multiples. Breastfeeding saves the time and energy that's so precious during these early months. Consider how much work it is to prepare a bottle, hold the bottle for the baby, wash the bottle, shop for the formula, and so on. Then you multiply that by the number of feedings per day an infant needs, and multiply again by the number of infants. . . .

Now, having said that, this does not mean that if you are unable to breastfeed, or have missed your chance, you should feel guilty about using formula. Sometimes a difficult delivery, the mother's own fragile health, or other problems make breastfeeding infeasible. If that is the case, remember that the most important thing for the babies' well-being is a healthy mother. You may feel bad, but be reassured that millions of babies have grown up healthy on formula.

Even though breastfeeding may seem like a solo act on the part of Mom, it is truly a team effort. You will need the support of your partner and your network of friends and relatives. Even if you are home and your partner works, his active involvement when he is home will make your efforts to breastfeed the babies much more successful. He can bring the babies, soothe them, and change them, along with his other contributions to the running of the household.

You'll need the support of family and friends even more if you have triplets or more. It's not easy, but it can be done with enough helping hands. If you can find a mother who has successfully nursed triplets, it would be helpful to establish contact with her before your babies arrive.

Finding out everything you can about breastfeeding ahead of the birth will help both of you build the confidence to start and persist through the awkward start-up phase until it all seems natural—and it will. There are excellent books on breastfeeding. There are also breastfeeding support organizations that can give you practical advice and encouragement when you need it. Many hospitals and community clinics offer the services of a lactation consultant. Find out about what community resources are available ahead of the birth so you will be able to find them when you need them (see Resources).

GETTING STARTED

Learning to breastfeed is a little like trying to ride a bicycle built for two—with twins, make that three! You keep trying until it all begins to click. If these are your first babies, you may want to nurse them one at a time until you master the basic skills. The nursing staff, your midwife, or a lactation consultant can show you how to position the baby and help him or her latch on to your breast correctly. The baby's mouth should cover about an inch of the areola around your nipple. You can help the baby readjust the position by inserting your finger into the corner of the baby's mouth to break the suction.

After the first week or so, the babies will have caught on to the correct mouth position and you will be getting a feel for how to help them. Now you can try feeding two together, if you haven't already. All it takes is pillows to help support their bodies and a little help from someone who can bring you the babies and help you to get them settled. Once you and the babies are more experienced at the process, you will be able to settle in for a double feed all by yourself.

If you have already breastfed older children, you have the tremendous advantage of experience. If these are your first babies, however, you'll benefit from the support of a mother who is comfortably breastfeeding multiples together. Ask your pediatrician or your local parents-of-multiples club for an intro-duction to a breastfeeding family. Ask if you can visit during a feeding. In exchange for their demonstration, you can offer to give a hand with the babies or some household chore. It will be time well spent. You will come away with a much clearer pic-ture of how to manage.

When the babies are very small and new to the whole process, they will need much more physical help supporting their bodies and directing their heads into position. This period passes quickly as they become accustomed to nursing and their bodies fill out so that they can support themselves.

BREASTFEEDING POSITIONS

Whether you are nursing twins, triplets in rotation, or quadru-plets in pairs of two, pillows will be your best friends. Make yourself a nursing station on your bed, on a couch, or in a big armchair. Position pillows along each side of your body to support each baby's body and another pillow across your lap to help support their heads. Or, you may want to purchase a nursing pillow, which is contoured to curve around you.

The idea is to reduce the strain on your back and to free your hands to adjust a mouth here and burp a baby there. Be sure there is a beverage for you within reach—you don't want to get dehydrated. And, believe it or not, there will be room for a picture book upside down on your lap to read to one or more of those older children while you feed the little ones.

Triplets can be nursed one or two at a time. The details will evolve as you become more adept and the babies get bigger. One mother of triplets tells about how she started breastfeeding the two who were well enough to come home, while the smallest remained in the hospital and was fed breast milk from a bottle. When he came home, she would nurse two, with the third propped in his infant seat as she steadied the bottle with her foot. She recalls with a laugh, "He bonded to my foot!"

Whether or not you use your feet, you will evolve a system that works for you and is comfortable and satisfying for all.

ARE THEY GETTING ENOUGH?

It is natural to wonder whether you are producing enough milk. There will be several clues that you are. Satisfied babies will usually be drowsy after a feed. Each will produce six to eight wet diapers per twenty-four hours.

At first each will produce loose stools three to four times a day. By six weeks or so, the number will decrease. Breastfed babies sometimes go three days between stools. As the number falls, the quantity of each rises. This is healthy as long as the stools continue to be soft.

The babies will regain their birth weights by the end of the first two weeks. They will continue to gain a little each week thereafter. Your pediatrician can give you more specific guidelines.

To keep going will mean braving the rough spots. Many mothers may develop sore nipples during the first week; the soreness usually eases on its own. It helps to check the babies' mouth positions. If the position is correct, their sucking should feel like a tug on your nipple but should not cause pain.

Another difficult period may be when the babies are having a growth spurt and want to feed more often. At these times well-meaning relatives may say, "See? I knew you couldn't make enough milk for both."

But that's not what is happening. It means the babies' need has increased, and your body will respond to the increased demand. You may be tempted to add formula feedings or to introduce solid food during these periods. Hold off as long as you can in order to build up your milk supply—at the very least, try to make it to one month without formula.

The more practice you have and the more stable your milk supply, the easier it will be to continue. However, your health comes first. If necessity drives you to add formula early on, it may not be optimal, but be comforted that some breast milk is better than no breast milk. You may find that you can manage only a morning feed and an evening feed, for example. Your milk supply will adjust to the lower volume; your babies will be getting some breast milk, and you will be giving your children the best start that you can.

Your babies' nursing styles may be similar or very different. One may have a very strong sucking reflex and another may be much less vigorous at the breast. One may want to feed frequently for short periods. Another may want fewer but longer sessions at the breast. You may be able to accommodate all of their different needs in a twenty-four hour period, but you may not get any sleep doing it. Survival requires that you streamline the feeding process as much as possible. Wear clothing that will make it easy to give a quick nursing here or there for the baby who wants a snack, but work toward combining their feedings as much as possible.

Here lies a major advantage of the simultaneous position. Your "snacker" can feed a little bit and rest in your arms, while your "deep feeder" nurses on. You will be with them both and they will both have their needs met.

There is an effective strategy for moving babies with dissimilar patterns onto the same schedule. When one wakes hungry before the other, wake the other one up for a feeding at the same time. When there are three or more babies to be fed, try to cycle them in pairs—wake the two you're going to feed, while the others sleep or wait their turns. It's practical to limit the number of babies you feed at any time to the number you can assist if one or more needs a burp or other adjustment. Although propping of bottles is best avoided (because the babies benefit from being held during feedings), there may be times when everyone is crying with hunger and propping bottles is an acceptable temporary solution. Naturally, you'll want to rotate the babies so that they all can get the breast feedings they need.

KEEPING YOUR STRENGTH UP

If you are breastfeeding your babies, you'll need the best nutrition possible—a high-quality, high-protein diet that includes at least 2,700 calories per day, and plenty of liquids. I've known mothers of multiples who were so tired during the early months that they forgot to eat or drink. You can't afford this.

Always have a thermos or water bottle at your nursing station. You can snack while breastfeeding, and certainly you should eat regularly throughout the day. The suggestions we gave earlier for eating during pregnancy can apply to your breastfeeding period as well.

A Word About Equipment: Breast Pumps, Nipples, Bottles, and Nursing Bras

If one or more of your babies has a prolonged hospital stay, or if there are times when you will want someone to be able to feed them by bottle, you will need to use an electric breast pump. (We have found that it's a good idea, even if you plan to breastfeed exclusively, to try to introduce an occasional bottle early on, before the babies are a month old, so that they will accept it later if you need to be away from them for any reason. It's especially important to help them learn to accept breast milk from a bottle if you plan to pump and store milk when you return to work.)

Manual breast pumps cost little but can be difficult to use. Some clinics and hospitals have electric breast pump loaner or rental programs. Pumps are also available from lactation consultants. The least expensive kinds are not particularly effective. It is a good idea to rent one first to try out. Then if you plan to use it for more than two weeks or so, it may be more cost effective to buy one.

A tip about freezing breast milk: Babies don't always finish their bottles. To avoid losing precious breast milk that way, freeze your pumped breast milk in small quantities so that you can defrost what you need for a particular feeding with minimal waste.

To help the babies adjust to taking the breast milk by bottle, test a variety of the bottle nipples available until you find the one(s) that are just right for them. It's amazing what a difference the right nipple can make!

If you are bottle-feeding, or expressing and storing milk, you can start out with eight four-ounce bottles and four eight-ounce bottles per baby.

If you are breastfeeding, you will need several nursing bras. It's difficult to predict your size until you get established, so start out just with one or two. You may also need disposable liners for the bras.

WILL I EVER GET A GOOD NIGHT'S SLEEP?

Probably the hardest thing about settling in with your newborn twins is the matter of sleep. And it's one reality that you can't really gloss over or prepare for. You will be tired—more tired than you ever imagined possible. But you will survive! Millions have emerged from that fog with their sanity—and their children—in good condition.

When new babies come home from the hospital, they may be awake all night and sleep all day, or they may have no pattern at all and be unpredictably wakeful or sleepy throughout the day and night. Gradually, over time, their wake-sleep pattern will become more regular, although it will be months before they consistently sleep through the night.

Most babies will adjust to a day-and-night schedule in two or three weeks, although they'll still probably want to be fed at least once during the night. Your task is to help this process along by minimizing stimulation at night and providing more play and company during the daytime hours.

After each nighttime feeding, hold and rock the babies, but don't be playful. Keep the light dim (that's why you have a nightlight). Then, during the day, move the babies around, keep them where the action is, and play with them to keep them awake longer.

Because you're unlikely to get your full eight hours for a while, do all you can to nap during the day. If it's difficult to find time when both babies are asleep, bring in one of your support people to stay with the babies while you try to sleep. Many mothers report that they can't sleep when they hear their babies cry, even if they know they're being looked after. If that's the case for you, try wearing earplugs.

If you are lucky to have someone who will do one of the wee-hours-of-the-night feedings, you can increase your sleep to a stretch of about four hours—no small blessing during these difficult first weeks. If that's not possible, have your helper do a late evening or early morning feeding, or one during the afternoon, when you're most likely to be able to nap.

Once your twins are on a more predictable schedule and wake up only once or twice a night, you'll feel a marked improvement in your sense of well-being. You can expect at least one night feeding for quite a few months. Many babies are able to sleep through the night when they are about seven months old and weigh at least fourteen pounds.

If you expect to feed two babies once or twice a night for months, you'll see why we advocate trying to breastfeed your multiples as much as possible. Feedings by breast are much less disruptive and less likely than bottle routines to fully awaken either baby or mother. Many mothers report that after a few months they can get up at three in the morning, feed and change two babies, and be back in dreamland without even fully waking up.

SUGGESTIONS FOR HELPING BABIES SLEEP THROUGH THE NIGHT

Once the babies are three to four months old, you can put them into the crib awake. Avoid waiting for them to nod off before you put them down. If your twins learn to fall asleep by themselves in the crib, they will be able to go back to sleep by themselves when they wake during the night. If they must be held in your arms in order to fall asleep, they'll need that whenever they wake up. Stay in the room and sing or talk quietly until they fall asleep. They may fuss, but they will learn. If one of the babies falls asleep more easily than the other, put that one in the crib first.

Introduce a security object (sometimes called a "transitional object"). This can be a small blanket, a cloth diaper, or a stuffed animal. Such an object helps your babies feel safe and relaxed when they are alone in their cribs, and makes them more able to fall asleep by themselves.

Consistency at bedtime is very important. Even when they're tiny, babies can benefit from a going-to-bed routine. Just like adults, they'll unwind and get themselves into a state of readiness as bedtime grows nearer. You can help them do this by following a simple routine every night.

Get the babies on a schedule as soon as feasible. Many child care experts deemphasize scheduling, preferring to allow babies to establish their own natural wake-sleep schedule. But they aren't writing about twins! For everyone's benefit, it's best to have some kind of coordination of sleep, play, and feeding times.

SIDS—MULTIPLES ARE AT GREATER RISK

All parents of multiples should be aware that sudden infant death syndrome, or SIDS, occurs more than twice as frequently among twins and higher-order multiples than among single-born babies.

This tragic syndrome, also called crib death, is characterized by the sudden and unexpected death during sleep of an otherwise healthy infant. It usually occurs in infants between the ages of four and sixteen weeks, and is thought to be associated with immaturity of the breathing reflex.

For years the syndrome was recognized but no clear advice for preventing it was available. In 1992, however, the American Academy of Pediatrics issued guidelines recommending that babies be put to sleep *on their backs*. Since then, the number of deaths from SIDS has decreased—a 50 percent decrease in 1995, from the peak year of 1989.

Often multiple babies are born premature and may have

poorly developed respiratory function at birth. They may be on ventilators until their lungs mature, and when they are ready to come home, they may require apnea monitors for a period of time.

Even if your babies have been given a clean bill of health, you will want to be mindful of the risk of SIDS and discuss sleep positions and related concerns with your pediatrician.

SO MANY TOENAILS, SO LITTLE TIME: KEEPING TRACK

With one baby, you never have to wonder whether you've fed your child or not. Your mind is free for thoughts a little loftier than "Did I just change you? Did I give you a bath? And which one *are* you?"

With twins, and especially with triplets and more, you'll need a system to keep track of whose is whose, and sometimes who is who. This is especially true in the earliest weeks, when you're less confident and less awake.

Your system should be both simple and flexible. As you establish a routine, you will find your own methods of organizing your babies' care. Here are some suggestions.

- Color-code any item that needs to be assigned to one baby. Before you use your precious time rushing out to buy colored markers and stickers, however, keep in mind that in the earliest weeks and months, it's not necessary to assign clothing and other items to a particular baby.
- If you need to give medication or other special care to one or more of the babies, use a notebook, or a chart if you prefer, to keep track. If you need to monitor one or more babies' consumption of milk or production of diapers, write these down or you'll all too easily forget.
- A safety pin that you transfer from one bra strap to the

other can help you remember which baby nursed on which breast last.

- A simple chart with labeled clothespins representing each baby may be helpful for keeping up with baths and other routines. Clothespins make sense since they spare you having to look for a pencil when you have your arms full of babies. You can move each child's pin to the tasks you're tracking—bath, vitamins, and such.

- Don't be overly concerned about one baby contaminating the other's bottles, pacifiers, and such. The babies share the same environment, including sucking one another's fingers. If one gets the other's bottle, no harm is likely.

HOW WILL I TELL MY BABIES APART? WILL I MIX THEM UP?

"My identical twins were so similar when I brought them home from the hospital that I worried about getting them mixed up." This is a practical worry. The best thing to do is keep the babies' hospital bracelets on when you come home. Just to be on the safe side, you can use colored nail polish on one baby's toenails until there is no doubt in your mind.

If you do this, make sure you remember which baby's toenails you painted! One couple was so exhausted they forgot. Distraught, the parents dug out the hospital footprints, bundled the babies off to the local police station, and got new footprints to compare.

GETTING AROUND WITH YOUR TWINS

"My main concern is going somewhere," one mother told me. "I am limited because I can't find an affordable twin stroller

anywhere. I can't find a used one, either. How can I go anywhere? I can't carry them both."

When your babies are tiny, the hardest part of moving
them from one place to another is having to pack them up all
the time, strap them into cars and strollers, and then get them
out again. You'll certainly look forward to the day when all you
have to do is tell them to grab their coats and jump into the car.

But look on the bright side: At least they can't run away
from you in two or more directions—yet!

Difficult as it is to move around with infant multiples, one
of the best things you can do for yourself is to try to get out.
Cabin fever is one of the occupational hazards faced by parents
of infant twins. At first your outings may not be very dramatic—
they may consist of a short stroller walk up and down the street
or a trip to the park. On bad days, just getting everyone out of
the house for a while can lift everyone's mood.

If getting out of the house with twins is difficult, getting
out with triplets is even more challenging. One mother told
me how guilty she felt because a week would go by and she
hadn't been able to take the babies out of the house at all.

I pointed out to her that although *she* may have suffered
from being cooped up, her babies probably did not. The reason
we take babies out (other than for essential trips to day care
or the doctor's office) is to give them fresh air and a chance to
get to know the outside world. With single babies, these outings
provide a change of scene and lots of interesting sights and
sounds. But multiple babies have a lot going on at home—they
have the companionship and noise and stimulation of their siblings, and may be getting plenty of changes of scene right where
they live.

When my daughters were little, we were able to set up
a play area near a large sunny window that had a wide view
of the trees and the street below. They were able to play
freely and watch the world go by. For your babies, it may be
an hour spent in playpens on the porch or in the backyard.
You'll work with your own environment to give your multiples

what they need within the limits of what you can reasonably do.

This is not to say you should never take your twins out, of course. You will, and as they get easier to handle, you will get out and about more.

For the latest in baby equipment and tips on how to use it, check your local parents-of-twins group and the Internet. Find a multiple-birth chat area and find out what other parents suggest. New products are coming onto the market all the time.

Here are some basic possibilities:

- Soft baby carriers, either standard single or specialized double.
- Baby backpacks (suitable for babies old enough to hold their heads up). Two of these make twin outings with parents much easier.
- A stroller big enough for all of your babies. The two basic styles for twin or more strollers are tandem, which seats the babies one in front of the other; and side-by-side, in which the babies sit next to each other. The seats should be capable of reclining, because babies should recline until they are old enough to hold up their heads. What kind of stroller you get will depend on how many babies you have and how you plan to use it—whether in a van, on public transportation, at the mall, or on a city street. You also have to consider whether you can lift the stroller to get it into and out of your car. There are quadruplet strollers, for example, but you may be better off with two double strollers.
- A safe car seat for each baby.
- An old-fashioned baby carriage (they're expensive, so consider borrowing one, if possible). A buggy will hold two or three newborns, and can be used indoors to move sleeping babies from one place to another, as well as outdoors for airings.

Suggestions for getting around with your twins:

- If you use a tandem stroller (with one baby in front of the other), vary which child sits in front so that each child gets a change of scenery. Side-by-side strollers have the advantage that all can face forward. In a tandem stroller, the baby in back may poke and pull the hair of the one in front.
- Consider putting one baby in a single stroller and the other in a soft baby carrier or backpack.
- For bus travel when babies are tiny, carry one in a front pack and carry the other in your arms. Backpack-type carriers are suitable for babies old enough to hold up their heads; when your twins reach that stage, you might carry one in a front pack and one in a backpack.
- Trips to the doctor are a three-ring circus, with all the carrying, waiting, and undressing you have to do. One mother of triplets arranged with her pediatrician's staff to give her the first appointment of the day, or the first one after lunch, so she and the babies wouldn't have to wait. The staff also arranged to have her bring the children directly into an examining room, so she wouldn't have to sit in the waiting room. If possible, arrange to bring a helper to doctor's visits. An extra pair of hands for dressing, playing, and soothing is a great help.

THE LIGHT AT THE END OF THE TUNNEL

As difficult as these early months can be, there is hope. As your body recovers and as your babies sleep for longer stretches and develop a schedule, your energy and mood will bounce back.

One mother I know recalls the morning when she and her

husband were startled awake by a strange new sound. "What was *that*?" her husband asked.

What they'd heard was the sound of birds singing. After months of waking up crying before dawn's early light, both babies had slept through the night. And the time will come when you too will wake up to the sound of birdsong.

CHAPTER SEVEN

ADJUSTING TO
TWINSHOCK

"*I'm a single mother with four-month-old twin boys. It has been very difficult, and I usually cry around six every evening. Yesterday, when I started crying at eight A.M., I knew I was in trouble.*"

In this chapter we'll examine the emotional and psychological dimensions of welcoming multiples into the family. Before the babies were born, you experienced moments of fear and moments of great joy as you anticipated their arrival. Now, as you settle in with them at home, you will continue that emotional roller-coaster ride. You sense that nothing in your life will ever be the same, and you're right. Becoming a parent does alter you and your world—your relationships, your household, your career choices. And when you give birth to two or more, the changes are more profound.

Surely the hours right after birth are among the most exhilarating times in our lives. As parents, we undergo a "peak experience"—a time when our emotions and sensations are heightened and we savor not only the new baby, but our own sense that we have come through a challenging experience. When the outcome is good—mother and baby doing well—the experience is one parents remember with delight for the rest of their lives.

For parents of multiples, there's an added sense of pleasure.

Heads turn as you leave the hospital with two, three, or four babies. Your family has achieved celebrity status during your stay, and doctors, nurses, and bystanders give you and the babies extra-special smiles.

You can't help but be proud of all you've accomplished, and be awed by the miracle of multiple births. You're over-come with tenderness toward your babies as you strap them into their car seats for their first ride home.

And now the moment of realization strikes—or it may be a bit later, when you lower them into their crib for the first time. Whenever it hits you, it's the same: "This is not a dream! This really did happen. These babies are *ours*—to take care of all by ourselves!"

Before we delve into the difficulties, however, let me say once again that it's easy to become caught up in the hardships of the task and lose sight of the satisfactions. There's a differ-ence between being realistic and being negative. Yes, raising twins can be difficult, but the challenges are matched with rewards.

For a number of years, Twin Services has used as a slogan the words of a proud but tired father who told me, "Twins are a hard happiness." This man had baby twins and three older children and was driving a cab two shifts a day to make ends meet. His words aptly illustrate our organization's mission of helping par-ents minimize their difficulties and maximizing their happiness.

As we discussed in Chapter Six, the work involved in caring for more than one tiny baby is daunting indeed. The fatigue, the lack of time for one's own needs, and the disrup-tion in the household all affect our emotional well-being and that of our families.

This "shock to the system" is caused by two elements: stress, which immediately affects our ability to cope and adjust, and the changed dynamics within the family.

Before we examine these elements more closely, let's look at how training and preparation help in both areas.

TRAINING FOR THE MULTIPLE OLYMPICS

In Chapter Two we discussed the importance of using the pregnancy months to prepare, physically and logistically, for the arrival of your babies. The value of preparation continues as you adjust to the reality of life with your twins.

I like analogies and find them effective tools in helping parents view their experiences in a realistic and positive light. Earlier in this book I compared the experience of raising twins to climbing a mountain—difficult, yet exhilarating, rewarding, and doable with proper training.

I also like to use a sports metaphor. After watching the last Winter Olympics on television, I began to think of preparation for twin care as something like an Olympic athlete's training. The physical training is combined with psychological preparation—for example, the athlete gets optimum nutrition and plenty of rest, and prepares emotionally for competition. A mother pregnant with multiples also follows a demanding training schedule and regime. She knows that the outcome may be good health for her and large, healthy babies, or she may have medical problems and one or more babies may be very small.

The athlete knows there may be setbacks such as training injuries on the way to the big event; the mother is prepared for the possibility of preterm labor.

Finally there is the much-anticipated event. No matter what medal is won, an athlete feels a sense of triumph and victory. And despite the outcome, the parents of multiples sense they will be able to cope because they planned ahead. Ultimately, participation in the event brings a fabulous array of emotions: exhilaration, relief, pride in accomplishment, coping with notoriety, and a sense that life will never be the same.

SOURCES OF STRESS IN
MULTIPLE FAMILIES

Most of us can imagine that having multiple babies is more stressful than having a single baby. As I discussed in the last chapter, just doing the math illustrates what an enormous workload caring for multiples is.

In Twin Services' study of fifty-three mothers, we found that the overall stress experienced by the mothers of twins was doubled compared to mothers of single infants.

The four most significant factors that the women identified were:

- No time for self
- No time for each individual twin
- Lack of sleep
- Having to quit work

Several elements in these women's lives increased their sense of stress. One factor, somewhat surprisingly, was the number of other adults in the home—the more adults, the more stress. The data did not suggest why this was true; perhaps the other adults weren't able to be helpful (such as might be true of an elderly relative), or perhaps the other adults were brought into a particularly difficult home situation *because* of a preexisting high level of stress.

What decreased the stress these mothers felt was the feeling that their partners were pitching in and helping adequately. The study indicates clearly that families with multiples can count on a period of high stress at the beginning, and that one thing that will help mothers cope is the supportive involvement of their husband or partner.

"The whole issue about how involved the father was going to be was moot," one mother recalls, "because he had to be or I would have been mad at him all the time. In terms of my temperament, I couldn't have taken on the whole load. He stepped right up to the plate, and there's no two ways about it."

Don't be surprised, though, if adjustment to your new reality takes a long time. My adjustment took three years. Until then, my first reaction when our two daughters woke us in the morning was disbelief, followed by amazement. "They really are real! It isn't all a dream," I thought as I staggered out of bed to take care of them.

In a large study in Great Britain, mothers of five-year-old twins had a significantly higher incidence of malaise, indicating depression, than did mothers of single-born children that age. The mothers of twin pairs in which one twin had died had an even higher incidence. So stress can be a continuing factor in multiple families.

MULTIPLES DON'T JUST ADD TO THE FAMILY—THEY CHANGE IT

Having twins or multiples throws all your relationships into disarray, changing them forever. And it changes *you* forever. This is true to some extent with any birth. But when single babies are born, the family can adjust to one newcomer at a time. Twins, triplets, or more put a greater strain on families, altering and complicating the interactions among family members. These changes can be both positive and negative; it's helpful to anticipate and plan for them constructively.

HOW HAVING MULTIPLES WILL AFFECT YOU AS A MOTHER

Certainly the one adult who is most affected by the arrival of multiples is the mother. Her body has undergone a grueling experience. Her postpartum experience is closely tied up with her level of fatigue, the difficulty of her recovery, and her hormonal status. This section deals primarily with mothers but is not intended to exclude fathers, because both parents can experience some of these feelings.

Mothers who had active professional or social lives before their twins were born can find it difficult to adjust to their new domestic status.

It's very easy to slip into isolation. Often the reasons are mundane—there's nobody to look after the babies while you go out, or the sheer logistical difficulties of going out *with* the babies are just too much.

Avoid isolation by keeping connected with other people in ways that you can reasonably manage. Don't say, "I'll just get the house cleaned up, and *then* I'll invite a friend over." Have your friends come over to visit and help out when the house is messy. Take the babies out to enjoy the sunset, or just go over and visit with the neighbor's cat when you're too tired to go far.

Another common problem is guilt about being a less-than-perfect mother, neglecting older children, bonding too slowly with the babies, or having a preference for one baby.

The key is to focus on what you are accomplishing now. Tell yourself, "I may not be perfect, but I'm taking care of twin babies, and we're all surviving." One mother I know worried about asking for help from her older children. Her husband pointed out that pitching in to help the family isn't bad for children. After all, he observed, if they lived on a dairy farm, the big kids would be expected to help by milking the cows.

Many mothers of multiples experience a kind of instant celebrity. One mother told me she had never stood out in a crowd before, yet now she was famous because of her triplets. Mothers of multiples also experience the "guru effect"—they are suddenly considered to be the neighborhood expert on all things related to babies and children, even if they've never had children before.

There's no harm in enjoying your celebrity status. We all enjoy being appreciated. But if you don't enjoy it, or you don't feel like interacting with strangers, just keep your head down and play deaf. Often a smile of acknowledgment as you push the stroller along may be all you need to protect your privacy.

In general, keeping yourself in good emotional health as all these experiences and feelings swirl around you is the best strategy for dealing with them. One of the most important ways to do this is by prioritizing. As we said in the last chapter, an essential part of managing the prodigious responsibilities and workload of raising infant multiples is to concentrate on what's important to you and your family. Just keeping everybody fed and rested and content may be all you can manage for a while. You will probably have to postpone or eliminate what's less important—such as having a tidy home, doing crafts or art projects, or giving formal parties.

Establishing priorities is also essential as you cope with your emotional changes. That means that worries, anxieties, and negative thoughts need to be put in their proper place. They are thieves of your emotional energy.

One of the best ways of dealing with this, I have found, is concentrating on one day at a time, rather than fretting about next week or next year. This doesn't mean that you shouldn't plan ahead, but rather that you should not seek to control things that lie too far ahead and seem overwhelming.

I've observed that many women who have been high achievers throughout their lives enter motherhood with exaggerated expectations of how perfectly they'll handle this new role. These are women who have excelled academically and professionally. They are ambitious and disciplined and have high standards. Yet when they experience the inevitable chaos of motherhood in a multiple situation, they may perceive themselves to be failures because they must inevitably lower their standards of "perfection."

For these mothers, it's important to think rationally about what their current task is and what parts of it deserve their energy. Certainly keeping the babies healthy and well fed is essential. But maybe looking perfectly pulled-together, keeping the house orderly, and pulling your weight in the church or community are things that can be postponed.

Here are some other suggestions for keeping yourself in good shape both mentally and physically:

- Make time for meditation, prayer, or other contemplative activity—what we at Twin Services call "sacred time." Whether it's yoga, visualization, or even listening to calming music, try to find an activity that gets you outside yourself and leaves you feeling emotionally or spiritually refreshed. It's important to keep this time for yourself—don't use it to do chores or go shopping.

- Adopt healthy living habits: walking, with or without the babies; maintaining good eating habits; and avoiding junk food, cigarettes, and anything else that saps your health and well-being.

- Think positively. Visualize your twins thriving and growing, and you growing more and more capable as time goes by. Remember that nobody is naturally good at being a mother right off the bat; it's something you grow into.

- Be flexible. Can you rearrange tasks, roles? Can you return to work while your partner manages the home? Some families make that choice with great success, as we discuss further below.

- Seek out other parents for get-togethers. If you can, find other families with multiples. Visit a Mothers of Twins club or other parents-of-twins group near you (see Resources).

- Talk about your feelings, and ask for help. Tell your husband or partner when you need more help or when you are feeling blue. When things are going badly, don't suffer in silence.

- Try to keep your sense of humor—often when the going gets tough, the tough get the giggles.

Ultimately, how you respond to this challenge depends on your own inner strengths and capabilities, your temperament, and your personality. People respond to challenges in highly individual ways (that's one reason I love to watch the Olympics), and the better you know yourself and how you handle adversity, the better prepared you'll be.

How Having Multiples Will
Affect You as a Father

Most of what we describe above about the impact of having twins and multiples applies to fathers, as well. You, as the father of multiples, also find your self-image altered. You find yourself doubting your abilities as a parent and looking for ways to keep your sanity.

But fathers have their own challenges—often because they tend to get overlooked as everyone focuses on the needs of the new babies and their mothers. There are likely to be times when your needs seem like an afterthought.

Like mothers, fathers experience both great joy and great distress as they adjust to their multiples.

First, the good news:

- Often, out of sheer necessity, fathers of multiples are more involved in infant care than fathers of singles. Consequently, you are likely to have a closer relationship with your babies than you might have had with a single infant.
- Fathers of multiples often receive adulation and admiration from friends and the community.

And the downside:

- Like mothers, fathers experience physical exhaustion and lack of sleep. Nowadays extended families are less common than in the past, and fathers are often the only regular source of baby care other than the mother. Remember that fathers need support, too. Acknowledge your own needs. Ask for help when you need it.

- You may become the only breadwinner and bear the burden of earning income along with household and baby tasks. You may feel you're in a double-bind situation: Your performance at work is more important than ever, just as you're needed desperately at home. When you feel anxious, talk about your concerns with your partner. Don't hide your worries behind a facade of strength.
- You may experience a sense of loss of your previous closeness with your wife, as you observe her preoccupation with the babies. Remember that this phase is transitory. Even in the busiest of times, you can feel close by sharing the effort, communicating, and giving (and receiving) lots of hugs.
- You may feel some resentment of the twins, and feel guilt over that resentment. This is normal.

If you are a father of multiples, recognize that your full participation will be essential. The babies' needs are so great that there's more work than two adults can handle. If you think you're doing 50 percent, you're probably not doing enough. Both parents have to feel that each of them is doing 80 percent!

In a family with sextuplets, the parents made a decision that the mother, whose income capacity was greater, would return to work while the father would supply child care. He and the children—who are four years old now—are doing well.

POSTPARTUM DEPRESSION

Whenever we talk about stress in new mothers, we must address the problem of postpartum depression, a condition that is particularly common in mothers of multiples.

It's important to point out that the "baby blues"—the mild sadness and anxiety that new mothers experience within the first days or weeks of birth—are common and self-limiting. More than 70 percent of new mothers experience these symptoms to some degree. Mothers feel weepy, excessively worried, or easily upset. Usually within days, as their bodies and hormones adjust to their nonpregnant state, their mood improves.

But postpartum depression is more serious. It affects about 10 percent of all new mothers—and 20 percent of mothers of multiples. Symptoms may be similar to the milder "baby blues" but persist for more than three weeks. They're usually more severe, and include feelings of despair and hopelessness. Often the mother loses interest in food and is unable to sleep.

One mother of twin daughters recalls, "On the fifth night, I suddenly developed this fear that if I went to sleep, I might not wake up for their feeding. I sat reading in bed all night. For seven nights I sat up listening to every sound they made, too frightened to sleep but unable to tell anyone about it."

The most severe form, called postpartum psychosis, is fortunately rare. But it is indeed serious. It affects only one to three mothers out of every thousand, but it can be debilitating or even life-threatening. These women become unable to function, and may hallucinate or be obsessed with thoughts of suicide or homicide.

Although postpartum depression and psychosis have many causes, including possibly a genetic predisposition and earlier bouts with mental illness, environmental factors figure largely. Mothers who feel isolated and unsupported and who have low self-esteem may be more at risk.

But there is one environmental cause that can be managed, and that is fatigue. This is another reason why you must rest as much as you can, especially in the early weeks and months. If you are young and healthy, you will survive the sleepless nights. But you need to pamper yourself (and be pampered by others) as much as possible during those early months when your body and your emotional state are fragile.

Here are some suggestions to help you keep normal "blues" from intensifying, and for coping when true depression strikes:

- Talk to someone about your feelings. In particular, talk to your obstetrician and ask for help, especially if your feelings of sadness persist beyond the first week or so after birth.
- Realize that your feelings are to some extent reasonable— you are going through a major disruption in your physical and emotional life. It will take time before you feel comfortable in your new role and feel good about your abilities as a mother.
- Seek immediate help if you have severe symptoms, such as hallucinations or thoughts of harming yourself or your babies. And seek help if insomnia becomes a serious problem.
- Seek help from a support group such as Depression After Delivery (DAD), a nonprofit information and support group (see Resources).

HOW THE ARRIVAL OF MULTIPLES
AFFECTS THE MARRIAGE OR PARTNERSHIP

During the first few months, parents have no sleep, no privacy, no time. All they can focus on is the endless round of feedings, diaperings, bathings. They themselves are unshaved, unfed, unshowered.

"You become very primal," recalled one mother. "The sleep deprivation was so severe, I think I would have killed for some sleep."

Just when you feel you have nothing left to give is likely to be the time when your partner is in greatest need. This is when you'll be glad you took some time to assess your communication skills, as we suggested in Chapter Two. Those imperfections in your marriage that you may have been able to skirt before will be unskirtable now.

Too, parents who previously communicated well may find that under their new routines, they hardly see one another. One parent may take the night shift and the other the day; or one parent may focus on the older children's needs while the other concentrates on the care of the twins.

Sometimes fathers in this situation withdraw into their work world, spending less and less time at home precisely when they're needed most.

What to do:

- It's important not to let resentments build up. Try to ask, every day, what your partner needs.
- Hug often. Sometimes the unspoken comfort of a hug (or lots of hugs) can comfort and soothe more than words can.
- Show appreciation for the other's efforts.
- Keep reminding yourself, and your partner, that this situation is transitory. It's helpful to remember that the first year postpartum is a continuation of the pregnancy; you and your babies are still in a state of adjustment. This process will eventually conclude.
- Find creative ways to make time just for yourselves— even if it's just for half an hour. You might pack dinner, then buckle the babies into their car seats and drive until they fall asleep. Park and have a picnic under a tree.

SEX AND ROMANCE

Sex? Romance? You may have only the vaguest recollection of such things. Certainly the months immediately after any birth—multiple or otherwise—are not conducive to passion. In the case of twins, however, that shortage of time and energy is greater and longer-lasting than with single babies. Mothers who are nursing several babies may feel they're getting more than enough physical closeness, while fathers may feel deprived.

In addition, you may have a house full of helpers, in-laws, nannies, au pairs, and assorted well-wishers (not to mention babies), so there's no privacy even if you had the time.

It's important to remind yourself—and each other—that this situation is not going to last forever. And even during those difficult early weeks, you can still hug one another, be close, and praise one another.

Sometimes the best thing to do is laugh. I remember when the subject of sex came up during one of our family meetings for parents of twins. One couple blushingly admitted that when they'd finally managed to arrange an afternoon away from home, they went on a picnic in a nearby state park—and promptly jumped into the bushes.

After they told this story, several other couples in the group began to smile. Soon they admitted having done the same thing—at the same state park!

HOW HAVING MULTIPLES AFFECTS SIBLINGS AND THE FAMILY AS A WHOLE

If you already have children, you have the advantage of experience, a sense of perspective, and an idea of what to expect.

But there's a downside, too—you have other children to care for, in addition to the new babies. And you have to worry about the well-being of your older children. You have to be concerned about their feelings as well. Sibling rivalry and jealousy of the new arrival are common with any birth. But with twins, there's a much more complex adjustment.

The arrival of multiples affects children in different ways, depending on their age.

TODDLERS

It's difficult for toddler siblings to understand what is happening when the babies arrive. It's not easy to prepare them for the coming event, since they may not be able to anticipate the future clearly. Yet they have less of a history as the only child than older siblings do.

Children this age are dealing with issues of independence and separation. They may suffer when their mother is absent giving birth, and cling (or withdraw) when she returns. They may regress toward earlier behaviors, asking to nurse or use a bottle again, or start having toileting accidents.

When you come home from the hospital with your twins, give your toddler two dolls or two bears to care for (or three or more, as appropriate). That way the child can care for the bears while you care for the twins. And he or she can role-play and act out feelings toward the babies in a safe way.

PRESCHOOLERS

I remember reading about a mother of triplets whose three-year-old came up to her one morning and said, "I got rid of the babies for you, Mommy!" After several moments of panic, the mother finally found the three babies safely nestled in the bedroom wardrobe. She never figured out how her daughter managed to put them in there, though.

This story illustrates that children can think of the babies as a mixed blessing at best. They can have trouble expressing negative feelings or, like that little girl, express them all too eloquently.

On the plus side, children this age—from about three to five—are learning skills at a great rate. Often they can understand more about what it means to have new brothers or sisters, and can take great pride in being helpers.

Parents can help by understanding how tough it must be on them. Remember that even though they seem big in comparison to the tiny babies, they're still very young and vulnerable.

Help them put the painful feelings into words in a way that helps them feel better. When your child says, "Send them back to the hospital!" or "I hate the babies!" it's tempting to deny the feelings with a statement like, "Of course you don't hate the babies!" It's better to say something like, "You're having a hard time right now because I'm so busy with the babies," or "Sometimes you wish they'd go away. They sure are noisy!" And suggest something constructive they can do with the bad feelings (draw a picture, come and ask Mommy for a special hug, get mad at a doll rather than at the babies).

In their book *Siblings Without Rivalry*, Adele Faber and Elaine Mazlish suggest dealing sympathetically with the older child when she's ignored by well-meaning friends and relatives who inevitably fuss over the new babies. You can say, "I bet it can be hard to watch everyone make such a big deal over the babies. Next time it happens, give me a wink and I'll wink back. Then you'll know that I know." Of course, you'll still want to stand up for your older child when people behave insensitively around him. You can praise the older child's contributions in his presence—for example, "Thanks for coming by to see the twins and Jonathan. I'm so proud of how Jonathan has been helping with them."

Encourage your children's creative involvement. Even at this age, children may be able to push the button on a Polaroid camera and take pictures of family events. Older children can take pictures more independently. Perhaps from time to time the pictures can be mounted into a scrapbook with text that the child narrates and the parents or an older child writes down.

SCHOOL-AGE CHILDREN

After the age of five or six, children are more ready to separate from their parents and home. They're making other friends. They have time away from babies, which gives them a break from the intensity of their feelings and inevitable noise and chaos of the home (not to mention having to be quiet so they don't wake the babies).

School-age children can be wonderfully helpful. Do, however, try to avoid leaning too heavily on them. You do not want to give them a reason to feel resentful. In fact, consider paying them appropriately for tasks above and beyond their routine chores.

If your school-age children can participate in family projects that are more fun than drudgery—such as making the photo scrapbook described above, or helping younger siblings with the task—they can experience an involvement that goes beyond that of helper. They can feel like an important part of the family unit, and they can experience the fun part of being an older sibling.

Children this age are developing other interests and have other sources of support and approval outside the family. They're better able to put feelings into words, to discuss and manage their negative feelings.

Often kids this age enjoy the celebrity that comes from having such an interesting family. Your child may even ask you to bring the twins to school for show and tell and let the other children ask questions—questions that the big brother or sister can answer proudly.

This is also the time to enlist grandparents, godparents, and other relatives to invite the older children out for some calm time with an adult who has the leisure to listen. Grandparents can be a crucial factor in a child's well-being while parents are so preoccupied.

ADOLESCENTS

Usually the older siblings of newborn multiples are younger, but certainly sometimes parents of teenagers have twins. I know of one mother with two teenagers who gave birth to triplets.

Teenagers may be appalled at the idea of their parents having babies (a result, they realize with horror, of having *sex*). They may be at a defiant or rude stage of their lives and may not seem supportive.

But teenagers are, of course, very capable and can provide

invaluable assistance. The most common concern with older siblings this age is that parents can come to rely on them so much that the older children don't have a chance to be kids.

The key is to find the right balance between expecting and appreciating a reasonable level of help, and not coming to rely on it too much.

Most siblings adjust eventually to the arrival of their younger brothers and sisters. But some have great difficulty and need help. Seek help for your older child if he or she shows signs of severe withdrawal and depression, or of serious physical aggression toward the babies. It is not uncommon for an older sibling to pinch or hit a baby, but it must be prevented. If you feel you can't protect your babies from an older child, you must seek outside help—for the sake of the babies, and for the sake of your older child.

FINANCIAL WORRIES

There is no question that the arrival of multiples puts a strain on a family's finances. We talk about how to cope with a serious financial downturn in Chapter Fifteen. For many families, decisions about the mother's career can be agonizing. They need both incomes, and the mother wishes to continue in her career, but her babies take up 200 percent of her time and energy.

For many families, careers can be postponed or redefined. They choose to consider these early years as an investment. You're better off sacrificing some financial security if it will pay off in later family strength. You can make up lost time when it comes to money, but not when it comes to children.

As you experience the joys and challenges of settling in with your new babies, make sure you give yourself permission to enjoy the good times. When you feel your heart ache with love for your babies, when others praise you and you feel justly proud, when you are having a particularly successful experience and are feeling capable and invincible, let yourself enjoy these feelings—they are rightly part of the rewards, and you deserve them.

CHAPTER EIGHT

TO EACH HIS OWN

UNDERSTANDING AND SUPPORTING YOUR CHILDREN'S INDIVIDUALITY

"*My twins have individual personalities and very different interests, but they care for and love each other very much.*"

The idea of twins inspires profound thoughts about the human condition and what makes us different, what makes us unique.

We bring to this process all the myths we referred to in Chapter Three, as well as other stories we hear about twin research, and then we wonder how they will play out in our own children. How does each multiple forge his or her own identity, individuality, and personality? How much do parents influence that process, and how much is it the task of the children? How do the twins themselves establish their own identities? How does their status as a couple influence them?

Parents need to understand what twinning is, how alike or different twins can be, and how their individual personalities develop. And they need to view their own role as that of coach or mentor, rather than as the creator of their children's individuality.

Individuality, independence, and the twin bond—these are recurring themes for multiples throughout their lives. And for you, their parents, these issues will arise again and again as you support your children's maturation as individuals and encourage a positive relationship between them as babies, toddlers, schoolkids, teens, and even adults.

In fact, we parents do not make our twins into individuals; they are individuals from the outset. Our job is to create an environment in which the children will forge their own identities as they grow.

IMPLICATIONS OF ZYGOSITY

As we've discussed in Chapter One, zygosity is one of several factors that influence how similar and how different your multiples will be.

If your twins are dizygotic, they will share the same degree of genetic similarity as any two siblings who are born singly. Consequently, they may have many traits in common and have a strong resemblance to each other, or they may have very different appearances and temperaments.

If your twins are monozygotic, they will share more traits, but they will show some differences as well. My own monozygotic daughters were not identical in appearance at birth. Krista, who was born first, weighed five pounds eleven ounces. She had a full head of hair, a birthmark on one leg, and a face slightly more narrow in appearance than her twin's. Kelda weighed six pounds eight ounces, had wispy hair, a birthmark on one arm, and rounded facial features.

Kelda, who had had much more freedom of movement in my womb, was relaxed. Krista, who had been scrunched into limited space, and who as firstborn had spent a longer time in the birth canal, was an alert watcher. It seems possible to me that her experience of having to contain herself in a very tight space in the womb had taught her to be strategic. Our family joked that she had more hair than Kelda because that was all the room there was for her to grow. Maybe we were right!

THE IMPORTANCE OF DIAGNOSING ZYGOSITY

If you have not discovered their zygosity before your babies are born, you will surely want to determine this after their birth—unless they are a boy and a girl, in which case they are of course dizygotic.

There are important reasons for knowing. First of all, it is the birthright of twins and other multiples to know their origins, and zygosity is an essential aspect of those origins. It is unthinkable to me that they and their families would not know. Obstetricians used to tell me that they thought it wasn't good for parents to know the zygosity of their babies, because it might influence the way they cared for them.

Yet maybe parents *should* be influenced by so important an element of their children's identity. In fact, there is evidence that zygosity influences parental care even when the parents don't know it.

Research has shown that even when parents were mistaken about their twins' zygosity, they cared for them in ways that reflected the children's true zygosity. Parents of true monozygotic twins treated them more similarly even when they believed they were dizygotic, because they were responding to their babies' similar needs. And parents of true dizygotic twins treated them more distinctly even when they believed they were monozygotic, because they were responding to their different needs.

But it makes sense for parents to know their children's zygosity. If your twins are dizygotic, for example, they'll have the same differences in developmental timetables and personalities as any two nontwin siblings. Knowing this about your twins means you'll be less likely to scrutinize them for similarities and more likely to celebrate their differences.

TWIN STUDIES—WHAT RESEARCH TELLS US ABOUT INDIVIDUALITY IN TWIN DEVELOPMENT

Until the birth of my own twin daughters prompted me to look for information about twin development, I had assumed that the "twin studies" I had heard about all my life were about twins. I soon learned otherwise. "Twin studies" in the usual sense refers to the use of twins as research tools.

Behavior geneticists and psychologists use twin pairs to study the relative contribution of genes and environment to human development. Since monozygotic twins have the same genetic makeup, any differences in their personalities and behavior can be attributed to differences in their environment. Many valuable contributions to our understanding of human development have come from this work, but much is not useful for parental guidance.

Research findings that might help parents raise their multiples are not only difficult to find, but are sometimes distorted. Often articles about twins and twin research in the popular media emphasize aspects of twinning that are eerie or strangely coincidental, such as reunited twins who have identical political party affiliations, clothing preferences, food preferences, and occupations. From headlines such as "Twins: Nature's Clones" and "Double Trouble," one would think twins aren't regular folks.

The insights that genetic research provides into twin development are largely by-products of the research, not the focus of it. And because it is the nature of genetic research to measure quantifiable characteristics and not the nuances of a particular family's life situation, even the findings that are relevant for parents may be too general to be of much use.

There are some notable exceptions, however, and we refer to the findings of these studies in more detail throughout this book. The Louisville Twin Study, for example, has conducted long-term research following hundreds of twin infants and children within the family context and has contributed much useful information. These researchers have found, for example, that toddler twins can reduce one another's separation anxiety when their mother leaves the room, and that twins who are developmentally delayed due to prematurity usually catch up with their peers by school age.

A study by Australian psychologist David Hay has done much to document the impact on families of having twins. This research has provided support for the idea that it is not necessary to separate twins in the early school grades, and have demonstrated how the twin relationship can provide mutual support and comfort during adolescence.

In my own early search for information about twin development, I was relieved to find Helen Koch's book *Twins and Twin Relations*. It reports on her groundbreaking research at the University of Chicago, which focused on twin development for its own sake. Koch's analysis includes discussion of major themes that concern parents, including school placement and the interaction between dominance and submission in a twin pair.

My search led me also to the National Organization of Mothers of Twins Clubs (NOMOTC) in the United States and Parents of Multiple Births Organizations (POMBA) in Canada. These national networks of parent clubs are a source of mutual support and information and resources for parents. Members are much courted by scientists who need a ready supply of twins to participate as subjects in their studies of nature-nurture questions. Unfortunately for us parents, many such researchers have little interest in looking at the aspects of twin development that affect their daily lives. In spite of the fact that "twin studies" have been ongoing for a hundred years now, we parents are still lacking a coherent picture of the complexities of twin development.

Much of the current work attempting to fill in the picture

of twin development is being accomplished not by the "twin research" community but by psychologists, linguists, obstetricians, pediatricians, and social workers who are seeking answers to the compelling questions asked by twin families—questions about practical care, the twin relationship, school placement, and ways that parents can help their children develop as individuals.

NURTURING TWINS ACCORDING TO THEIR NATURES

Any parent of a newborn baby can tell you much about the baby's characteristics. Each baby displays personality traits right at the beginning. Some are tranquil and easygoing. Some are sleepyheads. Some are hypersensitive and quick to startle, and have a difficult time settling down. And there are the watchful ones, easily distracted by everything going on around them.

Twins and other multiples may have many similar characteristics and many that are different. As we discussed above, similarities and differences in newborn twins are related both to their genetic inheritance and to their experiences in the womb.

What are we parents to make of this information? How much influence do we have on our babies' development and relationship?

There is a growing body of scientific research suggesting that the relationship between our genetic makeup and our environment is much more complex than first thought. It's no longer an either-or proposition when it comes to sorting out the relative influence of nature and nurture in a person's development. We are beginning to understand more fully that not only are children's inherited characteristics influenced by their environment, but the children themselves influence the environment, including their parents' style of caregiving.

We owe much of these insights to pioneering researchers such as Jerome Kagan, a psychologist whose research with babies and children has revealed much about temperament and its biological origins. In their decades-long study of children, psychiatrists Stella Chess and Alexander Thomas have demonstrated how consistent personality and temperament are over time.

We are also learning that genetic influences become stronger over time. Since the womb is the environment most likely to have the strongest influence on twin differences, it is natural to expect the similarities between monozygotic twins to increase as they mature. That has certainly been true for my monozygotic daughters, who in adulthood have more similar features than they did as children.

Scientists disagree regarding the relative impact of genes and upbringing on an individual's personality. Thomas Bouchard, director of the Minnesota Study of Twins Reared Apart, holds the view that about 70 percent of a person's personality is related to genetics and 30 percent to environment. Others, such as Adam Matheny, director of the Louisville Twin Study, which follows twins reared together, think it is a fifty-fifty proposition.

DIFFERENCES IN NEWBORN TWINS

In one of the Louisville studies, newborn monozygotic twins scored no more alike than dizygotic twin newborns on a range of variables including physical activity, attention, and temperament. After six months the monozygotic twins begin to show more similarities and the dizygotic twins show more differences.

Bouchard has found that monozygotic twins reared apart are more similar than some who were reared together. This suggests that monozygotic twins who grow up together make arrangements to divide up the territory, so to speak. It's possible that had they been separated, they too might be more similar.

PARENTAL RESPONSE TO DIFFERENCES

Ultrasound technology is giving us even more dramatic evidence of the genetic origins of behavior. Used to study the activity and interactions of monozygotic and dizygotic twin pairs in the womb, it has revealed that all of the babies, both monozygotic and dizygotic, have distinctive behavioral styles. And each pair of twins has its own distinctive style of interaction—some seeking contact with one another and some avoiding it. The babies then continue to display the same behaviors and styles of relating during their first year of life.

Parents respond to these differences in their babies, so that no two babies are treated exactly the same. For example, some mothers give special attention to the baby who has had the most health problems. Of course, it is natural to give more attention to an infant who needs special care. It is possible, though, for this to become a habit that persists well beyond the need.

All of these findings add up to good news for us parents. We are off the old hook that claimed it was up to the parents to engineer their children's behavior, and, in the case of twins, to "make" them different.

However, we also need to be aware of and readjust our responses to our children's differences as they grow and change. Here is an example of how the differences in my daughter's birth weights influenced me to unwittingly show preference for one of my daughters.

As a teenager, Kelda was reminiscing about when they were little. She asked me why I always gave Krista more jam on her toast. My first reaction was to deny that I had been so unfair. When I calmed down and thought back, though, I remember that whenever I noticed that I had spread more jam on one piece of toast than the other as I was bringing breakfast to the table, I automatically gave the one with the most jam to Krista, who had weighed thirteen ounces less than Kelda at birth. (Krista was perfectly healthy; she was just slight in comparison with her plumper sister.)

I'm glad that Kelda asked me that question, and she was relieved to hear my explanation. I hadn't meant to show favoritism. But from Kelda's perspective, I was favoring Krista. What I now see is that I was being influenced by the difference in their birth weights well past the time when it had any bearing on reality. Krista's weight had caught up to Kelda's in just a few weeks and has stayed nearly the same ever since.

TEMPERAMENT

Marilyn Riese, of the Louisville Twin Study, compared the predictability of temperament between twins of normal birth weight and those of low birth weight. She looked at activity level, intensity of reaction, distractibility, and other measures of innate temperament.

She found that the temperament qualities seen in newborns of normal birth weight predicted their temperament at thirty months. There was no such predictability for the temperament of babies of low birth weight. These data suggest that temperament traits are present at birth and tend to persist in babies who are of normal weight, but that in low-birth-weight babies newborn temperament is less fixed. This research supports other studies that have found a connection between temperament and birth weight, and it suggests that low birth weight may affect the development of temperament. This means that if your babies were of normal birth weight, you can expect their temperaments to remain relatively unchanged as they grow.

A study of happiness in twins found that the happiness level of monozygotic twins reared apart was more similar than the happiness level of dizygotic twins reared together. For the monozygotic twins in the study, each twin's degree of happiness was more likely to mirror the other's feelings of happiness, rather than their life circumstances. Such factors as income level and marital status, which we assume would influence the sense of well-being, appeared to have less impact. This suggests that feelings of happiness may be strongly related to our genetic makeup.

Happiness in dizygotic twins can be expected to be as similar or dissimilar as it is for most single siblings. Happiness in monozygotic twins can be expected to be pretty much the same over time. If one of your monozygotic twins shows a marked decline in happiness, it may signal a problem that needs to be addressed.

I know a pair of seven-year-old monozygotic boys, both gifted athletes, who usually are outgoing and cheerful. When one suddenly became withdrawn, their parents were concerned and investigated the cause. The boys were on the same baseball team, and their coach insisted that the entire team bat right-handed. The one major physical difference between the boys was that one was right-handed and the other left-handed (they were "mirror" twins), and this unreasonable rule put one boy at a distinct disadvantage in an area that meant a great deal to him. The parents would not have been as quick to get to the bottom of the problem if they had not recognized that the difference in the boys' moods signaled a problem.

RESPECTING THE TWIN RELATIONSHIP AMONG YOUR MULTIPLES

What is the twin relationship? Is it special? Is it good, bad, or a little of each? Why does it pervade family life?

Multiples are born with a special connection that is certainly physical: They have shared a womb for seven to nine months, something no other humans experience. The connection is also psychological. Newborn twins seem aware of one another's presence and show growing attachment to one another, as they do to their parents. When the multiples are monozygotic, their physical resemblance and shared temperament and abilities intensify this bond.

For dizygotic twins, who may or may not share similar physical characteristics and temperaments, the connection may be less intense, but no matter what their degree of compatibility, they too will have a lifelong bond.

The existence of the twin bond poses an unusual paradox for their parents, who must encourage the development of independence in their children while at the same time encouraging them to maintain a positive relationship. In the chapters that follow we will discuss the variety of twin relationships throughout the ages and stages of development.

You'll want to keep in mind that the relationship between your multiples is as dynamic as the relationship between the members of any other kind of couple. There will be times when their partnership is harmonious, and times when it seems more like a combat zone. Knowing that this ebb and flow of feeling is normal will help you enjoy the easy times and ride out the storms.

Once you have sorted out the zygosity of your babies and educated yourself about what you can expect in terms of differences and similarities, you are ready for the art of parenting your multiples. This is truly an art, not an exact science. It's good to keep in mind that you are not responsible for making them individuals, as we've noted earlier. They are born individuals. Your responsibility as a parent is to respond to each baby's needs and to respect the relationship between them, so that they each develop a secure sense of self and a positive view of their twinship.

HOW TO HONOR AND PROMOTE INDIVIDUALITY

"Which one of me is this?" three-year-old Kelda asked her dad as they pored over old baby pictures. Kelda's confusion was typical of what can happen when twins are so look-alike that even they can't tell themselves apart in photographs.

But it doesn't mean that twins don't know who they are.

Even though others may not know which twin is which from the outside, on the inside each twin knows him or herself as an individual.

As you prepare for the birth of your babies, you think about who they will be and how you will relate to both or all of them. And perhaps you wonder whether you will be able to tell them apart, and worry that you might mix them up.

Whether the babies are monozygotic, dizygotic, or, in the case of triplets or more, a mixture of both, you will recognize their individuality at birth, at least in a general way. You may not be able to identify all of the characteristics of their personalities, but each baby will display his or her own particular brand of behavior and temperament.

If they look a lot alike, you may not be able to tell them apart at a glance. But visual clues are not the key to their identities. Remember the old adage "You can't tell a book by its cover." When you hold them one by one, or even all together, you will begin to get a feeling for who each one is.

WHO'S WHO? AND WHOSE IS WHOSE?

"When I was growing up, I remember going to school with twins who looked alike and dressed alike. They had cute names that rhymed, and the other kids had trouble telling them apart. When I realized I was going to have twins, I wanted to think that other children would view them as individuals and make friends with them as individuals. We started by picking names that were clearly different. When they were born, we avoided dressing them in matching outfits."

Many parents are concerned about the choices they make regarding names and clothing for their twins. They know that those attributes do affect how others treat their twins, and how the children view themselves. One mother was surprised at the intensity of her own reaction when another child confused her toddler twin boys.

"I told him who was who, and he looked at me and said, 'What does it matter?' Even though he was just a child and didn't know better, I was so upset it brought tears to my eyes."

In Chapter Six we talked about how to tell newborns apart as you care for them in the early weeks. Such simple techniques as assigning each twin a color for some of their property serves not only to distinguish items in the early months but to help the children identify what is "theirs" as they grow older.

CLOTHING

Color-coding may be useful in the early months, and even the early years. As they grow older, the children might pick new colors at each birthday. But this technique makes sense only as long as it's useful and fun. Sometimes children begin to see their clothes as a uniform to be worn no matter what. Suppose both of your daughters want to wear pink? "Mom must like you better than she likes me. You get to wear the pink dresses and I have to wear the blue ones," said one six-year-old.

A major issue among parents of twins is whether, and when, to dress children alike. "I've heard I shouldn't dress my twins alike, but we've been given lots of matching outfits for them," said one mother. "I asked our pediatrician what to do, but she had no definite answers. Will it harm them if they're dressed alike?"

The answer to this question may sound complicated, but it's actually quite simple. When multiples are dressed alike, the individual babies or children are submerged in the identity of the group. They become "the twins," or "the quadruplets." When they are dressed individually, they stand out as individuals—to a degree, anyway.

When you are tempted to dress them alike, and everyone is at least some of the time, think about the impact. Can you tell them apart? Can you expect others to? Think about the "star" effect they will experience when strangers rush up to their stroller shouting, "Look, twins!" Sometimes you may feel like enjoying that reaction. It can be a pick-me-up to one's spirit

during a long, hard week to bask in the glow of public attention. But for day-to-day attire, let each baby have his or her
own wardrobe.

When they are newborns, of course, you can dress them to
suit yourself. In the early weeks it makes sense to keep all of the
babies' everyday clothes together within easy reach of the diapering station. Make sure, though, that each baby has at least
some items of clothing that belong to him or her alone. (This
also helps you identify the children later in photographs).

Once they become sensitive to the reaction of others, use
their clothes to help people tell them apart. Let them wear
those matching outfits on different days. They can each have a
cute pink dress, but they don't have to wear them the same day.

For preschoolers, a distinctive pin for each child that can
be worn with any outfit is another way to help others tell
which child is which.

The ownership of clothes and toys gives each baby a beginning sense of individual personhood. When toddlers are
mature enough to begin to dress themselves, they will be able
to exercise some control over what they wear. In making their
own choices about what to wear, each toddler has an opportunity to express his or her individuality.

Dressing is one of the few realms in which a toddler can be
safely allowed to have some independent choice. For twins, it
provides a nonthreatening way to demonstrate independence
from the twin relationship. Mismatched socks and plaid shirts
with polka-dot pants are a small price to pay for allowing flexibility in this area.

You may find that your children develop intense feelings
about owning specific items of clothing. When my daughters
were about five, an older cousin came to visit, bringing several
of her outgrown dresses for Krista and Kelda. I sent them
upstairs with the bag to divide the clothes between them.
When they rejoined the group, they were each wearing one of
the "new" dresses.

I noticed that Krista's dress was oddly puffed out. When I

asked her why, she showed me that she had put on two ordi-
nary dresses over her favorite, which had a Raggedy Ann doll
in the pocket. Her ploy was designed to keep Kelda from
seeing, and fighting over, the prize—and it worked!

When outer clothing is the same, you may not be able to
tell your children apart at any distance. This is a serious
problem when you need to call out a warning and you don't
know which name to use. You might consider giving them distinctive haircuts or hair ribbons or shoe laces.

TOYS

Another important area of ownership and choice is that of
toys. Children need their own toys. Twins and triplets and
more do, too. Of course, they can share blocks and Legos, as
siblings do everywhere. But each child must have some toys
that are his or hers alone.

There are powerful advantages to toy ownership. When a
child owns a toy, he or she can learn to share it. You can't share
what you don't own. It's better to buy smaller, less expensive
items for each child rather than to buy one big-ticket item for
them to share. The toys may be kept together in baskets or on
shelves, as long as each child knows which are his or hers.

Choosing toys for each baby is pretty straightforward at
first. In early infancy, and even early childhood for some, their
preferences and interests may be so similar that they will react
best if they are given the same toys. In our family, that was true
until each child was old enough to make her own wish list.
When Kelda and Krista were toddlers, we tried giving them
different but equivalent toys for presents, like a cat puppet and
a whale puppet or a dump truck and a fire truck.

It was always a disaster, because each believed the other
got the better gift. In fact, they did not even look at the
gifts they were opening. Each kept her eye on her sister's
package. When the contents were different, they were very
disappointed. They found a creative solution, however—they
traded! It became their standard practice. When the contents

turned out to be the same, they sighed with relief, because it meant each could happily keep her gift.

NAMES

Picking a name for any baby is a fascinating process that raises a number of questions:

Will the name fit the child?
Will the name sound all right with our last name?
Are we going to use a name already in the family?
Will the initials spell something funny? Will this name
    provoke teasing or jokes?
Does it lend itself to a nickname we don't particularly like?

The process of picking names for more than one is more complex because you have all these factors to consider, plus a few more. For example, do you want names that emphasize the fact that the children are twins or more? That would be the case with names that begin with the same letter (Ann, Albert, Andrew), or names that rhyme or sound very similar (Annie and Danny, Lateesha and Laneesha). Names that go together in some other context (Jack and Jill, Victoria and Albert) also emphasize twinship.

But there are plenty of distinctive names that sound good together and emphasize individuality. Distinctive names will help them and others have a clear sense of who is talking to whom.

You will also want to consider whether the names sound pleasing when said together, as they will be, and sound good with *and* in between. Hannah and Andrew, for example, may be difficult to pronounce.

If you're inclined to use family names, as either first or middle names, think about the selection from each child's point of view. It's better to give both twins a family name, or neither, than to name only one child after a relative.

Choose names that you like to say. And plan to use them

right from the start. It's a good idea to avoid calling them "the babies" or "the triplets" or "the twins" all of the time. I am embarrassed to remember how hard we were on our friendly neighbors when they called out warm greetings to "the twins." We scolded them and said they must use the girls' names. But they really couldn't tell who was who, so they referred to them as "the ladies" and do to this day.

TALKING TO YOUR MULTIPLES
ABOUT THEMSELVES

When you talk with others about your babies, use their names as a matter of course. When you describe them, refer to their positive qualities: "Donnie is wonderfully relaxed," "Sarah is high-spirited." Avoid labels that might lock them into positive or negative stereotypes, or limited roles. If you label one of your boys as an athlete at three and his sister as a musician, you add to their developmental challenges. Later if the "musician" wants to pursue a sport and the "athlete" wants to play an instrument, they will have to fight those labels and risk invading the other's terrain.

As your children grow, you'll talk to them about their identity as twins as well. In some families I know, the parents don't tell their children they are twins. Although these children generally figure it out when they get to school and learn that not everybody has the same birthday, they may feel that their parents haven't leveled with them or prepared them for all the questions and interest.

I know a family of triplet boys in which one asked, "Mom, how come people always laugh at us?" He knew he was a triplet; he just didn't understand why it was funny.

"He thought he and his brothers were being criticized," his mother said. "I explained to him that people don't often see triplets, and when they do, they are amazed and pleased."

As soon as your children are old enough to understand birthdays, you can explain to them that theirs are the same, and that most of their friends have birthdays that are different from those of the other children in the family. Later, as they understand more about reproduction, you can talk more about the two babies who grew inside you.

I believe parents should be straightforward and matter-of-fact with the children about their multiple status. However, I did avoid the use of "the twins" when talking about my daughters, referring to them by name or as "my daughters."

You will also have to decide how to discuss the issue of who is "older." Certainly being born a few minutes before your twin hardly confers any greater maturity, but the outside world seems very interested in the question of who was born first. I spoke recently to a mother of adult twins who to this day refers to her daughters as "my older one" and "my little one."

I avoided telling my daughters who was born first until later in elementary school. Very young children put a great deal of emphasis on age, and designating one as "older" can artificially confer dominant status.

PARENTING YOUR INDIVIDUAL BABIES

While it is true that their names and wardrobes are an expression of your attitude toward their individuality and their twinship, the ways you relate to them will have the biggest influence on their developing sense of individuality and as members of their "twin team."

But that's not easy. As one exhausted mother of triplets put it, "My pediatrician said to make sure I spend special time alone with each of my children every day. How can I do that? It's all I can do to get to the bathroom."

The basic formula to apply here is to give each child what's needed, when it's needed. When that isn't possible, say so, or let the child know you understand in other ways.

The best advice I received from our pediatrician when Krista and Kelda were newborns was to go ahead and care for them as a unit for the sake of our physical survival. How relieved I was to have "permission" to do what necessity was driving me to do anyway! I breastfed them together, bathed them one right after the other, and tried, not always successfully, to get them on the same sleep schedule. Even so, there were many nights when I had only two hours' sleep.

It may sound as if such "group" care will be impersonal. But in reality there are many ways you can bond with each individual while caring for them in a group. Whoever cries gets comforted. Whoever is hungry gets fed. Whoever has a wet diaper gets changed.

When both or all need something at the same time and you can't possibly respond to everyone at once, let them know. They'll learn to wait! You can sing a silly song about waiting, even when the babies are screaming. You can reassure them with a calm, soothing voice that their turns will come. And all the while you go on relating to the one you are holding or changing.

You address them by their names. You talk to each of them about themselves while changing them. You count their toes. You tell them what you are doing. "Mommy is changing your diaper. Andrew is screaming because he needs his diaper changed, too."

Of course they don't understand your words. But they do understand your tone. Gradually, day by day, the message seeps in: "Mommy (or Daddy) takes care of me. And Mommy (or Daddy) takes care of you. Then I have to wait." There is less fussing. All of the babies listen to what you are saying or singing while you are caring for one. You can be together one-on-one with an individual baby at the same time you are caring for the group.

You will get a lot of advice about making sure you have a special time alone with each of your babies every day. It's not likely that you will get that advice from a parent who has twins. They know that the idea is a good one, but in the early days it is seldom practical. They also know that opportunities for time alone increase as the babies mature and can safely entertain themselves. Then it will be possible to leave one baby in the playpen with a favorite toy while you carry one around on your hip as you cook dinner.

Of course, the babies' personalities will begin to affect the ways you spend time together—and apart. There may be some activities all of your babies or toddlers or little kids love to do together, such as blow bubbles or play with Play-Doh. But there will be times, too, when they want to be apart.

Make it a priority during their infancy to pay each baby individual attention and to respond to each baby's personal needs. Capitalize on opportunities that arise for spending special time one-on-one, but don't worry about manufacturing such times. In time you will have more and more opportunities to be alone with one or the other. One will wake up before the other and go to the supermarket with Dad. The baby who is still napping will stay home with Mom and have a special story time when he or she wakes up.

As they grow, you will reassess whether you are spending enough private time with each. Adding more time with each may take arranging—perhaps a walk together once a week, if there is someone else able to watch the other, or separate bedtime stories. It doesn't have to be much time. Just knowing that you are available privately will be reassuring and affirming of each child's individuality.

It may be an even bigger challenge to arrange, but you should try to make sure both of your children have some time alone—all by themselves. It may not be easy, and you just may not have the space available. But eventually they need to be comfortable with solitude some of the time. Adult twins, looking back, sometimes marvel that they were never alone for a minute in their entire childhoods.

If you have set the stage early, you will find that parenting your twins as individuals becomes second nature. You won't always be focusing on clothing and name tags. As your family grows and evolves, as you feed your children, help them with homework, and go on vacation, treating them as individuals will be as natural as loving them.

PART TWO

GROWING UP
TOGETHER

CHAPTER NINE

THE BABY MARATHON

YOUR MULTIPLES' FIRST YEAR

"*They hold hands and touch each other's faces. At night I put them in opposite ends of the crib, but they always end up snuggled together.*"

The first months with your infant multiples are likely to be a blur. You are recuperating from pregnancy and childbirth, and you're also suffering from fatigue and all the elements of twinshock we've outlined earlier.

This period of adjustment may range from a few months to a year or so. The sleep interruptions of night feedings may be replaced by the sleep disturbances of teething. From time to time, however, the fog thins and you can step back and take stock of your family and your babies' development.

Parents of one baby can easily become fixated on questions about their child's development. "Why hasn't she rolled over, when her older brother was able to at her age?" "Is she really smiling at me?" Questions about the baby's health, happiness, and accomplishments continue to dominate family discussions.

If that's the case for parents of single babies, it goes double (or triple or more) when there are several babies moving along the developmental path at the same time. Of course, parents worry about developmental delays that may be attributable to twinship or prematurity. But they also worry about the relationship between the babies and how they compare to one another. They have a built-in system for comparison, and worry about differences not just for the slower child, but in terms of the bond between the children.

Parents see differences between their multiples at birth, and each developmental step brings more areas in which babies may be similar or different. Differences in hair color or face shape are easy to accept and celebrate, but differences in the pace of development are more difficult.

As we discussed in Chapter Eight, twins may differ significantly even when they are monozygotic. Usually, however, monozygotic twins will follow a similar timetable with regard to sitting up, teething, walking, and toilet learning.

There are some exceptions, as we've noted earlier. Among monozygotic twins with very different birth weights, for example, the smaller twin may not catch up with the larger twin in size—there may be a "critical mass" of placenta necessary for adequate growth, and if one twin's placenta, or share of a placenta, was below this size threshold, that child may never fully catch up.

Among dizygotic twins, growth and development may occur according to very different timetables. Your twins may crawl or develop their first tooth at different ages, just as single-born siblings may. Those differences should not cause concern when they are within the normal range.

In this chapter we'll examine the developmental path your children will follow during their crucial first year. We'll look at normal developmental milestones in the context of twinship, and examine how being a multiple affects social skills, intellectual development, and emotional well-being. By looking at these landmarks, you will be better able to anticipate your children's progress. You'll be able to recognize—and delight in—what is normal, and take appropriate action when one or more of your children seems to be lagging. Sometimes "appropriate action" means simply waiting and having patience, but other times it may involve getting outside evaluations and assistance (to see if language delays are the result of hearing problems, as an example).

The age data in this chapter are for full-term or near-term babies. For preterm babies—which includes many twins and multiples—experts recommend that you use your children's *gestational age*, rather than their calendar age, for the first year or so. To get gestational age, subtract their lost time in the womb from their calendar age. Thus, if your babies arrived a month early, you would view them as eleven months old on their first birthday.

YOUR MULTIPLES AS BABIES

Many aspects of your babies' development will unfold in the same way that it unfolds in all children. They'll learn to roll over, crawl, and walk the way other children do, and they'll smile and babble and talk the way babies always have. We'll discuss these milestones below. For more insights into child development in general, you'll want to explore the many fine books for parents that are available. We mention some in the Resources.

In some areas, however, your multiples' development is unique. We'll discuss them here, and in the following chapters.

In particular, we'll discuss your children's social development. Their relationship to each other, how they influence one another, and how they operate as a couple are unique to multiples. Whether multiples or single babies, infants are busy laying the groundwork for their social development. They begin with the essential task of infancy—forging a secure attachment to their parents. In time their circle of loved ones extends outward, from the immediate family to grandparents, caregivers, and other adults and children.

THE EARLY TWIN RELATIONSHIP

Twins become trusting and attached to their parents in a much more complex context than single children. Because they are born together and need the same kinds of care at the same time, your twin babies relate both as a member of their "twin team" and as individuals: to each parent, to their siblings, and to each other. A pair of twins with one older sibling has *seven* relationships to negotiate; a set of triplets has *eleven*. A newborn single baby with one older brother or sister, by contrast, has just three relationships.

Remember that this is a team that has been together since before birth. The bond between twins is already an organic, established reality by the time the babies draw their first breath. That alone gives them a head start in developing as social beings.

The complexity of twins' relationships with others and the bond that exists between co-twins at birth define the differences in the socialization of multiples compared with children born singly. Fortunately, the special bond between twins provides comfort and makes it easier for the children to maneuver within this complex web of relationships.

Because your babies shared a womb, they are born companions. As newborns, they take comfort in the continuation of this companionship. Although newborns cannot state their preference for each other's company, they give clues. Observant parents who respond by allowing newborns to be together as much as is practical report tremendous benefits. A mother describes how she suddenly understood this need when her boy-girl twins were six weeks old.

"We had a bassinet at the foot of the bed, so I could reach down and scoop up a baby for nighttime nursing. One night our son was colicky and restless, so we put him in a different bassinet so his sister could get some rest. But then they both were making sad little grunts and groans—they were definitely missing each other. We finally put them back together, and they were fine."

As the babies mature, their own relationship will become more complex, as will their relationship with other family members. However, during the early weeks, their physical closeness (which is, after all, a continuation of their fetal closeness) is comforting and provides a strong foundation for the development of attachments with parents and siblings.

The physical care of infant multiples is so demanding in the early weeks that parents quite normally relate to the babies through a fog of sleep deprivation. You may find yourself caring for the babies as a unit, feeding, changing, and bathing them together. Through it all, the babies have each other's company, and a greater opportunity than single babies to give and receive comfort. They practice the dance of action and reaction, effort and response. They snuggle into their fetal position head to foot, hold on to one another's hair, ears, and feet, and suck one another's thumbs. From their earliest months they are reaching out—literally—to others, and feeling the comforting response of another little person reaching out to them.

Over the years, parents have sent us many pictures that show this attachment so vividly: three-month-old twins sitting side by side in their two infant seats holding hands, newborn twins lying side by side with the arm of one flung over the shoulder of the other, baby boys rolling on the floor with the hand of one in the mouth of the other.

By the middle of their first year, twins are sharing reactions— to the sound of thunder, for example—and helping each other cope. Soon they'll climb out of their cribs to comfort each other. Their ability to identify the distress of another and offer assistance is a natural outgrowth of their special relationship. No wonder, then, that by the time they are toddlers, twins are far ahead of single children in the development of empathy.

When you observe the incredible closeness between your babies, you may wonder how well they're bonding with *you*. Mothers often express some sorrow, even jealousy, when they comment on the strength of the babies' attachment to each other.

Although the bonding between the babies seems to have a head start, the parent-child bonding process is taking place at the same time. Because it's more complex, it may take longer. You may be so sleepy at first that you're not sure which child you're bonding with at any given time. Eventually you'll get better at taking advantage of opportunities for one-on-one time with each child. You'll talk lovingly to each as you diaper them and keep eye contact during feeding, and the parent-child bond will deepen.

PHYSICAL GROWTH AND DEVELOPMENT

During your babies' first twelve months, they will triple their weight—a staggering accomplishment, when you think about it. And premature or low-birth-weight babies who are otherwise healthy may grow at an even faster rate as they race to catch up.

It's understandable, therefore, that a major task of your babies is to eat—and eat some more. During those first few months, it may be difficult to view your babies as much more than little factories that take food in at one end and produce dirty diapers at the other.

Yet babies are busy in other areas as well. Newborns have functioning senses of sight, hearing, taste, smell, and touch, although these senses are not yet refined.

As you hold your babies for feeding, bathing, rocking, and play, you and they are communicating through your skin. The babies are organizing their internal and external sensations and getting to know you through your voice, your face, your feel, and your scent.

When twins are dizygotic, their differences may be evident—a boy-girl pair, for example. Their features and coloring may be similar or markedly different. Surprisingly, monozygotic twins often look quite different from one another at birth because their weights may differ, and their position in the womb or birth order may have affected their head shape.

As we said in Chapter Eight, monozygotic twins have a tendency to become more similar over time in terms of behavior as well as appearance. In a study we discussed earlier, monozygotic twins scored no more alike than dizygotic twins at birth on a range of variables that indicate temperament, including activity level and degree of alertness. After six months, the monozygotic twins began to show more similarities in these variables, and the dizygotic twins showed more differences.

At two months, babies begin to lift their heads. By four months, they may learn to turn over from tummy to back. By six or seven months, they may sit alone, especially if propped with pillows—a position that frees hands for play and the enjoyment of toys. Within the next few months, babies will become adept at crawling and creeping.

When that happens, you'll need to accept the change in your life that has occurred: You don't just have twins, you have twins who can *crawl*—and soon you'll have twins who can walk and run.

Toward the end of the first year, some babies begin to pull themselves up, and before long can stand alone or with support from a convenient piece of furniture.

By their first birthday, most babies are either in the early stages of walking or getting ready to walk. However, many children don't walk independently until the beginning of their second year. My own daughters didn't walk until they were fourteen months old—but I was relieved, rather than worried, because I knew the delay put off the next stage of havoc.

FINE MOTOR DEVELOPMENT

During their first year, babies are also developing their fine motor skills—particularly the muscles and coordination of their hands. You can see the blossoming of your babies' abilities as their hands unfold from the curled fists so typical of the newborn into the dextrous instruments of the one-year-old. Babies' ability to hold and manipulate objects appears to parallel brain development during these months. By the third month, hands open and may be able to cup an object. At around five months, babies learn the palmar grasp that allows them to hold an object with the whole hand.

Soon babies are able to hold objects securely, although they have difficulty letting go. They either fling the object or let it drop when they forget it. Controlled release of an object develops around nine months. As grasp develops, so does interest in self-feeding—you'll find your babies reaching for the spoon as you hold it to feed them. Tempting as it may be to feed them yourself to minimize the mess, letting them practice enhances their physical development and their sense of mastery.

Between seven and nine months, babies become adept at picking up small objects with thumb and forefinger, opening opportunities for manipulation of their environment.

Single babies practice all these activities on their own, or with other family members. Twin babies have a convenient partner for practice. "I think they are ahead of the norm in motor skills development," one mother of five-and-a-half-month-old boy-girl twins told me. "I think it's because they have the opportunity to observe each other and learn from each other's progress."

Around seven to eight months, babies sprout their first teeth—and in the case of monozygotic twins, they may do so at almost the same time.

INTELLECTUAL AND LANGUAGE DEVELOPMENT

During your multiples' first year, their brains will grow in size, and the neurological connections will increase and become refined. This growth makes possible the amazing skills your babies will demonstrate during this year. In the earliest weeks, they will pay attention to sights and sounds, and they'll focus their gaze on your face. During the next few months they will begin to smile at the sight of you. You will become attuned to what each of your multiples responds to—if they are dizygotic, one may focus more intently, and the other may be more dreamy. If they are monozygotic, they may give similar responses.

When your babies cry and whimper during their early months, they are communicating—they are expressing their feelings of hunger, discomfort, or pleasure. You'll learn to recognize which cries mean what, and respond appropriately.

Babies around six months of age are famous for the repetitive babbling sounds that resemble speech in cadence and intonation. Infants practice the "music" of speech, through their babbling, before they learn the "words." You and the rest of your family will enjoy eavesdropping on your multiples' crib conversations at this stage—it's as if they are playing jazz riffs. One baby will say "bah bah" and "bo bo," and the other will repeat it back. Then the second twin will vary the sound, perhaps to "bah bo, bah bo." And the game—and the learning—goes on.

This babbling evolves into words during the second half of the year. But for this to happen, babies must have a language partner. Single babies usually use parents as their language partners, as do multiples. But when parents aren't handy, the co-multiples will do nicely.

Although your babies will benefit from talking with one another, they still need to hear adult speech in order to develop standard language. That's how they'll gradually acquire grammar and vocabulary. And this adult speech can't just be the words and images on television—it needs to be intimate communication with a loved one. The words you say lovingly to each of your babies, and the words their other caretakers and relatives use, are the ones they'll be most responsive to and learn the most from.

That's why it's so important to talk each day with each of your multiples. It's not necessary to complicate matters by setting up "speech lessons" at a time when you're barely able to get through the day as it is. What you can do, however, is work language and conversation into your daily routines. As you change each baby, say his or her name; talk directly to your babies as you bathe, dress, or feed them.

As your babies develop the rudiments of memory, they will enjoy games of peekaboo, which indicates their comprehension of object permanence. They're beginning to understand that an object, like you or a teddy bear or a ball, still exists even if it isn't actually visible. They will respond joyfully to your voice and face. They'll begin to name objects, and they'll start to call you—and their co-multiples—by name.

By the time they turn one, your multiples will have developed an extensive facility with language, although they may not produce many recognizable words. That's because comprehension vocabulary normally develops before productive vocabulary. Thus, your ten- or eleven-month-old twins may not yet produce the word *bunny*, but they might well be able to point to the right stuffed animal when you say, "Show me your bunny."

Before they can talk, multiples evolve highly sophisticated nonverbal communication skills. They point and screech and nudge one another (especially when they are fighting over a toy) and make themselves quite understandable to each other and to family members. As they become more mobile, preverbal toddler twins move around a play area like participants in a choreographed dance. I recently watched two monozygotic boys move wordlessly from the drapes, which they tried to pull down, to the picture books, which they both put on their heads, to the toy trucks, which they both shoved under the couch. They took turns leading and copying, but they also moved in unison, taking up similar projects at the same time without any apparent copying.

This unspoken coordination may reduce twins' motivation to use words, and their mutual conversations may reinforce each other's immature pronunciation and baby talk. But their twinship gives them the advantage of having a partner with whom to practice alternating the leader-follower roles and the art of taking turns. This art is essential to the development of conversation skills. One will babble or practice a word, while the other is silent. Then they switch, with the second twin chattering and the other listening. Without words, they make rules about sharing parents and sharing toys. They use facial expressions, gestures, and a lot of noise to enforce their rules. And you will probably understand them quite well.

EMOTIONAL AND PSYCHOLOGICAL DEVELOPMENT

Babies don't generally seem particularly sociable during their first few weeks, but by the time they are a month or so old they will begin to show alertness in facial expression when you speak to them. By about two months, this expression becomes a smile.

Later these smiles are directed at specific people. There's nothing quite like seeing your children's faces light up when you enter the room. It's truly amazing to think that your babies, small as they are, are capable of recognizing your face and translating that recognition into an appropriate emotion (delight) and facial expression (a smile). And by about four months, babies are laughing and chortling with delight.

Single babies usually reserve their first smiles for their parents, but multiples also share their first smiles with each other. I started Chapter One with a journal note about the moment when I first sensed that my twins recognized each other. It was as if they said, "Oh, hello! It's *you*!" This "discovery" of the other twin typically occurs around the age of four months.

During the second half of the first year, babies become much more discerning. They make a distinction between their loved ones and people they don't know, and may show wariness or even anxiety in the presence of strangers. They show an expanding emotional range—delight, fear, anger, affection. Twins frequently pick up on the emotions of the other, crying when the co-twin cries or shows distress.

For example, around the age of eight months, it's typical

for previously mellow babies to become frightened at the sight of an unfamiliar or unexpected face. Although you may be disturbed that your babies scream at the sight of their grandfather (when a month earlier they smiled joyously at him), their response is a sign of intellectual maturation, as they become more able to distinguish between faces and assign emotional meaning to each.

Twins may share this response, or they may not. "My boy is indifferent to public reaction," one mother said, "but my girl is going through stranger anxiety. She acts scared and cries when people she doesn't know rush up to her."

As I said earlier in this chapter, twins and higher-order multiples have a complex web of relationships to negotiate very early in life. And they do so admirably. What they require most from parents is an admiring eye for the social skills (such as turn taking) they learn so well and so young, and patience when an area of language development (such as productive vocabulary) lags just a tad behind that of a single baby.

CHAPTER TEN

TODDLER DILEMMAS AND DELIGHTS

YOUR TWINS, AGES ONE TO THREE

"*By the time they're one or two, they're like an old married couple. They fight, but they love each other. They know that they have to live together. They have a connection that is deeper than we can comprehend.*"

If attachment is an essential task of babies, the main agenda for children from one to about three is to become autonomous—to become separate and independent, on one level, but to remain attached and supported at the same time. It's not an easy task, either for the children or for their parents. Defiance, loud protests, and occasional tantrums are a natural and predictable by-product of toddler life.

Between the ages of one and three, children master a striking array of skills—and that mastery brings a powerful sense of accomplishment and helps enhance the sense of self. There's nothing quite like the look of giddy pride on the face of a one-year-old who has just begun to walk, or the joy of a two-year-old who is exploring her world and has the words to share it with you.

Because toddlers have the ability to walk on their own, they are able to follow their interests. They can run toward and away from other people. They use both their physical mobility and their burgeoning skill with language to assert their independence, on one hand, and to demonstrate affection, on the other.

The toddler years usher in the cycles of distancing behavior that recur for all children regularly throughout childhood and climax during adolescence. Typically, toddlers cycle between intense affection and closeness to parents, and hostility, protest, and testing behavior.

HOW TWINS ARE DIFFERENT

Multiple children do all these things, but in a much more complex setting. They must learn that they are different from Mom and Dad, from their older brother, and from their twin. Along with growing autonomy, children experience insecurity and anxiety about separating from parents and from each other. Twins have the buffer of their relationship to soften the stresses of separation when Mom goes back to work or when it's time for the challenge of separating from each other as well. Of course, the separation process is very gradual.

For twins and other multiples, the distancing behavior so typical of toddlers is complicated by the children's need to distance themselves both from each other *and* from their parents.

Rachel Biale, a licensed clinical social worker with Twin Services for many years, has observed that there are two phases in the process. Twins join forces as a team while they are in a phase of separating from their parents. No wonder it is an exasperating time! Two tornadoes shouting, "No! Won't!" and running away can quickly bring parents to the end of their patience.

Just when parents are thinking dark thoughts about sending their two-year-olds off to boarding school, the children become loving and compliant. They smile, hug Mom and Dad, and seek their approval.

But this pleasant period is simply the lull before phase two, Biale says. Here the children, fortified by positive relationships with their parents, can take *each other* on. Just as the twin situation provides early opportunities to learn empathy, it also provides early opportunities for aggression—hitting, hair pulling, and biting.

"My two-year-old girls bite each other's arms until they're black and blue," a mother wrote to us at Twin Services. "I try to stop them, but nothing seems to work for long. Will they ever stop?"

Yes, we told her. They will eventually stop. But this kind of aggression is understandable. Such "violent" behavior usually starts innocently enough and does not signal true anger or aggression, but rather develops from the easy access to another child or children. Babies may be teething and gnaw on whatever is close at hand. They hit and pound their sibling, just as they hit and pound objects. When the victim screams, the villain is just as shocked and begins screaming as well. How the family reacts sets the tone and influences whether the children will begin to use aggressive behavior as a strategy for attention and control.

We recommend a three-point technique for handling infant and toddler biting and hitting:

- Comfort both children—the biter as well as the "bitee."
- Try to determine whether the biting tends to recur in certain situations or at certain times of day (we've found it often happens in the late afternoon, when children are tired and hungry).
- Change the routine a bit during peak times. Perhaps move bath time into that slot, or serve a predinner snack, or find a way to get the children to play separately during those hours.

As your twins learn to control their aggressive impulses, their struggles for independence will become increasingly verbal.

This early shared companionship and empathy, and the

early opportunity for physical aggression, make the socialization process different for multiples. They practice a range of social behaviors, both positive and negative, within their unit. As toddlers, they begin to apply their advanced ability to share and cooperate as they socialize with other children.

"My two boys always were more at ease in new situations, because of each other," reports the mother of monozygotic boys. "They were much better at sharing toys than single children." She observed the same thing to be true of the other twins in their toddler play group.

In the 1920s child development pioneer Jean Piaget based his theories of early child development on the play dynamics of his own children. In this way, he observed the phenomenon of "parallel play," which he characterized as the earliest stage of play. A baby or toddler will play side by side with another child, rather than in a cooperative way.

But Piaget's children were singles, not multiples—and he apparently didn't study twins! Yes, twins too will sit back to back amid their toys, building their own individual block towers. But twins and other multiples begin to engage in cooperative and interactive activities far sooner than single-born children.

I remember my two would rummage through their pile of alphabet letters to help each other find the particular color one of them wanted. "Here you are! Here's da orange!" the finder would shout as she handed it to her sister.

Dianne Thomas, a marriage and family counselor, has for many years held toddler classes for both single and twin children in Palo Alto, California. She observes that twins display advanced social maturity. They separate from Mom more easily to go into the playroom, for example. They respond to their co-twin's distress by going to help, and they also go to the aid of any child in the room who needs help or seems upset, whereas the single toddlers tend to keep right on playing undisturbed.

Dramatic evidence of twins' precocious ability to collaborate is their tendency to circumvent the best security measures.

While one toddler cannot hope to breach a safety gate all by himself or herself, twins can help each other to climb over it or (as my own did) unscrew the hinges holding it in place at the top of the stairs.

Cooperation and collaboration can be positive, too. Multiples share information, rely on each other, and explain the world to one another. They do this so naturally that they are seldom troubled by their own lack of knowledge. I remember listening as one of my daughters told her sister all about helicopters, after seeing something about them on television. Kelda chattered on about "helicops," what they did and how they worked. After she was finished, she paused and then asked her sister, "What's a helicop?"

All that cooperation is great, but it can result in young multiples sharing their ignorance. Naturally, parents need to be intensely involved in helping children develop an accurate picture of the world.

PHYSICAL GROWTH AND DEVELOPMENT

Except in the case of premature and low-birth-weight babies, twins will follow the same schedule of development as single children. By their first birthday, babies who seemed insatiable eaters just a few months ago may slow down. Their growth rate is slowing; between the ages of twelve and twenty-four months, average weight increases from about twenty to twenty-seven pounds, and height increases from about twenty-eight to thirty-two inches. On average, boys are a bit bigger and heavier than girls.

By around fifteen months most babies are walking. Late walking is not usually a matter of concern, especially if the child has accomplished the preliminary steps that precede walking: crawling, standing up with support, cruising along furniture. A child who is not standing alone at the end of eighteen months, however, or walking by the second birthday should be evaluated by a specialist.

Babies gradually become more surefooted throughout this year until, by age two, they walk like children, rather than babies—and with great speed at times.

Often during the first part of this year, the thrill of walking and running overshadows the development of fine motor skills. Yet those less spectacular skills are developing. At one year, babies are often able to stack one block atop another, which is a quite remarkable skill when you think about all the systems—visual, intellectual, and muscular—the baby must control in order to make it happen.

By about eighteen months, babies may begin to show a preference for the right or left hand as you hand them a spoon or they reach for a toy. Soon babies are holding spoons or cups, although they may not use them in particularly agile ways. By their second birthday, they may be able to stack a tower of five or more blocks.

Between the second and third birthday, children continue to grow fairly slowly—the huge growth spurt of infancy is over and won't be repeated until adolescence. The average weight gain is only about four or five pounds. Height increases about three inches, from about thirty-four or thirty-five inches to about thirty-seven or thirty-eight inches.

From now on, children concentrate on organizing their abilities and developing their skills, rather than accumulating size and weight. They walk more smoothly, skip, walk backward, climb stairs. As their muscles develop and their bodies thin out, they become more like children, rather than roly-poly toddlers.

SPECIAL ISSUES

In dizygotic twins, physical growth and the development of skills may vary. One twin may be smaller and less agile, while the other is surging forward. Monozygotic twins usually develop along similar timetables.

Even when parents understand developmental differences among twins, and when the twins themselves seem fairly comfortable with them, it's hard to avoid the intrusions of strangers and family members who make a fuss because one twin is walking and the other isn't. This is manageable when it's a private discussion between you and a well-meaning aunt, for example. But when adults make disparaging comments in front of the children, it can cause stress unless you defuse the comments.

A stranger may ask one of your twins, "How come your sister's so much bigger?" Or Uncle Ralph may say, "Are you still in those diapers? Your twin brother's already wearing underpants." Your toddlers will be too little to respond effectively, but you can say something like, "Andrew's just the right size for now." Or you can tell annoying Uncle Ralph, "Jonathan is learning how to use the potty, too. He'll get his big-boy underpants when he's ready."

INTELLECTUAL DEVELOPMENT

Your multiples' first birthday is a momentous occasion. Not only have you gotten through the challenges of round-the-clock baby care, but you and they are poised on the brink of a great new adventure as their newfound ability to walk and talk opens new vistas for them.

Once again, intellectual milestones are only different for twins, as compared to single-born children, in cases of prematurity and/or low birth weight.

By now, children's brains have developed to nearly full adult size. The functional areas of the brain have sorted themselves out by this point, so it's possible for them to process sensory data and regulate motor activity fairly efficiently. The brain is now busy forging links and associations between different regions; this process is not complete, but as the brain matures, your children's ability to remember, recall, create, and plan will evolve.

From now on, learning is not so limited by biology; behavior and culture begin to assert more influence. Thus, in their first year your babies got smarter as their brains grew and matured. Now they get smarter as a result of their own play, observation, trial and error, and what they learn from you through language.

By the time they are two, your children are beginning to understand abstractions such as time, future, past, and the difference between what's real and what's pretend. Over the course of the year, this play becomes more imaginative. Instead of piling blocks and knocking them over, they will incorporate blocks, cardboard boxes, and dish towels to make a castle, then spin complex, imaginative games. They'll develop the rudiments of humor, enjoying silly songs and nonsense words.

Children this age are beginning to recognize shapes. They are able to sort objects according to categories, such as size and color. Some children this age can name several letters.

LANGUAGE DEVELOPMENT

Between their first and second birthdays, your twins will name the objects they see around them—their toys, clothing, animals—and in the books you read to them. This acquisition of nouns is called *labeling*, and your children will acquire anywhere from a dozen to a hundred or so by the time they're two (the normal range is very wide). By that time they will also have combined two or more words together into a simple noun-verb sentence, such as "Daddy go" or "Jamie cry."

Between the second and third birthdays, vocabulary increases to as many as a thousand words. Now you're able to enjoy the way your children put words together into original sentences. Those sentences may not be sophisticated, but they demonstrate an awareness of the rules of grammar. Even their mistakes demonstrate a consistency that is quite amazing. For example, children this age know that in English we add -s to a noun to form the plural, and -ed to form the past tense of a verb. That understanding can result in a sentence like, "The mouses goed down in the hole."

SPECIAL ISSUES

As we said in Chapter Three, it is often assumed that twins are fated to have delayed language acquisition. While that's not necessarily true—multiples are no less able to learn to talk than single children—there are factors that may lead to delay.

Twins and other multiples who are born early often exhibit delays in physical and intellectual development during the infant and toddler years. However, their growth during these years is faster than in full-term nontwins, and the gap narrows. According to one study, an intellectual gap is likely to close by age six; physical disparities disappear by age eight.

But there is also a different way that twins acquire language. It has to do with their language partners—the people they spend the most time talking with when they're little.

An Australian study that measured the duration of mother-child interactions found that mothers averaged about two minutes with single children, ninety seconds with each twin, and twenty seconds with each triplet. The more children there are, the less time each child spends listening and responding to adult speech—an essential element in learning to speak. Because toddler twins tend to use more mature language when speaking with an adult than they do with their co-multiples, they need to converse with adults in order to develop language on schedule.

Your twins may also use baby talk in a way that is hard for adults to understand but is perfectly clear to the kids. Twins are more likely than single children to communicate effectively with baby talk, since they have one or more constant partners who are likely to understand it better than adults. The use of "invented words" is universal in children this age; most toddlers say things like "bah" for *book* or "gakter" for *tractor*.

The use of these invented words among multiples is not a secret language, but a shared baby-talk vocabulary. When you listen to your one-year-old twins "conversing" in this way, you'll be convinced they understand each other. This seemingly "secret" language is in fact something called "autonomous language"—an imperfect version of adult language that is often developed and reinforced by close siblings. It often develops in twins—perhaps 40 percent of twin pairs—but is not limited to twins; it occurs whenever children in a family are learning language at the same time and have reduced contact with adult speakers as models. Invented words, autonomous language, and baby talk may continue through the toddler years, but gradually fade as children communicate more with friends outside the family—perhaps by age three or four.

It's important to keep in mind that it is quite normal for children at this age group to acquire socially understandable language at different rates. In any group of two- and three-year-old children, whether multiples or singles, the children will be speaking to one another with a wide range of sophistication. Some will speak in complete paragraphs, others in two- or three-word sentences. Some will speak clearly, while others will mispronounce words.

It's hard not to compare your twins as they learn to talk. At twenty months, Josh speaks in sentences and Matthew still says one word at a time—yet both boys are normal. Language differences that would be seen as perfectly normal in two siblings not of the same age assume magnified significance in twins and multiples. You will find yourself comparing—but it's best to compare your children to other children the same age, not just to one another.

The differences in the rate of language acquisition are greater in dizygotic twins, who may exhibit the same variability that all children display at this age. And boy-girl twins in particular may vary considerably, because girls on average acquire language earlier than boys.

Barring the presence of profound speech disorders, therefore, children (whether multiples or not) with language delays will still be part of the social world of other children and will probably catch up with their peers by early elementary school.

It is important, however, that toddler and preschool-age

multiples develop the ability to communicate fairly well with peers outside the family. Sometimes, because of their closeness and empathy, they develop such an effective nonverbal communication system that their ability to be understood easily by others outside the family develops slowly.

Language delays in any child make peer interactions more difficult; in twins, they can also isolate the children and lock them into their couple status. Twins may find it easier and more comfortable to focus their verbal communication toward their sibling, rather than struggle to communicate with other children who may not understand.

If your twins are slower than their peers to communicate verbally with friends, the following strategies can be helpful:

- Continue to provide opportunities for play that include other children.
- Intervene tactfully to translate when your children seem frustrated, or when they are having difficulty making themselves understood by another child.
- Do not criticize poor grammar or pronunciation. If your children can ask for things, approach others verbally, and take part in activities, they are using social language effectively.
- When your children make mistakes, resist the temptation to correct them. Instead, model the correct word or phrase. For example if one of your twins says, "Bear hurt hisself," you could reply, "Poor bear! How did he hurt himself?" Following your example, your children will correct themselves in time.

If you are concerned about your children's language development, it's wise to ask for a professional opinion. Either your pediatrician can reassure you or a specialist can evaluate your children's speech and language.

Whatever your twins' level of language skill, it's important to create a language-rich environment in your home. You do this informally as you bathe and diaper and care for them. You point out and name objects in the household and out in the world—birds and cats and trucks and airplanes. You read aloud with your children, talking about the pictures and asking questions as you go.

EMOTIONAL AND PSYCHOLOGICAL DEVELOPMENT

One-year-olds often begin the year with particularly affectionate and charming behavior—but it's a stage, and it soon degenerates into fussiness and negativity at midyear. Often, toddlers around their first birthday are so entranced with their own ability to move about that they seem to ignore others, and are uninterested in social interactions.

About six months later, toddlers become highly negative, even as they feel intensely attached to their parents. Their task at this stage is to separate and define themselves, even as they yearn for closeness with their parents. They assert their independence by shouting "No!" and refusing to cooperate.

Certainly all this defiance can be taxing to parents, but it's important to recognize that it's a positive sign. Try not to take these cries of independence personally, but rather make use of the toddler-management techniques we discuss below.

At the same time, they will show their need for closeness by clinging. During this stage, tantrums may become evident. Nightmares may begin as the children's ability to imagine develops.

Single babies do not often show evidence of empathy during these early years; they seem to view other people as objects—interesting, lovable objects, but not people with feelings like their own.

In contrast to single babies, twins often show remarkable empathy. If one is upset and crying, the other will quickly join in. In one study, mothers left the room with one twin, leaving the other behind. The "abandoned" toddler cried and ran to the mother for comfort on her return. The other twin—

the one who had been with the mother all along—showed distress at the other twin's unhappiness, and also turned to the mother for support.

During this year, most children exhibit signs of separation anxiety—crying or other distress when separated from loved ones. With single children, this usually means the mother or father. The Louisville Twin Study looked at attachment in twins and found that at age one, twins adapted calmly when their mothers left them with a stranger—as long as they were with their twin.

They were much more upset if the mother left with the other twin, leaving one alone with the stranger. This suggests that being with one's twin provides an impressive protection against anxiety in new situations; it certainly suggests that parents should be careful about separating toddler twins when making child care arrangements.

At age two, children are often fairly cooperative—a condition that belies the famous "terrible twos" image. They usually engage in parallel play with other children—side by side rather than together. Twins often play cooperatively earlier than single children. As we said above, even preverbal twins synchronize their play in a way that foreshadows the true cooperation of later toddlerhood.

During this year, children develop a fondness for routine and a delight in rituals, from welcoming Daddy at the door to an elaborate bedtime routine full of stuffed animals and storybooks. These rituals and routines help children learn and retain what's expected of them; they also are immensely soothing and comforting.

By about two and a half, children frequently become more difficult, more oppositional with adults, and more grabby and bossy in their interactions with other children. Tantrums reach a peak during this stage. Children this age often develop fearful behavior. At midyear, fears are fairly concrete—loud noises and big dogs, for example; toward the third birthday, they give way to the more imaginative fears of the preschooler: ghosts, witches, scary images from television.

By the third birthday, most children are much better-behaved. They are beginning to understand rules and family expectations, and can make an effort to behave well. This effort is often imperfect, however, and slip-ups and backsliding are par for the course.

TWIN-PROOFING

Child-proofing is important in any household, but even more so when there are two or more potential collaborators up to risky business. Your multiple toddlers will get into trouble according to their own temperaments. Sometimes they'll work as a team; at other times, they'll play follow the leader.

"When I was pregnant and envisioning what it would be like when they were toddlers," said a mother of triplet boys, "I imagined they would all go for the light sockets at the same time. It never happened. They always got into danger one at a time."

The child-proofing strategies for multiples are similar to those needed to keep a single child safe, and that's why you'll want to refer to a good baby-proofing guide. However, read those guides with the assumption that your multiples will get into trouble *sooner* than single children because they will help one another into trouble.

That brings us to three essential ways that child safety issues are different for multiples. First is the distraction factor. One child can crawl into trouble while you are changing the other, or might head for the hot iron while you are coping with the other twin's tantrum.

Second, two or more children are physically capable of more than a single child is. Two very short toddlers can climb higher than one average-sized toddler, because one can boost the other onto a high shelf (or up the chimney, as happened in one family). Three triplets working together exert three times the force on a baby gate that one child can.

And finally, twins collaborate. A single child might never dream of climbing out a second-story window, but two schemers might well plan such an escapade. If one twin has the brilliant idea of tasting the dishwasher detergent, the other twin is likely to copy the first.

In the beginning you will want to be sure you have safe places for the babies to sleep, be bathed, and be changed. This includes having a safe spot to leave one baby while you are feeding or changing the other. Sometime during the second half of the first year, your multiples will develop mobility, and at that point the fun begins.

Never underestimate your toddlers' ability to move heavy furniture or tip it over. They also climb and boost one another up. I finally had to take all the shelving and bureaus out of my daughters' room, using low cubbies for storage. Another option is to bolt bureaus and heavy furniture to the wall. One family with sextuplets has no furniture at all in the children's rooms, except the cribs. Everything is stored in baskets.

Make sure any upper-story windows are secure. I know a family whose daughters quietly moved their crib across the room to their second-story bedroom window. They used it as a ladder to climb up to the sill of the open window. There they sat, with their arms around each other, looking up at the moon. They survived because their vigilant dad saw them and swept them to safety before they could fall.

Be mindful of where your children are when you are getting them into and out of your car and buckling them into their car seats. Leave one baby in the playpen while you carry the other out to the car, then return for the other. Later you might assign a safe spot next to the car for the children to stand and wait as you are putting them in the car or letting them out.

Difficult as it is to keep two or more toddlers in hand, they do need to be restrained in some way when you are in public or near traffic or other hazards. Use strollers and backpacks when the children are small. If necessary, use harnesses when they're older.

The Triplet Connection, a support group for parents of higher-order multiples, has suggested designating one room in the house for the babies, and then baby-proofing it thoroughly. Of course, they still need to be watched, but in this room there will be very little danger for them.

One family with triplet boys did just this. "We had a room for them right next to the kitchen," the mother said. "It had no furniture—just appropriate toys and nothing else. Some might think I was depriving them of stimulation, but I had to have a place where they could be safe when I couldn't be watching them. And they had each other's company."

COPING WITH THE TODDLER YEARS

"Well, today, the kids put Rice Krispies in the air-return vent, and now we get Rice Krispies floating out of the hot-air registers," said a mother of two-year-old twins.

"Things don't get better with toddlers," another mother explains. "They just get different."

It does get better, of course, but it's true that toddlerhood brings a new set of challenges. Now you have little ones who can run and jump and climb. And your babies begin to talk—and talk back to you!

Toddlers are notorious for noise, defiance, spills, and all manner of behavior that takes a toll on parents. But they also can be sweet, loving, funny, creative, and delightful. In the case of multiples, both the negatives and positives are, well, multiplied.

HELPING YOUR CHILDREN LEARN LIMITS AND SELF-CONTROL

Although some misbehavior is to be expected, the wisest course is to design your home and routines to minimize conflict. For example, if you want your twins to stay away from your collection of valuable porcelain, it's wise to put it away rather than leave temptation within reach of busy hands.

The rules for a safe home that we've just considered have a value beyond keeping your toddlers safe. The safer the environment, the more the children can move about freely and learn from it. If they can touch and move and manipulate physical objects, they begin to understand cause and effect. If they have some autonomy, they can learn to control their impulses.

Minimize squabbles by changing the scenery. For example, when toddlers try to push each other off your lap, put them both down and start over. Stay calm (or at least pretend to), even if they scream. If they are unable to share your lap or wait for turns, change the setting. Lie down on the floor to read to them for a while, and there won't be any lap to fight over.

Try to anticipate trouble and redirect before things get out of hand. If you know, for example, that your children always fight over who gets to pick the first bedtime story, work out a turn-taking arrangement. And remind the children about it: "John picked first tonight. Sarah, you'll get to choose first tomorrow."

Remember that fatigue and hunger can set kids off, especially late in the day. Head off trouble by having snacks available, and try to get the kids to nap before they're entirely exhausted.

Use assertive but positive language when guiding your children. In practical terms, this language should grow naturally out of the chatter you and your twins have engaged in all along ("Now we're putting on Joseph's shoes, and next we'll put on Brian's shoes"). Let's say one twin is mistreating the family cat. You might guide him by saying, "Joseph, the kitty wants you to pat her gently. It hurts her when you pull her tail."

It's best to minimize the times when you have to say no. If you limit it to truly dangerous situations or major infractions, it will be less likely to inspire rebellion. One father I know has good results with "Stop!" rather than "No!" in emergency situations. When two twins are scampering off in two directions, there's a good chance at least one of them will actually stop.

In addition, using positive commands takes advantage of the fact that toddlers tend to hear the last part of a phrase or sentence. If you say "Don't run in the street," they may hear, "Run in the street." But if you say, "Stop," or "Come here," they are more likely to understand.

When toddlers disobey, time-outs are a better solution than harsher punishments. These sessions can be very brief at first. As your children mature, they will begin to understand that when they can't behave themselves in a social situation, they must go and be by themselves until they can rejoin the group.

The American Academy of Pediatrics has recently issued guidelines opposing the use of spanking as a method of discipline, recommending other approaches, such as time-outs and, for older children, the loss of privileges.

ENCOURAGING HELPFULNESS

As soon as they can manage, toddlers love to be allowed to help with chores. They love routines and showing that they know where things go and how things are done.

Their "help" isn't always truly helpful—helping with the laundry probably means dumping all of the clean clothes out of the laundry basket onto the floor. Watering the flowers may mean soaking the whole backyard and themselves. And yet by allowing your toddlers to try, you are introducing them to the *idea* of helping. As they grow older, they'll do more, and they'll do it with less complaint.

During the toddler years, your children's "jobs" should feel like play to them—helpful play. Your children may enjoy doing the same job at the same time, or each may enjoy "owning" a job. One child may be responsible for putting groceries into the cupboard, while the other prefers setting out silverware for family meals.

Your multiples are learning from everything they do with you. As they set out a spoon for each member of the family, they're learning elementary math concepts. They tear lettuce leaves and learn about cause and effect. They mix batter, watch the muffins rise, and learn about physical states.

Best of all, their activities are teaching them that they are part of a family, and everyone—even the tiniest members— can contribute.

POTTIES, POTTIES EVERYWHERE

Believe it or not, those diapers that seem to dominate your life will eventually recede. Your multiples will learn to use the potty all by themselves! One adult twin who grew up during the era of cloth diapers remembers family members joking about the "White Forest" in their basement—acres of diapers dripping on clotheslines.

The trick is to wait until they are truly ready and eager to start the learning process. There's no greater waste of precious energy in a multiple family than trying to toilet-train toddlers who aren't ready and motivated. It's been said that twins potty-train about six months later than singletons; yours may be earlier or later, but hurrying them is definitely inadvisable.

It's true for single babies, and doubly so for twins: The earlier you start, the longer you'll spend trying to train them. If you allow your babies to remain in diapers until they show signs of readiness, the process will go quickly and you'll spend less time in that transitional period when everyone is making puddles on the floor.

And how will you know when yours are ready? Sometime between their second and third birthdays, most children have acquired enough maturity and interest to begin the process. You'll know they're ready when:

- Your twins are able to understand and follow simple directions involving two or three steps.
- They have a basic understanding of cause and effect: "If I go in my diaper, it gets wet."
- They are emotionally at a stage where they wish to please and cooperate with their parents. Don't try to start training at the height of temper tantrums, or the "No!" stage, or during a time of unusual stress or changes in family life.
- They are physiologically ready to learn to control their excretions. They need to know what it feels like to be about to go, and recognize and control the sensations of elimination.

When you think your twins are old enough, try to begin the process at a time when they are enjoying doing things together and copying each other, rather than fighting and competing. This way they'll be partners in the effort.

I remember when mine were learning. One would rush to the bathroom and get there too late, leaving a puddle on the bathroom floor. Her sister would rush after to watch, running through the puddle. Meanwhile, the puddle drifted toward the toys lying on the floor, and I'd have to clean up the floor, clean up the toys, and clean up the kids—including four little feet.

Once they get started, twins often master this developmental milestone sooner than single children because they have each other to observe and learn from. It's not uncommon, however, for the process to last beyond the toddler years and past the age of three. By three and a half, most children will be dry at night as well as during the day.

It is quite likely that twin children will not reach this milestone at the same time. If this is the case with yours, resist the temptation to make a big deal of the differences. The child who is behind is certainly aware of it. Be matter-of-fact and accepting. Encourage "big-kid" behavior, but don't scold when there are the inevitable lapses.

Do, however, pay attention when a child who has been dry slides back into bed-wetting on an ongoing basis. This can be a signal of stress, so you will want to review factors in the child's life that may be causing the stress. Then you can understand and can help.

TODDLER MULTIPLES AND SLEEP

Adequate sleep is essential to good health and a positive outlook on life—for both parents and twins. You will be more relaxed and adaptable in your dealings with your children when you are rested, and they will be more cheerful and cooperative when they've had enough rest.

Yet toddlers often resist bedtime and nap time, even when they're clearly exhausted. With twins, this natural balkiness can create more difficulties because they wake each other up or keep each other from falling asleep in the first place.

Children don't all have the same need for sleep. One may become sleepy earlier in the evening or wake earlier in the morning than the other. One may fall asleep quickly and easily, while the other may be more keyed up and require a longer going-to-sleep ritual before settling down.

NAP PATTERNS

If you are lucky and your multiples have similar sleep needs and similar developmental patterns, their nap times will be easy to coordinate. They'll probably take a midmorning nap and another in the midafternoon until they are fifteen to eighteen months old, eventually phasing out the morning nap. They will probably both be ready for bed at the same time, soon after dinner or bath time.

However, it's quite likely that your twins will have different patterns. One may be sleepy after breakfast, while the other is up and running until noon. If one of your children clearly needs more sleep than the other, you'll have to accommodate those needs by putting the sleepy one down for a nap.

On the plus side, you'll have some time to spend one-on-one with your wakeful child. The downside, of course, is that you'll have less quiet time for yourself.

When twins nap at the same time and place, one may keep the other awake. Often twins "nap" by emptying their bureau drawers or rearranging the furniture in their room. If naptime consistently deteriorates into playtime, you may want to separate them for naps.

Another option is to define nap time as "quiet time"—the children must be in their room, looking at picture books or playing quietly. Although they may not sleep, they will have the benefit of some rest. And so will you.

NIGHTTIME SLEEP PATTERNS

At our house, Kelda was always ready to go right to sleep at night, but Krista was geared up to talk about the day. "Talk more!" she would shout over at Kelda. "Not," Kelda would sigh in response. Sometimes Krista would climb out of her crib and into Kelda's, where she would sit on her despite her protests of "I'm asleep!" Sometimes Kelda won, and Krista would fall asleep; sometimes Krista won, and they would converse for another half hour or so.

I'm not sure if we would have separated them even if we'd had the space. Over time, these nighttime talks, during which they "debriefed" one another about the day's events, became a special benefit of their relationship. On the other hand, separate sleeping arrangements are a reasonable approach if these disturbances are continual and debilitating and you have room to accommodate it. Parents often tell me, however, that they have given each child a separate bedroom, only to find them sleeping in the same room in the morning.

TOYS AND PLAYTIME

We talked in Chapter Eight about the importance of individual gifts and individual ownership of toys. Your toddler twins will benefit from owning their own dolls, teddy bears, trucks, and other treasures. Even as they cherish these toys, they may choose to share, to take turns, or to swap with the other twin's possessions.

From a practical standpoint, some toddler toys will be held in common—blocks, Duplos and other building sets, climbing equipment, games, and certain big-ticket items. These shared playthings provide learning opportunities as well, as your twins take turns and compromise in their use.

Some playtime suggestions for toddlers:

- It's easy to get buried under toys, trucks, blocks, dolls, and puzzle pieces in a twin household. Not only is it hard to keep everything tidy, there's also the likelihood that the children will get bored with toys that are accessible all the time. It's a good idea, therefore, to cycle your children's playthings in and out of storage. Every week or so, you might quietly pick up the items that are less used, and bring out a fresh box from before. A doll or game that your children rediscover is as exciting as a new one bought from the store—and much cheaper.

- Children thrive on "gardening"—watering the flowers, digging in the dirt, playing in sand or mud.

- If you have a handy sidewalk or concrete porch or patio, give each child a small pail and an old paintbrush on a summer day and let them paint with water. Their "pictures" will show clearly until they evaporate.

- Set large cardboard cartons on their sides, as playhouses, one for each child. You can cut out doors and windows and draw curtains and other embellishments. Children love to have their own space, and twins benefit from a chance to practice being all by themselves.

YOUR TODDLERS AND THEIR SIBLINGS

We talked earlier about how siblings react to the arrival of newborn multiples. As the babies grow into toddlers, the older children are growing, too. Family routines will evolve accordingly. Your older children can help in new ways, and they can also find new ways to become annoyed by the little ones.

If you're able, try to protect your older children's territory. If they can be trusted behind locked doors, allow them to lock their rooms; alternatively, supply them with safety gates.

Continue to validate their role as big brother or big sister, and praise their contributions. However, find ways to encourage their involvement in ways that aren't just related to their status as helpers. When possible, find occasions for them to share in the fun of living with multiples. When your older children play with the little ones in ways that are fun for both, and not just baby-sitting, everyone benefits. For example, those cartons you set up for your twins to use as houses can be decorated by an older child, who might draw curtains or shutters or other details.

CHAPTER ELEVEN

NEW FRIENDS, WIDENING HORIZONS

YOUR MULTIPLES DURING THE PRESCHOOL YEARS

"*My daughters are the best of friends, and the best of enemies. They can be fighting one moment and really angry at each other. Then the next moment, one says to the other, 'Let's go play princess.'*"

Between the ages of three and five, children learn about the wider world beyond their family, and their place in it. As they embark on this adventure, twins have a lifelong companion—and occasional adversary—at their side.

As their minds and spirits blossom, as they learn and think and imagine, they pool their information, or lack thereof. They provoke each other to try new things, and they exert a restraining influence as well. They teach, comfort, annoy, and challenge.

Often this is a "golden age" for parents of twins. The challenges of the toddler years are behind them, and the children are able to do more for themselves and accept household rules and limits.

In this chapter we'll talk about the development of your twins' social and intellectual skills, their evolving self-concepts, and how their relationship with one another unfolds.

189

THE BROADENING OF THE
TWIN RELATIONSHIP DURING
THE PRESCHOOL YEARS

When multiples are very young, they may thrive on each other's company. But around the age of three, your multiples—like all preschool-age children—are typically ready for cooperative play, and for friendship outside the family. I remember my daughters coming to me one day and saying they were bored. "We doesn't got nobody to play with," they said. Krista told me, "I don't want to play all by myself with just Kelda."

During these years, children are becoming more interested in other children and more comfortable about separating from parents. If they have spent their early years at home, they are usually ready for a preschool experience, although children certainly differ in how easily they take this step.

Whether they're in a nursery-school setting or at home, they begin to apply their social skills to a broader realm. As they play more with children outside the family, they develop distinct—if often short-lived—preferences for certain children and gravitate toward their favorites.

During these years, twins socialize individually with other children some of the time and socialize as a team at other times. Their playmates are beginning to notice their unique relationship. Sometimes the power of the twin unit can tempt other children to try to drive a wedge between them. One day when I picked up my daughters and another girl at nursery school, Kelda was chewing gum. When I asked where she got it, I learned that the third child had bribed her—in exchange for a stick of gum, she had demanded that Kelda be her friend and never speak to Krista again!

When other children play favorites with one of your twins, pay attention to the feelings of both. The "chosen" child can't help but be pleased with the special attention. If she is old enough, however, she may be able to understand the unfairness of a friendship that is based on the deliberate exclusion of her twin, and she may choose to withdraw from the friendship on her own.

Although twins and other multiples continue to cooperate and collaborate more than single children during the preschool years, the extent of this cooperation varies depending on the children's personalities—and on their zygosity. Nancy Segal, director of the Twin Study Center at California State University in Fullerton, has captured the cooperative play of a series of pairs of young twins on video as they work to complete a puzzle. The dizygotic twins divide the puzzle pieces into separate piles, both trying to do the puzzle on their own and—inevitably—arguing over the pieces. The monozygotic twins pool the pieces and work on the puzzle cooperatively.

As we've discussed, twins develop a sense of empathy much earlier than do other children. They bring each other toys. They go for help in emergencies. They comfort each other. Your praise when they are kind to each other will encourage them and make them feel good about themselves and their relationship.

This thoughtfulness flourishes among preschoolers. If one of my daughters woke up with a scary dream, the other would comfort her. One would help the other remember a poem, or teach the other how to tie a knot.

One mother described her three-year-old boys giving and receiving comfort. "Matt was sad. He went to his brother and said, 'I need a hug.' Brian gave him a hug and said, 'It's okay, Matt. I'm here.' "

As they get older, twins refine the kind of support they give one another. I recall my own daughters, at the age of about three and a half, discussing whether to get out of bed at night for a drink of water. Krista said she wanted to get a drink, but she wanted Kelda to come with her and hold her hand in the dark. Kelda agreed, but drew the line on holding her sister's hand—"You don't need to hold on to a hand. You know you're not afraid of anything."

Along with their expressions of caring, your twins will

continue to squabble and fight. But often the disputes are short-lived or are balanced with genuine caring.

As one mother of four-year-old boy-girl twins said, "My daughter is a real fireball and beats up on her brother like nobody I've ever seen. She doesn't hold back. But if he goes somewhere without her, she wants to know what he is doing every minute, and when he will come home."

MULTIPLES BENEFIT FROM PLAY DATES, TOO

Sometimes parents may not take advantage of opportunities for their multiples to play with other children, because the twins "have each other." Since multiples often do play well together, overstressed parents may not find the time or energy to orchestrate play dates, especially if the children want to play with different friends. Yet it is important to arrange play opportunities so each child has a chance to get the social experience he needs.

A group of mothers I know created a no-hassle twin play group at a local park. The five mothers and ten kids gathered there monthly. The children had a grand time, plus had the opportunity to get to know other children, while the parents enjoyed a much-needed chance to socialize.

Pairing up with another set of multiples can be valuable in a different way, too. I know of a set of dizygotic twins in which one girl is big, outgoing, noisy, and energetic. Her sister is smaller, quieter, and seems to fade into the background when they're together. Her parents found another set of twins with similar dissimilarities and arranged "matched" play dates—the bolder twins would play together at one house, and the quieter ones together at the other house.

Sometimes an even number of children in a play group works best, because it reduces the likelihood that one child will be excluded. For some children, however, a threesome actually works better. Twins may be accustomed to playing as a unit, and they delight in having a third child to play with. That child had better have plenty of energy, however. My own daughters had a friend named Thomas, whom they took turns playing with. One would get tired and rest, and so then the other would play with Thomas. They'd go back and forth like this until it was time for Thomas to go home—and by then he was a very tired little boy.

OFF TO PRESCHOOL

Saying goodbye to parents and going off to nursery school can be an exciting but sometimes painful transition for children who have spent their early years at home. The start of preschool may introduce you to the issue of classroom placement for your multiples. If there are several classrooms in the nursery school, you may wonder if your children should be together or separated.

This is a theme that runs through the school years, and we address it in detail in the next chapter. With multiples this age, a good rule of thumb is: Keep them together for now. Let them benefit from their relationship during this transition into a wider world. When twins make their first journey beyond the shelter of family together, they have the support of one another. Ideally, the activities and other children encourage them to play individually, yet in the comforting presence of the other.

"At first my twins stuck to one another's side," a mother recalls. "But later, after they'd been in nursery school a few weeks, they didn't have to be with one another. They'd do their own thing, but if something happened to the other across the room, they'd be right there.

"I've seen that again and again with twins. They react that way with other kids, not just their own twin. If someone cries or is upset, they go over and try to help. They're so used to doing that."

PHYSICAL DEVELOPMENT

Sometime between two and a half and three and a half, your toddlers become less babylike and more like children. They walk and run with increasing mastery and confidence. They are developing "big-kid" bathroom habits.

In their first few years, your babies mastered fine and gross motor skills so rapidly and dramatically that changes in their abilities could be measured almost daily. From ages three to five, however, children refine their new skills through daily practice. Their ability to manipulate objects—from spoons to toothbrushes to crayons—makes them able to care for themselves more, and to express themselves through play.

Now they can handle paintbrushes and crayons. Artwork becomes more and more realistic. They can use silverware at meals and set the table. They can take things apart to see how they work. They can open and close Velcro fasteners, undo buttons, handle zippers. Soon they'll be able to tie their own shoes.

Your twin pair may be well matched in energy level. Or they may be very different—one always on the go and the other content to play quietly. They may also be matched or mismatched in athletic ability. Here is another area where their individual gifts begin to shine. Your job is to praise, whether they are the same or different, and avoid negative comparisons.

By this age, your children will become much more aware of these differences. Even if you accept and celebrate these variations in your children, strangers and acquaintances may not. I know a family with triplet boys who are trizygotic and thus quite different in size and appearance. One of the boys is much smaller than his brothers.

"Total strangers would notice this," his mother recalls, "and comment right in front of him. They'd say things like, 'Oh, he's the runt of the litter.' Physical differences like this are harder on multiples than on single siblings, because they're the same age and are all traveling in the same circle." When people make unkind comparisons in front of your children, consider a rejoinder such as, "All my boys are doing beautifully, thank you."

INTELLECTUAL AND LANGUAGE DEVELOPMENT

Sometime around your children's third birthday, a marvelous shift takes place. It's as though they are standing on the threshold of an exciting new world—a world full of wondrous things to explore, to try out, to imagine. You'll see it in the questions your children ask and the way they listen to your answers.

During these preschool years, all children make spectacular progress in their ability to think, to reason, to speak, and to express themselves. Your children will be able to remember the past and anticipate the future (as they'll demonstrate by using past tense and future tense in conversation). Their thinking will be more abstract and no longer limited to the physical world.

Of course, there will be limits to their cognitive abilities. Piaget refers to this period as the "preoperational" stage of intellectual development, during which children are able to manipulate symbols (such as words and pictures that represent reality) but are not yet adept at distinguishing between what is real and what is not.

In the last chapter, we talked about the early process of learning language. By age three, most children will have a fairly large vocabulary—perhaps nine hundred words—and are speaking in sentences. Pronunciation improves but may not be perfect. Speech becomes less and less babyish.

Apart from any developmental difficulties related to prematurity, twins and triplets and higher have the same intellectual capacities as single-born kids. Because so many multiple babies are born premature, they may exhibit during their early years the delays that are associated with prematurity or low birth weight. Even so, most catch up by the time they are ready for school.

But multiples develop their intellectual and language abilities in a different context than do single kids. They are growing up with one or more siblings the same age, and therefore usually have less individual interaction with adults. This has advantages and disadvantages.

In order to develop language, children need good models of the language they are learning. They need practice in speaking it in a relaxed, pressure-free environment. It's easier for parents of a single child to provide these necessities; parents of multiples may need to make a conscious effort.

Multiples often have to compete to get a word in edgewise. Some common tactics are to speak loudly, talk at the same time, interrupt, and talk very rapidly. These behaviors can become habits that make conversation outside the twin pair or family more difficult and may in fact affect their social lives.

On the other hand, as we said in the previous chapter, multiples usually have a language or conversation partner handy. They can practice conversation, share information, ask and answer questions, and help one another remember words and ideas.

In spite of the oft-repeated stories of twins making up their own language, there has been little systematic research on how twins learn to talk. We do know, however, that the twin situation affects the language-learning environment. Most of the research focuses on documenting language difficulties in twins.

A recent Australian study found that twins had mild delays in pronunciation and mastery of grammar but had normal conversational skills for their ages. Triplets were delayed across the board. No connection between language delays and birth weight or zygosity were found. There was a correlation, however, between language competence and multiples who were conceived with the help of infertility treatments. This may be because parents with the resources and sophistication to pursue such treatment are likely to have more education, and more support in caring for their multiples.

Some research findings indicate that early studies reporting language deficiencies in twins were flawed because they used standard measures of language that do not account for the twin situation. For example, twins are adept at finishing each other's sentences. This sophisticated linguistic process reduces the amount of time each twin is speaking during a conversation. Yet language development is often measured by the length—in terms of the number of words—of what is said. Such tests would report a deficiency, instead of the advanced ability that the twins showed.

From the beginning, twins and triplets have to engage in conversation with more than one person at a time—parent plus other child (or children). Consequently, they learn early how to direct their conversation to a particular person. When given the opportunity, a twin child will direct his or her speech to the adult rather than the twin.

LANGUAGE AS A WINDOW ON THE TWIN WORLD

KELDA: What do you think *to* means?

KRISTA: I don't know.

KELDA: *Two* means when you're growing much bigger than the ceiling.

KRISTA: No, it means you can crawl.

KELDA: Oh.

KRISTA: *(sings)* Happy birthday to you . . . oh! *Two* means "baby," and "happy birthday to you" means . . . That's what *to* is! That's the same word!

Your children's increasing mastery of language lets you understand their evolving intellectual development. Now your children can talk about ideas and abstractions, and you will be able to understand their evolving view of reality.

In the above exchange, my daughters were figuring out the meaning of words and how one word can have more than one meaning. They had the benefit of working out these concepts together. Together they were able to consider intricate subjects at very early ages. Like all twins, they taught and learned from each other. They discussed, disagreed, considered, reassured, and sometimes schemed.

It is important that the adults in the family stay tuned in to the children's conversations as a reality check. Although none of the children has more life experience than the other, one twin will often give the other an undeserved authority. I call this phenomenon the "rule of the tribe." By the age of three, all children have had enough contact with older children to admire and try to emulate their "sophisticated" ways. Watch any small child gaze admiringly at the big kids at the playground. Children who have older siblings have models for more mature behavior close at hand, and older siblings usually become the primary authorities on the ways of the world and on you, their parents.

This is true for twins and triplets, too, but with a twist. Twins will certainly respect the authority of older siblings, but they are liable to give primary authority to their co-twins. Whatever their twin says and knows comes first. This is fine when they share accurate information. It may not be so fine when they share distorted or inaccurate views of reality, or when they share a fantasy as if it were a reality—a common element of the preoperational thinking of the preschool-age child.

One day my daughters came home from preschool very upset by the prospect of a fireman coming to visit the school the next morning. I finally figured out what was going on: They believed that since our mailman brought mail and our milkman brought milk, the fireman would bring fire.

Nothing I said could convince them otherwise. In the morning they refused to go to school until I promised them each an ice cream cone after school if the fireman showed up. He did, we got the cones, and a family ritual was launched. Every time there was a visit by a fireman or there was a fire drill at school, we went for ice cream afterward.

"TWIN EFFECTS"

In my own research on language development, I have identified what I call "twin effects," which are related to the children's concepts of themselves as a team. These are adaptations of standard English, used to express the special reality of twinship. They parallel the development of standard usage but don't necessarily replace it.

Such twin effects include:

- The use of a team name, like "me and me too" or "we guys" (the opposite of "you guys"), which the children use to refer to themselves when they are together.
- The use of singular verbs with their team name: "Is Krista-Kelda going to the park, Daddy?"
- The use of *me* to refer to themselves as a team: "Sit between me, Mom."

In a survey I conducted about twin effects in twins and triplets ages two to five in 166 Canadian families, 44 percent of their parents reported some kinds of twin effects in their children.

Several parents responded that there were no twin effects in the language of their children because they "didn't allow it." Apparently fear of language delay had prompted these parents to forbid this creative use of language to express the twin relationship.

When and if your children use "twin effects," such as a double name, appropriately to refer to themselves as a team, don't worry about it as long as they each know and can use their own names. Their use of a team name will diminish as their social horizons expand beyond their team and will give you an idea of how they are maturing.

If, however, your children appear confused about their own names—if Sarah calls her sister "Sarah," for example—do everything you can to help them grasp their own names as their individual property. Review all of the arenas in which you can validate their individuality—be sure each has ownership of some clothes, toys, and space. Use each name individually as much as possible when you address them.

Team names are not to be confused with substitute names. Sometimes the children are not able to pronounce the letters of one of their names, so they make up a substitute. One two-year-old pair named Jessica and Phaedra could not say "Jessica," so Jessica called herself "Not Phaedra." This did not mean Jessica had a negative view of herself. She was making creative use of *not* to give herself a distinctive name, different from her twin's.

As your children's language matures, they will give you more insights into their views of themselves as individuals and as a "couple" or "tribe." Kelda, at age three, told her sister, "You and me are the same, because people tell you that you and me are the same." Yet they knew they were different, and they explored those differences in their conversations.

As they mature, expect to hear less babyish pronunciation, fewer twin effects such as a team name, and more and more complex sentences and ideas. Now you can talk with each of them about their needs and wishes and discuss their relationship.

CREATING A LANGUAGE-RICH ENVIRONMENT

The challenge of finding enough time for language-building conversation with each of your children is really not difficult to overcome. Think about the many times during the day when you have contact with each child: helping with buttons, combing hair, washing hands, serving a meal.

You can make each contact count linguistically by talking about what you are doing. Ask questions—always an excellent stimulus to language—and listen respectfully to each child's answers. Instead of saying, "Michael, I like the red buttons on your jacket," ask, "Michael, what color are your buttons?" Encourage your children to respond in sentences. If you say, "We had fun at the playground, didn't we?" you may get a response of "Yes." If you say, "Tell Daddy about our trip to the playground," you're likely to inspire a description of the day's activities.

Other suggestions:

- Make trips in the car a time to play with language: make up songs together, talk about yesterday and tomorrow, make up silly rhymes. One mother I know improvised a song about a whale, to which she added salient bits about each child as they drove to nursery school every morning. The children listened hard for the parts about themselves and added some of their own words to the tune.

- Encourage other adults to spend talking time with each child—grandparents or other relatives can be a wonderful help. Especially if you are finding that the demands on your time are overtaxing your ability to have meaningful conversations with each child, figure out a way to get the help of other adults.

- Insist that each child speak for him or herself: "No cookie if you don't ask."

- Resist responding to interrupters. Reward turn-taking and patience. When one of your children interrupts, you can respond calmly by stating what you observe: "I hear Carlos trying to talk. But Andres is showing me his picture. Carlos, when Andres is finished, you'll get your turn."

- Read to your children every day. Fifteen to thirty minutes of story time just before bed or a nap provides a wonderful opportunity for enriching your relationship with the children. Make it a quiet, relaxed time. Turn off the television and the phone, and settle in. You can read to the children one by one or all together. Just be sure each child has a chance to choose a story and has a chance to look at the pictures and to comment. In the process you will be modeling good language and will be able to detect and correct any misconceptions and misinformation they share. When they fight over who gets to sit on your lap, stop and work out a solution together.

Remember that there is a tremendous range in language development. When one of your children seems to be lagging behind the others, compare that child's language to that of other children the same age. It may be in the normal range for the age, just different from the rest of his or her brothers and sisters. Most variations are just that—variations.

You needn't worry about every mispronunciation, lisp, and stutter. Those are parts of the learning process. If, however, you develop any anxiety about one or more of your children's language, seek help through your school district or a private counseling service.

The first step is to have the child's hearing checked. If there are no hearing problems, have all of the children's language evaluated by someone familiar with multiple-birth children to be sure no correctable problem is overlooked. If a problem is diagnosed, be sure that all of the children understand the goals of any speech therapy you undertake for one or more of them, so that they can help rather than hinder the process.

Generally, by the time children are four, their speech should be clear enough so that they can be understood when they leave the family setting for preschool and other social experiences.

If your three- or almost-four-year-old multiples are doing

the following, they're probably within the normal range of language development:

- Speaking in sentences of five to six words
- Listening with interest to stories
- Telling brief stories or sharing their own ideas
- Referring to themselves as "I" or "we"
- Counting to three
- Saying their first and last names

HOW YOUR ROLE AS PARENT CHANGES WITH YOUR MULTIPLES

During the infant and toddler years, you have had to be the rule maker and rule enforcer. Before two and a half or so, few children internalize the rules well enough to be able to set limits on their own behavior. You can't trust them not to cross the line. With maturity comes more and more internal control. They can stop themselves (and each other) from going too far.

All children need guidance about fair play in board games and in sports, sharing toys, and taking turns. At this age they learn many lessons from their playmates and siblings. Things are a little more complex for twins. By the age of three they will probably have experimented with several different ways of balancing the power in their relationship. They will have tried out different roles: leader and follower, bully and victim, model citizen and anarchist. And they will have evolved their own set of rules about sharing, taking turns, and what is fair and what is not. Now they are reconciling their rules with yours and the larger society's, and in this they will need your guidance.

This means that your role evolves from the intense supervision you exercised during your twins' toddler years. Now your role is that of coach or referee.

YOU AS COACH AND REFEREE

As your children's coach, you will set the family rules of fair play, teach the required skills, encourage the players, and help them negotiate the rough spots.

As a referee of the family turf, you make sure your children understand the rules and the consequences of breaking them. You arbitrate disagreements, call for time-outs when needed, and apply appropriate penalties when rules are broken.

There is an art to coaching and refereeing within the family context. You will need a sense of humor about the children's drive to test your and one another's limits. You will need flexibility and patience. Above all, you'll need to remember that maintaining a healthy, functioning family system is a process. Sometimes nothing will seem to work right. You will have to regroup and try again. As you do so, your children will learn important lessons: that it is okay to make mistakes, and how to keep going.

Suppose you and your twins have established a job chart to assign chores. Even so, the children start squabbling over whose turn it is to set the table. You're coming down with a cold. As the kids argue, your head begins to pound. Then your partner calls to say he'll be home from work late. You may simply run out of patience, and in the heat of the moment, you might be tempted to snap that the job chart isn't working and from now on you'll decide who's supposed to do what. Even though such a shortcut seems like a time saver, it's bound to backfire.

A better approach might be to say, "Kids, I know this is important, and I really want to help you figure this out, but I can't right now. Just for tonight, let's get our own silverware. We'll try to solve it tomorrow."

TWO (OR MORE) AGAINST ONE

By now your multiples are past the challenging toddler stage, when defiance and resistance are so much a part of normal development. You can expect your preschoolers to have more control over their behavior. You can expect them to talk to you more about their likes and dislikes, rather than act them out in tantrums.

Still, your children are in the process of moving toward more mature behaviors, and they haven't arrived yet. Keep your sense of humor handy for when you are confronted with a double or triple rebellion. Your twins or triplets may announce in unison that they hate spaghetti, won't play with their cousin, or won't dress up for the party.

True, their rebellion may cause you some inconvenience, and it must be addressed as a serious breach of family etiquette. But it's important to remember that this is a thrilling experiment from the children's standpoint. They are exerting their collective power and testing limits in a new way—as a team. There's nothing like a common enemy to unite the opposition. Of course, you don't want to become locked into position as their "enemy."

Let's take a look at some of the other negative behaviors that you might observe in your twins. While all preschool-age children may exhibit some of these, they're points of particular concern with twins. Because the children are the same age, and because they share so much time and so many activities, negative behaviors in twins can become more of a problem than in other sibling pairs.

Be alert to the following:

• *Bossiness.* One mother of monozygotic girls telephoned Twin Services with this question: "My four-year-old bosses her twin all day long. She even decides what her sister can and can't play with." This mother had heard that this kind of bossiness on the part of one twin eventually works itself out on its own, and wondered if she should intervene or not.

While it is true that twins experiment with different roles and may take turns being dominant, if one seems to be settling into the role of boss for life, you will need to intervene.

Perhaps one of your twins is ordering the other about—for

example, demanding that she stop playing with her horses and play ball instead. You can say, "Erin, I don't like to hear you telling Molly what to do. Molly has told you she wants to play with her horses right now. If you can't wait until she's ready, you'll have to find a different place to play."

If Erin persists, you can escalate the consequences to a time-out. If Erin does a better job of negotiating with her sister, you can praise her efforts.

You might find another strong-willed playmate for your bossy one. As she grapples with a stronger adversary, she may learn the value of compromise. Likewise, finding a docile playmate for your "follower" twin might give her an opportunity to lead.

• *Overnurturing*. It is not uncommon for one twin to "mother" the other in a way that may seem kind but is actually quite controlling. One may always tie the other's shoes, remind him to take his jacket to school, help him buckle his seat-belt, or jump in and answer questions before he can speak for himself.

Quite often, the girl in a boy-girl pair takes on the nurturing role, because girls frequently are more mature than boys of the same age. In this case, the imbalance will eventually correct itself as your boy catches up to his sister developmentally.

If one twin does seem to be taking over, however, this smothering may hinder the less forceful child's development. Of course, you don't want to discourage kindness and helpfulness in your twins, but you can remind the nurturer that there are certain activities that her twin must learn to do for himself, such as tying his shoes or answering questions. She can understand that she will help him more by allowing him to learn.

• *Bullying*. It's quite natural for children to experiment with the role of bully—getting their way by means of physical force, verbal put-downs, and threats. Before they can communicate verbally, twins experiment with physical aggression. By three, those baby experiments have usually given way to more mature manners.

Sometimes, however, the behavior persists and can cause great distress in the twin situation because it's so hard to escape. If your child has a playmate who bullies, she can at least escape when she returns home. When the bully is a twin, the child can feel overwhelmed. I knew one little girl who was so intimidated by her twin brother that she grew fearful of other children—so much so that she was afraid to sit next to her preschool classmates during circle time.

If you find your child or children using bullying tactics, intervene at once. Prohibit intimidation of any kind. Enforce the same rules with visiting children: If a visiting child continues to bully, cancel the play date.

• *Low self-esteem.* Everyone has some unhappy days. But if a child does not feel good about who he or she is on a daily basis, self-esteem will sink. The child withdraws from social contact, becomes listless, and perhaps may seem sullen and quick to anger. If you see this happening in one of your multiples, look for possible causes, including problems with the twin relationship. Does the child have enough opportunity to act independently? Are there problems with other family members? Does the child feel hemmed in by the twinship in some way? Are there difficult relations with other children in the neighborhood? In school?

If you aren't able to identify a cause and make a positive difference fairly quickly, get the help of a professional who is familiar with twin dynamics. Don't let this situation drift unattended. Take preventive action as soon as possible.

SUPPORTING YOUR TWINS AS INDIVIDUALS AND AS A TEAM

Several years ago, a school principal asked me to help a family whose kindergarten-age twin boys would not leave each other's work alone. If one built a block tower, the other raced across the room and knocked it down. If the other drew a picture, the other scratched it out. The parents, the teacher, the principal, and the school psychologist had tried everything they could think of to stop this rivalry.

Together the boys' mother and I reviewed the household environment, looking for clues. The twins had their own beds. I asked if they had their own clothes and their own toys. "No!" she said with a gasp. "We keep all of the clothes handy in a big basket, and the toys are all kept in common as well."

Once I pointed out the importance of ownership to the development of identity, this mother was eager to make changes. She helped the boys divide their toys and clothes between them, and she rearranged the storage areas so that each could have his own things in his own place. Within a week, the mother and the principal called to tell me that the children had changed dramatically. Instead of putting each other down, they were cooperating and collaborating and a pleasure to be around.

If you notice that one of your twins is bothering the other at work or play, pay attention. Are they just kidding around? Does it happen occasionally, or is this an everyday occurrence? If it happens regularly, at the same time of day, it may be related to hunger and fatigue; in that case, you may be able to ease the situation with snacks and a change in the schedule of activities that includes quiet play at the end of the afternoon.

If food and rest do not calm things down, it's time to take a close look at their environment. You want to be sure both children are getting what they need to feel a sense of growing mastery of their destiny. Does each have enough personal space or territory? Do they each have an assigned bed, clothes of their own, individually owned toys?

I have found that lack of ownership and control is usually the engine driving this kind of ongoing interfering behavior. But ownership does not mean that the children cannot share some possessions or enjoy the same things. It's okay if both children want another story or enjoy going out for ice cream. There will be many times when they don't. You don't have to manufacture differences. In fact, if you do, you will be putting unnecessary stress on your children and giving them the unspoken message that something is wrong with their similarities.

Do respond to their differences. I know a family whose dizygotic girls are as different as oil and water. One, outgoing and theatrical, dominated their play and upstaged her quiet, contemplative sister at every turn. After much struggle, their parents came up with a neutral device that ensured each girl would have a chance to make some decisions: The girl whose time of birth was an even number got to call the shots on days with even-numbered dates, and her sister, whose time of birth was an odd number, was in charge on days with odd-numbered dates.

The method wasn't magic. It didn't erase all their differences, but it did calm down their daily conflict and helped everyone survive their tumultuous childhood.

STRATEGIES THAT HELP

Here are some other suggestions to help honor your multiples as individuals and as a team:

• *Help your children speak up about who they are.* If they look very much alike, encourage them to tell their friends and relatives their names. And teach friends and relatives to ask when they aren't sure. Twins have told me that they are used to other people's confusion and would rather be asked their names than become the objects of yet another guessing game.

• *Plan special time with each child.* By the time they're five, children have a much greater understanding of time, and this understanding will help them agree to take turns having special times alone with you. Start gradually with brief special events, like reading a story or going out to the park or library. Make sure you follow through with a special time with the second child as soon as possible. If some emergency interferes, explain it and schedule a makeup date right away.

A mother of triplets said she and her husband started taking one child out for a special time when the kids were about three. "Even though they had each other's company, the two at home would get upset. At that age, they didn't understand it. But the more we did it, the more they got used to it. I made sure to keep the special times short and close together, so no one would have to wait long for his turn."

• *Structure some time and space for each child to be alone.* Make sure each has the opportunity to be alone if he or she wants to be. If you are short of space, make a quiet spot in one room and designate that place for alone time. Make a rule that anyone who wants to be alone can go there and no one is allowed to interfere. Allow them increasing freedom to decide when and how to play together. And, of course, referee when necessary.

Of course, it's easier to provide each child with space when they have their own bedrooms. In families with single-born children, an older sibling often will want his or her own bedroom by preschool age; in families with twins, the children may be content to share a room. The decision whether to keep your twins in the same bedroom or not should hinge on two factors: whether you have enough rooms available, and whether your twins want to be separated. There's no need to rush. But if yours are boy-girl twins, they'll need privacy sooner than will same-sex multiples.

• *Give them gifts according to their interests and requests.* Help them make a wish list of presents for their birthdays, and abide by the requests. If they each want the same robot, get two. If one wants a robot and the other a ball, give those as gifts. By responding to their expressed wishes, you are helping each to form his or her identity on his or her own terms. Resist the temptation to give them different gifts if they want the same thing.

Remember, it is their internal processes that establish their sense of individuality and self-worth, not their external belongings. If you and your mate use the same kind of tennis rackets or wear the same kind of sunglasses, no one thinks you are losing your sense of individuality. You just made similar choices.

• *Allow your children to make some clothing decisions.* When twins are able to choose the clothes they wear, they are also deciding whether or not to dress alike or differently from each other. This is an important step in developing a sense of mastery of their fates. By asserting their individuality and testing the effects of dressing alike or differently, they are making decisions that affect their sense of self and their awareness of their relationship.

When you can, encourage each child's individual choices in clothing and appearance, but try not to be overly concerned with whether they look alike or not. Explain matter-of-factly that it is easier for other people to know which is which if they wear different clothes and hairstyles.

• *Help your twins channel competition in healthy ways.* Competition is a natural aspect of growing up. When it is balanced with genuine concern for others, when it doesn't overwhelm, it can spark interest and enterprise. Your twins will compete in many ways right from the start—for your attention, for the attention of big brothers and sisters, even for your lap. When your responses to this natural urge are calm and reassuring, you are guiding them toward a balanced relationship. Acknowledge their feelings and set limits on aggressive behavior.

When preschoolers accuse you of favoring one over the other, begin by asking, "What makes you think so? What can I do to make you feel better?" When they argue about who gets to sit next to the window on the bus, ask them to make up a rule for it. Some situations call for taking turns; in others, flipping a coin settles matters.

When you're helping your multiples resolve disputes, discourage the idea that one twin succeeds at the other's expense. Sometimes your children will have different and even opposing needs. To satisfy one, you will make the other miserable, or so it seems. If you find yourself caught in this kind of bind, step back a minute and look for alternatives. Try to find a way to make whatever you do a win-win situation for each child. Although in an inequitable situation, the child who is having his or her way may appear content, the lesson the children are learning is that one's success depends on the other's failure. You want them to learn that there is plenty of room for both—or all—to succeed.

• *Stand firm against favoritism.* Twins are particularly sensitive to adults who play favorites, because so much of their daily life is shared—including their birthday. When an older child gets a special privilege, you can always explain to your younger child, "Jeremy can stay up until ten o'clock because he's older. When you're twelve, you'll have a later bedtime, too."

Not so with twins. Your twins are bound to scrutinize any differences in treatment with the eyes of accountants. That's why you need a firm stance when other adults forget this. An adult twin I know tells about an elderly aunt who gave gifts to her twin sister alone. She laughs about it now, but it was hard on her as a child, even though her sister would later share the presents.

If your friends or family play favorites, try to help them understand how important it is that they be fair to all your children. If they continue to single out one child for favors, give serious thought to limiting their contact with the children.

HOUSEHOLD MANAGEMENT, PRESCHOOL-STYLE

Three-year-olds are mature enough to be helpful members of the family. For example, they can empty the dryer, help clear the table, and put their toys into baskets or onto shelves.

If they are given tasks that they can accomplish easily, preschool-age children will gladly help out. They will love having responsibilities and will profit from the feelings of accomplishment that come with a job well done. Here is an arena where each child can shine, especially if your children have a say in what jobs they are assigned.

The family system for designating chores will evolve. As the children become more competent, their toys will become more sophisticated and so will the family system for regulating them. You may hang a chart of jobs on the refrigerator door on which each kid signs up each week. Or you may evolve an automatic rotation. One week Jeremy feeds the fish and puts the silverware into the dishwasher after every meal; Catherine brings in the morning paper and helps set the table for dinner. Next week they switch.

As coach, you will provide lessons in fish feeding, table setting, dishwasher loading, and newspaper fetching. You will assist when there are difficulties, and cheer each child's successes: "Catherine, I like the way you set the table tonight." "Jeremy, you have a real knack with the fish food."

Of course, the day will come when somebody forgets to do their job or balks at doing it. When this happens, the other child will be the first to let you know. All of a sudden you become a referee in two directions. There is the wayward child who doesn't want to feed the fish. And there is the child in front of you, telling on her brother.

Your child who reported her brother to you may be delighting in the prospect of getting him in trouble, or be sincerely upset about the unfairness of doing her job while he slacks off. She will learn from your response. If you invite both children to state their wishes and feelings calmly, they will learn to do this on their own.

YOUR NEW ROLE AS EDUCATOR

During the preschool years, your children spend more time outside the family—in the neighborhood, in the playground, in the park, in day care or preschool. As multiples, they will draw considerable attention and comments from others.

Most parents of multiples adjust to their status as "celebrities"—they accept it, or they even enjoy it. It's certainly not easy to ignore it. But as you move out into the world more with your preschool-age twins, you will be asked more questions and hear more comments. Sometimes you will be given lectures by total strangers.

The range of questions from parents, teachers, and strangers grows wider and more challenging. Even such an innocent question as "Are those twins?" may cause parents to brace themselves, because it's invariably followed by a flood of other questions: "Are they identical? Did you have fertility treatments? How come they're dressed alike (or not dressed alike)?" One mother was asked, "Did you have to have sex three times in one night to have triplets?"

Depending upon your energy level and how much time you have at the moment, you will find yourself fluctuating between ignoring the comments, giving a neutral response, or rolling up your sleeves and delivering a little lecture on twin development. All of these are perfectly fine reactions.

If your preschool-age children are with you, they'll hear these exchanges and pay close attention to how you respond. You may want to talk about it with them later, explaining why you said what you said or why you wish you'd said something different.

This kind of discussion is an excellent training ground for the children themselves, who will have to develop their own styles of dealing with the same kinds of comments.

One mother I know let her three-year-olds decide what to wear every day, so that they could have the experience of making decisions. On the days the girls dressed themselves alike, their mother faced scolding from other parents when she dropped them off at preschool. "I thought you weren't supposed to dress them alike," people would say.

Some days she took the time to explain that the kids were experimenting. Some days she just smiled and kept going. Eventually, though, she made sure the girls wore name tags with whatever outfits they chose, and the criticisms died down.

Whether or not you ever wanted to, you will have the opportunity of becoming a public educator about twin issues. Whether or not you talk about twin topics, other parents will be observing and learning from the ways of your family. It will be important that you stay grounded in the reality of your family and the needs of your children, so that you do what's best for your children—regardless of what others say.

CHAPTER TWELVE

TOGETHER AND APART

YOUR SCHOOL-AGE MULTIPLES

"*Our seven-year-old sons fight a tremendous amount. A large part of their relationship since they turned six has been fighting. They argue about issues of fairness, who gets more and who gets less. And they fight physically, but don't hurt each other. They're like wrestling lion cubs.*

"*Along with all the battling, there's a lot of touching and physical connectedness. There's a teasing quality, a joy and comfort between them, a closeness and intimacy that I don't see in their friends.*"

The school years—from about five or six to twelve—can be both exhilarating and frustrating as multiples move out into the world, forge friendships, become involved in school activities, and restructure their relationship with their family members and co-multiples. They learn to shoot baskets, play the piano, do long division. They compete, drive one another crazy, and then turn around and support each other lovingly.

During these elementary school years, children develop an array of skills and interests. The school-age child takes on challenges—learning to read, dance en pointe, or pitch a baseball accurately. Friendship and social interaction blossom. Children forge attachments that range from the closeness of the "best friend" to the more casual camaraderie of sports teams, school activities, and shared interests.

Children are also learning the language and behaviors of courtesy and social discourse. They learn to extend and receive invitations. They also, of course, learn the language of rudeness and teasing. They exclude others from friendship as well as include them. So these years can lead to hurt feelings in any child, whether part of a multiple group or not.

This is that middle stage of childhood that falls between two periods of greater turmoil: the toddler years, and the development of mature sexuality during adolescence. It is a time when children can concentrate more easily on acquiring knowledge and learning skills—the common activities of the elementary-school-age child.

This period may be calmer in families with single-born children. Parents of multiples often report more bickering and squabbling during these years as children apply their increased knowledge and cognitive abilities to their relationship.

In this chapter we'll examine how school-age developmental issues play out among multiples, and then we'll examine in depth the sensitive issue of how to determine whether children should be placed together or separately in school.

YOUR TWINS' RELATIONSHIP WITH EACH OTHER

By now your children have had five years or more to establish and negotiate their relationship. They have experimented with different possibilities and combinations of dominance and submissiveness, of mentor and mentored, of comforter and comforted. Usually they are close friends according to their own style, which may be sunny and cooperative or stormy and combative.

CONFLICT COMES WITH THE TERRITORY

Around age six or seven, and for the next two years, it's common for twins to engage in battles, as powerful as for toddlers, but usually more verbal than physical. The twins may go toe to toe and eyeball to eyeball as they argue from sunup to sundown. "I hate your face!" they shout at each other.

Typical topics for these explosions may be fierce rivalry, jealousy and hurt feelings, social disparities, or abandonment of one twin by the other.

What's going on here is a preliminary separation process, like a trial separation prior to divorce. They are practicing for the more mature separation that comes with adolescence.

"They fight a lot," said one mother of seven-year-old boy-girl twins. "Always. He is a pest, and he bothers her. They're having to learn about fighting and conflicts and how to solve conflicts."

On the other hand, she said, her children support each other some of the time. If one doesn't understand something, the other will explain it.

"And they do play," she said. "They play Barbies together, along with toy animals. They call the Ken dolls 'boy Barbies.' "

COMPETITION AND COMPARISONS

Competition, whether social, academic, or athletic, can develop during these years, as it does among siblings who are not multiples. School-age children take great interest in making rules and keeping score. Your multiples will do this as well, but they'll have much more opportunity for scorekeeping than single-born siblings. Because they're doing the same things at the same time, any perceived distinction or unfairness becomes a major issue.

"It's right in their face," says one mother. "I try to tell them that life isn't fair, that it's not really about what your brother's got, but about whether you have enough. This concern with fairness is a big thing for seven-year-olds, and it's exacerbated by their being twins."

A mother describes her monozygotic sons, who share some interests and skills but are developing different ones as well. One is active in drama; the other is more interested in painting and drawing.

"There is competition, but not for friends," she says of her children. "Now it's competition for grades. I tell them not to compete with each other—if they have to compete, go for the top person in spelling or math in the class."

Here's what to do about conflict:

- *Teach your children to handle it.* That means accepting that some degree of conflict is inevitable, but that there are ways of managing it. Children can learn to "fight fair" about their disagreements and to avoid hurtful name-calling.
- *Teach them to use "I" statements rather than "you" statements.* For example, praise your children if they say "I don't like it when you come into my room without asking," rather than "You always mess up my stuff."
- *Help them negotiate what things to share and what to own individually, and sort out "together" time and "private" time.*
- *Fight the temptation to solve their disputes for them.* Sometimes you have to let them work it out themselves.
- *Try to help your twins focus on their academic performance in relationship to their class or grade, rather than just in terms of the other twin.* Help them focus athletic competition toward the other team or the record they hope to beat, rather than toward their brother or sister.

YOUR TWINS' RELATIONSHIP
WITH THEIR PEERS

Whether multiples are in the same classroom or not, they still need to learn to make their way as individuals, academically and socially. They continue the process of separation and differentiation from their fellow multiples, as well as from parents. During their school years they will develop a range of interests. Based on these interests and their own personalities, they will gravitate toward some children and away from others. As is often the case with monozygotic twins, they may gravitate toward the *same* interests—and that's fine, too.

Friendships may evolve naturally in multiples as the children's interests expand. Thus, the child who is passionate about drama naturally spends more time with other children who enjoy theater; science or athletics draws another sibling in a different direction. This kind of friendship building is natural, sound, and tends not to drive wedges of jealousy or competition between or among multiples. During the elementary school years, multiples may have not only friends in common but also other friends that "belong" to one or another. Not all play situations work effortlessly. One mother with boy-girl twins found that her son, who is more outgoing, tended to monopolize the play when his sister had a friend over. "This was true even when they were playing with dolls," she recalls. "He'd join in, playing in a way that made the guest pay attention to him. And he'd end up monopolizing the friend, excluding his sister."

Concerned that her daughter was being deprived of valuable social experiences, she began arranging to have Matthew play elsewhere when Laura had a friend come over to play. This arrangement allowed Laura a chance to develop and enjoy friendship at her own quieter pace.

As the children make more and more independent friendships, it is inevitable that they will have different opportunities. One may have a friend who invites her to the family's beach house. It may be that her twin brother is so involved in his baseball league that he doesn't notice her absence. But if he doesn't have a passionate interest of his own, he may mope around the house and feel sorry for himself when his twin is absent.

As parents, we want so much for our children to be happy that we may be tempted to equalize their fun—by denying one twin an opportunity, or by giving up our own weekend plans to manufacture a fun event for the child who is feeling at loose ends.

The best strategy, however, is to step back and help your children realize that life has its ups and downs and that not everyone will have the same opportunities for fun at the same time. Encourage both your children to take advantage of the opportunities that life offers, and support them when they have a chance to do something fun, whether it's at the same time or not.

THE MULTIPLE ADVANTAGE

Multiples are especially well prepared to enter the social world outside the family. Their experience with the changing balance of their own relationship within the family has given them an advantage, as have the comfort and confidence they find in one another.

"They had the edge socially," one mother said of her sons. "They had each other. It's very natural for them to make friends. The other kids were very curious about twins and wanted to be friends with them. They've used their twinship to their advantage in making friends."

When twins are very different from one another, these differences can actually help the children broaden their social experience. "By having an outgoing brother," a mother of dizygotic boys says, "my quiet one is more involved with the 'boy world' than he would be if he didn't have a twin brother like this."

THE MULTIPLE CHALLENGE

However, there are ways that being a multiple can hinder or complicate social development. For example, other children may not treat multiples as individuals, but rather lump them together, as though they weren't complete human beings in their own right. As parents, we want others to respect our children's unique relationship, but we want them to be seen as individuals as well.

Also, social competition (like all kinds of competition) can be a problem. That's especially true when relatives or others focus on social differences between the children, or point out one child's successes at the expense of the other. Feelings of competition, jealousy, or being left out may be more painful than they would with other siblings, because of the powerful intimacy and bond between the twins. This may be a particular problem if one child is clearly more outgoing than the other.

Sometimes older children will make "pets" of younger twins, including them at their school lunch table or inviting them into their games at recess. While your twins may bask in their celebrity status and the attention of older children, they do need the chance to socialize with their own classmates. If this becomes a problem, enlist the help of a playground teacher to steer your children toward activities with their own age group.

BIRTHDAY PARTIES AND OTHER EMERGENCIES

The issue of individual invitations is a problem for twins. Before the age of about five or six, it's difficult for preschool multiples to understand an invitation extended to one member of the group, especially when the multiples are same-sex. By the time they are in elementary school, however, most multiples are mature enough to understand that both of them won't be included in every social event.

Parties—and birthday parties in particular—can be a source of delight as well as a source of stress and hurt feelings in multiple families. Certainly those family videos of three cakes, each with three candles, are a treasure. But as the years go by, there is the nagging question of which party is whose, and which friend is whose.

Often party planning can be worked out to everyone's satisfaction. "I wanted them to have separate birthday parties," a mother of boy-girl second-graders said. "I wanted people to respect that yes, they're a couple, but they are also individual children and are developing different interests. There was a lot of overlap in the guest lists, but they had the chance to invite their own friends."

Another mother who had arranged combined parties for her boy-girl twins agreed to give separate parties when her children were about to turn seven. But the children kept changing their minds—one day they wanted to share the party, and the next day they wanted them separate.

It's often difficult for young multiples to fully understand that the social world of nonmultiples isn't geared to couples or groups. Usually an invitation is extended to just one friend, but when the host knows the family, often both twins or all multiples will be invited. "I really appreciate the offer, whether both of the kids accept or not," said one mother.

Difficulties with invitations can probably best be avoided by knowing the parents of the children's friends and talking with teachers in preschool and kindergarten about how to avoid awkward situations.

The parent whose child issues the invitation may not know that the invitee has a twin. When that happened with my daughters, I would usually talk with the parent and explain the situation; if it was a casual affair, such as a backyard birthday party, the other twin was usually invited as well.

Other situations can be negotiated so that both twins can take part without imposing on the host. For example, parents can offer to chaperone, or to help with driving.

By school age, multiples are usually beginning to branch out and forge independent friendships. By now they should be able to understand separate invitations. You can explain to the other that most people invite guests as individuals, not as family groups. One twin may be invited this week, but the other will get a chance another time.

Same-sex multiples have a harder time understanding when an invitation does not include them. Boy-girl multiples may be better able to accept the idea of all-boy or all-girl parties and outings.

"Last week Christine went to a party that was all girls," said a mother of second-graders. "This is the first year they've been invited to birthday parties separately. Adam didn't like the idea of missing anything, but when we explained that it was a girls' party, he understood."

Adam's father made a point of planning an activity for that day that Adam really wanted to try—in this case, helping work on a house the father was renovating. The key was to pick something that seemed like a treat arranged just for Adam.

Ultimately, the beginnings of separate social lives provide opportunities along with the hurt feelings. When the children's social lives begin to diverge, there's more room for one-on-one activities between the parents and one child at a time.

GROWING BODIES, GROWING MINDS

PHYSICAL DEVELOPMENT

By the age of six, children are capable and comfortable in their bodies. Children in this age group vary in height and weight, but the growth spurt of adolescence has not begun. If your twins were small at birth and lagged behind their peers in size and strength, they have likely caught up by now, or will within a year or two.

By late elementary school, girls typically outstrip boys in height and weight, a situation that causes consternation to both the taller girls and the shorter boys. For boy-girl twins, this disparity in size may present difficulties, especially when the twins have many friends and classmates in common who are likely to observe and comment on it. The best course for parents is to continue, as before, to accept and support both children, to admire their unique qualities, and to assure the twins that their growth is normal and will even out in adolescence.

Coordination can vary considerably, especially with dizygotic twins, so athletic ability may not be the same. One twin may be agile and a great success on the soccer field, while the other may have trouble with athletic skills.

By kindergarten, children are looking forward with considerable excitement to their first loose tooth and the associated celebrations and rewards. Monozygotic twins often lose their baby teeth at the same time; dizygotic twins may differ.

Generally, by the time they enter school, children are beginning to take care of themselves in a number of ways. They can handle their coat buttons and tie their own shoes. They no longer need afternoon naps. Most are using the bathroom independently, and accidents are rare. Sometimes a child may revert to bed-wetting during times of stress. If bed-wetting has a physiological cause, it is likely to occur in both twins of a monozygotic pair. If it affects one child in a monozygotic pair but not the other, it may signal unusual stress in that child's life.

INTELLECTUAL AND LANGUAGE DEVELOPMENT

During these years, school changes the way children acquire knowledge. No longer are they limited to their own immediate experience and play. Now they also learn from teachers, from classroom projects, from texts and other books, and from television and peers.

Children's ability to distinguish between real and pretend is refined. Abstract thinking and the manipulation of symbols are rudimentary in the early grades but blossom as children approach adolescence.

This is what Piaget called the "concrete operational stage" of cognitive development. Children can classify objects according to categories, and apply logical thought to their physical world. They can understand and apply rules, whether those rules apply to mathematics, grammar, soccer, or distribution of household chores. But they tend not to think abstractly about concepts beyond their experience.

In fact, rule making and rule following loom large in the lives of school-age children. In a few years they'll philosophize about the meaning and ethics of rules; during these years, however, they're mostly interested in keeping score.

Is there any truth to the common view that twins are at a disadvantage intellectually? All children vary considerably in their abilities at this stage. Your twins will vary as well. If they are monozygotic, their school performance will be more similar than if they are dizygotic. Boy-girl twins are especially likely to differ in language and reading ability.

Some studies, but not all, show twins having lower reading scores than singles; in most cases the delay is linked to low birth weight, rather than to the twin situation itself.

However, there is some evidence that twin boys are more likely to score lower on reading tests than either a twin sister or single children, possibly because of a higher incidence of attention deficit hyperactivity disorder (ADHD), which occurs more often in boys than in girls and more often in twins than in single children.

Parents naturally worry about differences in academic ability between their twins, but it's sometimes challenging, too, when twins are very similar in ability. If they are in the same class, they'll have the same assignments, and they may have to use ingenuity to make their schoolwork distinct from one another's. My daughters were careful to read different books for book reports. Sometimes they'd make a point to choose different essay questions or topics; otherwise their work would be remarkably similar.

Academic comparisons are difficult to avoid when children are in the same grade or in the same classroom. When twins are similar in their abilities, even tiny distinctions in performance can seem highly significant to them. I know a monozygotic girl who scored in the ninety-seventh percentile in a test of mathematical ability. When she learned that her twin scored in the ninety-eighth percentile, she said, "I always knew I was dumb in math."

It can be awkward for twins, and monozygotic twins in particular, when one is placed in a gifted or enrichment program and the other is not. Usually when this happens, it is not the result of any difference in the children's innate abilities, but rather the outcome of having different teachers who assess students differently when recommending them for enrichment.

YOUR MULTIPLES IN SCHOOL: TOGETHER OR APART?

"Our fraternal twin boys appear very independent and play separately at school, as well as engage in 'twin business,' but a lot of that independence is built upon the security of the presence of the other. On one hand, we'd like them separated so that their cutting up would not distract them from learning; on the other hand, it seems a double burden to impose two major developmental tasks at once. This is clearly not a simple either-or decision."

This parent's concern is echoed by thousands of parents of multiples as their children are about to enter school. They sense, correctly, that the decision about whether their children are together in one classroom, or separate in two or more, is crucial. In fact, it is the single most important event in the expansion of their children's social environment (after preschool or day care), and signals a major separation from parents and home. No wonder parents and school administrators give it so much attention.

But the decision is complicated by a persistent myth on the part of the general public and some, but not all, school administrators.

THE CONVENTIONAL WISDOM: "SEPARATE FOR THEIR OWN GOOD"

Nowhere in the course of twin parenting does mythology have a stronger influence than in the arena of school placement. Perhaps because so many school administrators believe it, the myth that it is "good" for twins to be placed in separate classrooms no matter what their ages or stages of development lives on.

During the past two decades I have conferred with hundreds of school administrators regarding school placement of multiples. Time and again administrators have told me that research supports the policy of placing multiples in separate classrooms, but none has ever produced a single reference. Nor have I ever been able to find any proof in the research literature that early separation is beneficial.

However, there is research that does support starting multiples in school together. When they are making their initial adjustment to school, their lifelong relationship is too important an asset to be overridden.

When you are deciding about school placement for your children, your goal is not to prove that they can be independent as soon as possible. Instead, the goal is to do what's best for them as individuals, in a way that respects their relationship.

The forced separation of twins who would be more comfortable together not only is difficult for them but also sends them a negative message. One six-year-old whose principal was bent on separating her from her sister asked, "Are we bad because we're twins?"

So why, then, does this practice persist? In my view, there are three basic reasons. First, school personnel believe that separation of multiples makes them just like the other kids, so the school won't be troubled by "twin problems" such as competition, showing off, or acting out.

Second, they believe that physical separation supports the growth of independence, so it's better to do it as early as possible.

Third, perhaps school officials are overreacting to practices, common a few generations ago, of dressing and treating twins alike throughout the grades. Separation in school was seen as a necessary way to counteract the overdependence fostered in some families. There have indeed been cases of twins whose relationship was pathologically close and who did benefit from separation. But those were rare cases in which the twins had been raised in dysfunctional families; it makes no sense to apply the same policy to normal children.

In addition, teachers may oppose having multiples in their classroom because they are afraid of upsetting the twins if they cannot tell them apart.

WHAT TO CONSIDER WHEN DECIDING ON SCHOOL PLACEMENT

It's important to remember that the twin relationship is not a "problem," and you are not creating "problems" for the school when you insist that it do what is best for your children.

When they first start school, multiples have a well-established connection to each other—a strong bond that can provide them with a marvelous sense of security when they move out into the wide world of school.

The classroom *is* the wide world to a child. Can you

remember how big your kindergarten classroom seemed when you were five? Maybe you and a friend stuck together until you began to know some of the other children.

How wonderful when your multiples can enter the classroom in the company of a best friend or friends. How scary when they must leave not only you and the security of home, but also their twin or triplet siblings. Indeed, many multiples are traumatized by forced separation from each other at a time when all children are very vulnerable.

At Twin Services we hear every year from parents whose twins show signs of stress when they are separated. They exhibit physical aggression, bed-wetting, loss of language, sudden shyness, nervousness, clinging behavior, and anxiety, along with difficulty learning in class.

One parent asked to have her twins reunited after one of the twins was clearly suffering from the separation. The school refused to place the children together, but referred the suffering child to a psychologist.

In one case I remember, monozygotic boys were separated in first grade as a matter of school policy. A month later one of the boys lost all his hair. Doctors couldn't find a medical cause for the hair loss, but stress appeared to be a likely factor. Finally a psychiatrist suggested putting the boys in the same classroom. The school agreed, and within a week the child's hair had begun to grow back.

Seldom do we hear from parents whose twins suffer from having to be together in the early grades. On the contrary, twins placed together seem to benefit from the security of ready access to each other. We do hear often about the successful adjustments of twins placed together, where each readily becomes involved in work and play groups with other children.

Even twins who are very different in abilities and personality seem to benefit from initial placement together. This is true as well when the twins are competitive; separation as an antidote to extreme competition is not always the most appropriate response.

Here's what we at Twin Services have recommended:

- Place co-twins together when they start school, unless there is overwhelming evidence, such as successful independent placement during nursery school, that their relationship is ready for day-long separation.
- When in doubt, place them together. If it doesn't work well, it is easier to fix than forced separation.
- When monozygotic twins are placed together, take simple steps to help the teacher and the other students tell them apart and call them by name. Name tags at the beginning of the year, or specific colors for each child, usually do the trick.

Ultimately the decision should depend on the children's circumstances and personalities. One mother of two sets of monozygotic twins placed her daughters in separate kindergartens, because that was the school's policy, and the girls had no objections. They did fine. Two years later, when her sons began kindergarten, she decided to ask to have them placed together.

"The boys were so connected at that stage, I wanted them to be together," she said. "They get bothered if they don't see one another. It's as if something is missing. And that's a distraction for them. You give them what they need, according to who they are."

COPING WITH UNSYMPATHETIC SCHOOL OFFICIALS

In the United States, school policies on the placement of multiples vary from one district to another. Some districts have a policy either to separate multiples or to honor parental preference; others leave the decision to each principal.

If your district wants to separate your twins and you want them together, your first step is simply to make a request. Some schools will accommodate exceptions to their policy if the parents request it.

The mother of two sets of twins quoted above believes that the best approach is to be polite, firm, and prepared when you make your request. "If parents tell the school in a confident manner, 'This is what I want, and I can tell you why,' there will be less resistance," she says.

Sometimes it's best to begin by approaching a sympathetic teacher, counselor, psychologist, or other staff member who will be on your side as you work your way through the administrative channels.

If your district insists on separating your twins, you can ease the children's adjustment by working closely with both teachers to ensure that the children are able to see each other during the school day. It may be possible for them to play together at recess or to join each other for lunch. However, this should be a temporary solution; in the long term your children will be better off using their lunch and recess periods to expand their social horizons and share activities with other children.

As a last resort, consider enrolling your children in a more understanding private school, or an adjacent public school district to which you can pay tuition.

A final consideration that should enter into your deliberations is the question of school readiness. In recent years the trend has been to delay starting children in first grade if they are immature or lagging developmentally. Boys in particular often benefit from an extra year of maturity before they begin first grade, as do children with autumn birthdays, which in most districts makes them the youngest.

If one of your twins seems ready but the other is less so, you have a dilemma. Should you start both children together and hope one catches up with the other? Start one in first grade and hold the other until the following year? Or delay both children another year?

In this situation your children may benefit from waiting, then starting together the following year. An extra year of kindergarten can be enriching and productive for your advanced child. And starting both children when both are ready reduces the risk that one will be held back later on (we discuss that issue later in this chapter).

THE IMPORTANCE OF REEVALUATING PLACEMENT EACH YEAR

Once multiples have adjusted to school, it will become clear when and if they should be in separate classrooms. Every year consider whether your twins would benefit from being in the same classroom or not. This evaluation will include the school's recommendation, and should also take into account of your children's wishes.

As the children move through elementary school they may wish to be in separate classes at some point. This is a natural evolution of their relationship, especially when they have been permitted to begin their school experience with the support of their twin in the classroom.

Sometimes when consulted by their parents, one twin will ask for separate placement and the other will want placement together. In this situation it is important to explore the causes for the discrepancy. Does one feel overburdened by responsibility for the co-twin? Is he or she parroting what they've heard others say—that twins are supposed to be apart?

Usually it's best in this situation to keep them together. The one who asks for separation may have a change of heart. And even within the same classroom, an enlightened teacher can be sensitive to the children's need for "space" and see that they occupy themselves with different projects or sit at different tables.

In a situation when one twin is socially adept and the other is immature, it is important that they have help with balancing their relationship. Placement in the same classroom with a sensitive teacher can enable them to adjust their relationship to account for their individual differences and strengths without making one feel responsible for the other.

For example, a teacher who takes a relaxed, accepting approach to the children's differences can draw out the shyer one and steer him or her toward manageable activities and friendships. The more social twin can feel free to make friends without feeling responsible for the other twin's social life.

Separation in a case like this, or in other circumstances where they have great differences, can give the message that only one twin can succeed and must do so at the other's expense.

WHEN SEPARATION IS THE BETTER COURSE

Although I strongly recommend starting twins out together in school, there may be some situations when it is apparent that they will benefit from being in separate classrooms even as early as kindergarten. Here are some possible scenarios:

- When both, or all, of the children themselves initiate the request
- When they're quite different in personality or abilities, and one twin is paying too high an emotional price trying to keep up
- When there is a concern that the twins are getting locked into different roles that may restrict them

One mother recalls a positive experience with her boy-girl twins. "I think it's worked out very well," she said of her children's placement. "They're in separate kindergartens now. What was happening was that they each had clearly defined roles—one was the 'social' one, and one was the 'intellectual' one. The other one was intimidated in those areas. In separate classes, my daughter was able to respond to questions without the sense that her brother was standing over her shoulder, knowing the right answer before her. And my son, who is less social, can go out and make friends on his own.

"My children are very close, but totally different," she added. "It was so clear that one had the role of getting new friends and the other the role of learning. And now that they're separated, they can each develop their own individual talents."

Another parent whose boy-girl twins were separated for kindergarten found that while their girl was delighted with her teacher and thriving in her orderly classroom, their boy was unhappy and not learning in his class, where his teacher presided over a loose, chaotic atmosphere.

The parents debated about what to do for first grade. They considered putting the children in the same classroom, but finally decided that the children really needed different teachers. They kept them in separate classrooms for first grade but gave particular attention to the match between the boy and his teacher. His first-grade teacher was kindhearted but organized; the boy blossomed into class leadership and within a month was bringing home achiever-of-the-week awards.

A father of dizygotic boys said he and his wife took the same approach. "Because our twins are so different," he said, "we tried to pick out which teacher matched with which twin. And it's really worked out well. We put the twin who needs a relaxed atmosphere with the teacher who was more laid back, and the one who's more social with the teacher who would keep the lid on more."

WHEN ONE TWIN IS PROMOTED AND THE OTHER HELD BACK

Sometimes the school may recommend promoting one twin but keeping the other back to repeat a grade. This is a particularly difficult aspect of the school-placement issue. It's hard to justify promoting a twin who is not keeping up, but holding one twin back is a serious strain on the twin relationship.

Before concluding that separation in different grades is the only solution, however, we recommend you consider the causes for the recommendation.

Often the twins are both within the normal range for their age, but because one is ahead of the other, teachers overreact and think the slower twin may not be able to handle the challenge. Quite frequently the "slower" twin is the boy in a boy-girl pair. He may be behind when compared with his sister, but it's important to ask how he compares with boys the same age. Is he within the normal range? And even if he is somewhat behind, might he catch up within a few years, as so many little boys do?

In cases like these, separating the twins by grade may be a permanent solution to a temporary problem. It's normal for boys to mature more slowly than girls. Often they catch up by the upper elementary years. Given that, it seems a shame to give twins permanent academic labels (the smart one, the dumb one) when the difference might resolve on its own.

Retention is hard enough for single children (and recent evidence suggests it is overused as a policy). With twins, however, promoting one and retaining another is particularly troublesome. A single child may adjust, and the retention will be more or less forgotten over the years. But with twins, the comparison (and the inevitable questions and judgments) is forever as the children progress through elementary and secondary school. Despite the best efforts of parents, the held-back twin will tend to be perceived as "the dumb one," even when the developmental lag has been narrowed.

When the school suggests this, parents can meet with the school staff and ask for specifics. Is the "slower" child just less mature in terms of classroom skills and deportment? Is the difference between the twins substantial? Are both twins within the normal range? What support (short of retention) is available for the twin who is behind?

We at Twin Services recommend doing everything possible to keep the children in the same grade. Extra support, either within the school or tutoring privately, may be advisable. This may be a situation when separate classrooms are the best solution.

As a last resort, consider placing the children in the same grade in separate schools, if that's the only way to give both children the education they need in the same grade. Later, if the developmental gap narrows, they can be reunited at the same school.

CHAPTER THIRTEEN

GROWING UP
AND AWAY

YOUR MULTIPLES
AS ADOLESCENTS

"*The first thing I thought when they were born, two months early, was not 'Will they live?' but 'How will I survive having two thirteen-year-old daughters at the same time?' Well, I did. Now they're fifteen. Somebody's always not speaking to me these days!*" says one mother.

Another comments, "*Oh, they do bicker. Sometimes I just go outside. And last night it got so noisy that one of my daughters asked, 'Mom, can I just go sit in the car?'*"

And a third says, "*She's busy designing her prom dress, and trying to talk her brother into going because she thinks he'd look so good in a tux. So far he is resisting. I'm really enjoying it!*"

During the years from about twelve to the late teens or early twenties, your children will change in ways that are as dramatic as those early years of infancy and toddlerhood, when they outgrew their clothes and learned new skills overnight.

Once again your children will morph before your eyes—boys changing into men, girls into women—in ways that startle, frighten, and delight you. All children move through predictable stages in this process and struggle to acquire the same skills. But the struggle in multiples is even more complex.

In this chapter we will explore the increasingly complicated nature of the twin relationship during this stage of development, and examine how adolescence alters social, school, family, and parent-child relationships, as well as the twin relationship itself. We will talk about how you, as parents, can weather the inevitable confusion and changes, and how you can guide your teenage multiples toward a healthy adulthood.

It's helpful to begin by taking a look at the stages of adolescence. Although your children will change from year to year (and sometimes from week to week), scholars have generally agreed that the two stages of early and late adolescence are distinct enough to provide a useful framework.

Children vary, of course, but generally the years from about twelve to fifteen are considered early adolescence; late adolescence extends from about age sixteen to twenty-one or beyond.

The early stage is defined by the dramatic changes of puberty. Usually, but not always, an eleven-year-old looks and acts like a child. During the next few years, however, the child's body develops into the body of a man or woman.

This adult body is still occupied by a child—someone whose judgment, experience, and self-control are not yet fully developed. By age fifteen or sixteen, however—the beginning of late adolescence—teenagers are becoming more mature. Not only do they look like adults, but they begin to *behave* like adults.

Often the early stage of adolescence is marked by strife and withdrawal—early teens have emotional ups and downs, spark arguments with their parents, slam doors, and challenge rules and expectations. Older teens do calm down, and often reestablish rapport with their parents on a more mature level.

YOUR TWINS' RELATIONSHIP
IN ADOLESCENCE

If the major task of adolescence is to complete the psychological separation from parents and become an independent adult, that task in multiples is twofold: They must separate from the parents and separate from their co-multiple(s). In each case, a close relationship that has been nurturing and valuable needs to change. It doesn't need to end, but it must move to a more mature level.

That means that your multiples have a more complex task than their single-born friends during these years. They must stake out their "differentness" from you, their parents, as all adolescents do. And they must redefine their relationship in a way that affirms their "differentness" from their co-twin.

Often children who have been comfortable being together through elementary school, and comfortable being thought of as twins, change in early adolescence. There will be times when your twins want to be close to each other, and times when they want to be apart. There will be times when they get along famously and have great fun together, and times when they drive one another crazy. Sometimes (more commonly in early adolescence) they'll imitate one another; other times they'll dress and behave as differently as possible to advertise their individuality.

It can be hard to maintain that distinction of dress or style. One sister in a set of triplets got a trendy new hair style so that she could stand out from her sisters, and was infuriated when her two sisters immediately got the same style.

This natural ebb and flow is complicated by the expectations of others—in particular, peers. All adolescents feel they are under heavy scrutiny—they're convinced that everyone at school notices every pimple, every embarrassing mistake. In twins, this feeling of being on center stage is intensified.

Thus, multiples often allow peers' perceptions of them to

push them together or apart in ways that may not always seem logical. One boy who needed glasses, when his twin did not, refused to wear them. His perplexed parents finally learned that their son's friends had decided that since twins are "the same," this boy's need for glasses must be a sign of weakness, and they teased him about it.

More frequently, this sense of scrutiny pressures adolescent twins to accentuate their differences. They may choose separate activities just to be different, refuse to dress or cut their hair similarly, refuse to be in the same classes, or change their names or nicknames.

This need to be different is intensified by typical adolescent sensitivity—especially when one twin feels less competent or capable than the other.

"One of our twin boys takes karate with their younger brother, and his twin has decided he can't do karate," said the mother of monozygotic sixteen-year-old boys. "I pointed out that since his brother is talented at it, he might be, too. But he doesn't want to talk about it or do it."

A pair of monozygotic girls who both excelled at gymnastics came in first and fourth in a competition. Because the top four prize winners would share the podium, the second girl said she wished she'd actually come in fifth so that she wouldn't have to stand next to her twin.

This delicate balance between closeness and distance, sameness and difference, is something your twins will have to work out. You can help by supporting the decisions they make. You can remind them that being similar is fine, and being different is fine, too.

As time goes by, your twins will be negotiating their own differences and similarities. Sometimes one twin will prefer to be more independent, and sometimes it will be the other.

One study of Australian twins tracked through questionnaires the decrease in the amount of time the twins spent together through adolescence. At ages eleven and twelve, they said they spent about 80 percent of their time together. This figure dropped to 53 percent at age seventeen, and 35 percent at eighteen.

PHYSICAL DEVELOPMENT

The changes in appearance between your school-age multiples and their adult selves at the end of adolescence will be truly stunning. During the earliest years, the changes of puberty occur. In boys, facial and pubic hair appears, voices crack and then settle into their adult tones, and sexual organs grow and become functional. Girls develop womanly figures, see pubic hair appear, and have their first periods. Both boys and girls grow in height and weight. During early adolescence, boys may shoot up five inches during one school year.

The hormonal changes of puberty bring physical and emotional changes: acne, surging interest in—and confusion about—sex, weight concerns, and emotional volatility and irritability.

In the later years, adolescents settle into their new bodies. The gangly fourteen-year-old develops muscle. The chubby girl grows out of her baby fat. Complexions clear up somewhat later in high school. And the moodiness really does abate.

Monozygotic twins generally go through these physical changes in tandem, except when one has had a developmental delay from the beginning. Dizygotic twins diverge more in the age at which they experience puberty or rapid growth in height.

The issue of comparisons becomes more painful in adolescence. Early in adolescence, when physical growth is so dramatic and self-consciousness is at a peak, twins who develop at a different pace can suffer. Even the one who is "ahead" may feel awkward, whether it's the girl in a boy-girl pair of thirteen-year-olds, the boy whose voice has changed faster than his brother's, or the girl who has developed a womanly figure while her sister is still coltish and flat-chested.

INTELLECTUAL DEVELOPMENT

The academic progress your multiples made in the elementary grades continues in adolescence. But there is a qualitative change in your children's ability to think that goes beyond their ability to do math problems that are increasingly more difficult.

Piaget argued that around age twelve, children move from the concrete operations stage of childhood to the mature thinking of the adult—what he called the formal operations stage of intellectual function. As we said in Chapter Twelve, school-age children are capable of understanding fairly complex intellectual concepts and can manipulate information and symbols. But in adolescence these abilities evolve further. Teenagers become capable of greater abstraction, greater objectivity, greater ability to see moral issues from differing perspectives, and a greater ability to put themselves in another's shoes. In other words, they are beginning to think like the mature human beings they are becoming.

However, the ability to think this way doesn't mean they always will. Your young teens may be capable of logic, but they may not always act logically. They may be capable of empathy and moral reasoning, but they may still act with cruelty and use poor judgment at times. That's because their judgment and experience are not fully developed.

One of the major tasks of later adolescence, then, is the application of these new intellectual abilities to their lives and actions. And when older teens tackle this task, they continue their challenging and questioning of parental values and authority—but they do it in a new way. In early adolescence, your twins may be defiant and sassy toward you. As older teens, they are likely to sit down and forcefully outline their positions on an issue, citing chapter and verse to support their arguments.

It's interesting that a key element of formal operations is empathy, a trait that multiples develop much earlier than single children. Other twelve-year-olds are just becoming adept at thinking about others' feelings, while your multiples have been doing this since they were toddlers. They've always been attuned to the other's feelings; they know what's going on in the other child's mind. And now they're able to put rational argument behind those insights.

All that insight, and all that intellectual ability, can cut both ways. Multiples can be exceptionally supportive of one another, or their comments can cut to the quick. Two or more teenagers who join forces against you can be intimidating (and noisy). They may go on strike and refuse to do certain chores. They may argue on the other's behalf, defending their twin who has violated curfew or some other rule.

Then these allies can turn on each other in a moment, pointing out each other's foibles. A mild criticism about behavior or appearance—"I hate when you make that face" or "You look really weird in a turtleneck"—carries more weight when it's issued by a twin.

EMOTIONAL DEVELOPMENT

In all fairness, teenagers do have something of a bad rap when it comes to their emotional lives. Certainly young teens are often emotionally volatile, and the drive toward independence is not smooth—it veers between defiance and rebellion, on one hand, and dependence and vulnerability, on the other. But overall, the teenage years can be enjoyable for the entire family, as the kids develop new skills and enjoy new experiences. For multiples, becoming teenagers can have particular advantages, as we discuss below.

The most fevered period of adolescence is usually at the beginning, when moods soar and plummet wildly. Pimples erupt, puppy love blossoms, doors slam, and moodiness and daydreaminess send teens into their rooms to moon and listen to music by themselves.

Peer pressure is at its strongest at this stage, when children have not yet developed enough independence to assert their own opinions and tastes. Another hallmark is self-consciousness—the sense that the whole world is noticing and commenting on every flaw, every dumb mistake.

In the case of teen multiples, that exaggerated self-consciousness has more basis in fact than it does for singletons. After twelve years of being compared with one another and showered with attention for their multiple status, they often become fed up with being noticed as twins.

In the later teen years this volatility subsides, but new difficulties arise. The issue of privileges and freedom becomes acute as adolescents negotiate, or demand, privileges such as driving or dating. As high-school graduation approaches, teens are facing the most profound separation from family they have experienced—and multiples must also consider their separation from each other.

Despite the conventional wisdom, teenage rebellion to the point of rejection of parents is not inevitable or necessary. Certainly some defiance and challenge is typical and healthy. But most teens do grow toward independence successfully while still remaining attached to their parents. And multiples, too, can become independent of one another without totally rejecting or damaging the twin relationship.

THE CHALLENGE OF BEING ADOLESCENT MULTIPLES

When teenagers are at their most difficult, certainly having multiples means the unpleasantness is multiplied. One mother of monozygotic triplet girls is dealing with all the volatility that being thirteen brings, times three.

"Currently they hate being triplets. They can be the best of friends and the worst of enemies," she says. "It's very normal.

Their bodies are changing, their minds are changing. When they get sassy, it's very challenging. They're much more emotional than before. We take one day at a time."

Squabbling, fighting, bickering, and hurt feelings go with the territory among young teens, whether they are multiples, siblings close in age, or members of a peer group. Often teenagers whose conduct is exemplary individually can sprout horns when they're in a group. Higher-order multiples thus can try the patience of parents when they fight—because they're usually in a group.

"As a parent, you have to pick your battles," the mother of triplet girls says with a sigh. "You kind of have to block things out. I don't like to hear them say, 'I hate you,' but is it worth making a battle out of it?"

The shyer of a set of twins, who may have used their twinship as a shelter, may be less mature socially than the other twin and their peers. The more socially outgoing twin has had the role of finding friends, and the shyer twin has not had to develop that skill. A sixteen-year-old dizygotic girl, for example, muses on the issue this way: "My sister has been making friends with my friends, and that worries me. It's hard when one person is more shy than the other. I want someone to say something to *me*.

"At summer camp we would be walking together and my sister would do all the talking for both of us when we were meeting other people. Sometimes I think we shouldn't spend so much time together, because she pushes me around. I'll admit I'm happier being the passenger. But even though I'm happy having her be a leader, I'm not happy feeling taken for granted."

Both parents, and the twins themselves, run the risk of viewing the twins relative to one another, whereas they would view a single child with more flexibility. Thus the single child may be shy one year and outgoing the next as interests and friendships evolve. But at each stage, the twin is sized up in relation to his or her co-twin.

THE GOOD NEWS ABOUT
ADOLESCENT MULTIPLES

At a time when teens may not turn to their parents for advice and counsel, they have their twin to turn to—and many do, especially girls.

In the social whirl of adolescence, being a twin can add to the fun. Certainly it's an icebreaker for many teens. According to sixteen-year-old Mark, who has a twin sister, "It's kind of fun to tell someone we're twins when we're just getting acquainted with them—it opens up a whole new topic, and they are always more interested in us then."

In addition, twins provide one another with emotional support, which is precious in adolescence, and which is often difficult for teenagers to seek from their parents. Just knowing you have someone who's always there, who understands you completely, and who is going through the same peer experiences can be a great source of comfort.

Twins often take considerable pride in the strength of their relationship. They are old enough to understand that a good, solid relationship with another person is a precious commodity, and something they have because they worked it out themselves. "We get along really well," says sixteen-year-old Jennifer about her relationship with her twin sister. "We didn't used to when we were in the same school. Now we're in different schools, and we're not thought of as the twins anymore. So I'm kind of proud of how our relationship has developed. Most people don't have the kind of relationship we have."

Time and again, parents of teenage multiples have repeated what I observed in my own daughters: Multiples frequently develop friendships as part of a larger social circle than single children do. They may be more inclusive and less insistent on one-at-a-time relationships. This experience extends into the teen years in healthy ways. Rather than dating right away, multiples often socialize in large groups that include boys and girls.

"In elementary school," a mother of fifteen-year-old girls says, "they were in a large pool of girls and boys who were all friends. It gave them a chance to get over that initial 'boy-crazy' thing, because they had boys as friends. Now, in high school, when one makes a new friend, that friend gets absorbed into their large social group."

My daughters say that having a twin kept them in touch with that larger social group. If one was dating and spending less time with the group, she could still stay up to date with everyone's news, because her twin was involved. Then she could rejoin the group more easily than a single child who hadn't had that link.

TWIN CELEBRITY—IT CUTS BOTH WAYS

Like it or not, twins get noticed. Triplets and other higher-order multiples get noticed more. This social visibility is a double-edged sword, as we've said. Some adolescent twins enjoy using their twinship to social advantage, while others hate the sense that they're being scrutinized and compared. They may complain, as many have to me, about having to answer the same questions over and over, year after year.

Often adolescent twins develop keen and spirited responses to these questions. Here are some they've told me:

When asked what it's like being a twin, one responds, "I don't know. I've always been a twin. What's it like *not* to be a twin?"

Another common question is, "Which one of you is older?" (Usually the "younger" twin resents this question.) An eighth-grade boy puts it this way: "People always want to know who's older, and by how much. What do you say? Daniel is older by a minute. They always think I'm older, and are surprised that I'm not. I wonder why. I don't see how you can really tell."

A lot of people ask, "Do you have ESP? Can you read your

sister's mind?" A sixteen-year-old dizygotic girl says, "I just kind of roll my eyes. If it's my friends, I ask if *they* have ESP with their siblings. Sometimes you joke around and say you do. I don't think anyone has that kind of thing. People ask, 'Do you look alike, do you think alike, do you swap places to fool people?'"

Another question twins get asked is whether they're identical. (Boy-girl twins find that question particularly silly.) One monozygotic boy said he and his brother have always enjoyed teasing people who ask silly questions. "If someone says, 'Are you twins?' I'll say, 'I am, but he's not.' People say, 'Which one's which?' And I say, 'I'm him and he's me.' They'll ask, 'How do your girlfriends tell you apart?' and we say, 'They don't—they just take the closest one.'"

Some multiples, when they're in the mood, take the questions as an opportunity to educate their friends about twinship, about what's myth and what's truth.

"If you're going to get mad at stupid questions," says one girl, "you're going to live a life mad all the time. It's not worth it."

HOW TO SUPPORT YOUR ADOLESCENT MULTIPLES

Despite their growing independence and their occasional negative comments, adolescent multiples have great need for the support of their parents. Here are some ways you can provide that support:

• *Recognize your changing role.* With every passing year, you do less direct coaching, less refereeing. Instead you'll serve as a resource and mentor. You'll toss out ideas, raise questions about alternatives, then back out and accept their choices. But realize that despite the change in your role, you still need to set limits and keep talking with your multiples.

• *Recognize that your children's feelings are changing.* This is especially important if you've enjoyed the celebrity and "glamour" of having multiples, and if your children have enjoyed it as well. Chances are they will want to present themselves to the public in a more independent way.

• *Recognize their need for privacy.* All teens need some time and space separate from parents; multiples need it not only from parents but from each other as well. Sometimes multiples vary in how much privacy they want. One might want to socialize alone or go to camp by himself. When this happens, help your children use that remarkable empathy they have in positive ways, and remind them to consider the feelings of the other while they honor their own right to decide what they want. You can say, "It's okay for you to want to be separate for summer camp. It's also okay for your twin to feel sad about it. Why don't the two of you talk it out?"

• *Help them cope with differences in physical and social maturity.* As their interests and abilities develop, strive to be supportive of both—whether those abilities are similar or different. One mother of boy-girl twins says she always tried not to define her children in terms of their differences because she didn't want them to feel that their roles limited them. Now, as teenagers, her children are dramatically different in terms of their interests and their degree of maturity, and she and their father have accepted that. "My son has been the classic anti-school, antiauthority, antiparent kid," she said. "He has a rock band and composes music. My daughter is more mature and working hard in school. They take wildly different positions. But we struggle to be unconditionally supportive of each of them."

• *Do continue to observe and monitor their development.* Intervene appropriately when one, for example, is hogging the leadership role at the expense of the other. If one of your twins is trying to run the other's life, speak up about your feelings. Say, "It makes me uncomfortable when I see you making decisions about your sister's social life. You know as well as I do that that's not fair."

In the teenage years, it's not usually effective to give orders and solve problems the way you might have when they were little. It's more profitable to help your children come up with strategies for change on their own. You might call a meeting and discuss your concerns with both, and then talk to each twin privately as well.

• *Establish important rules (those related to safety and well-being) individually, according to each twin's maturity.* If one twin is mature enough to have a late curfew and the other isn't, they'll have to deal with the consequences. The less mature twin may accuse you of favoritism or unfairness when the rules are different. But your less mature child should expect to demonstrate maturity as a condition of greater freedom.

• *Pick your battles.* Hold firm on the important issues and be more flexible on less important matters, such as clothing tastes.

LEAVING HOME

If ever there is a time when multiples need to follow their hearts, it is in the matter of their transition from home and family into the outer world. Whether these leaving-home decisions lead to college, a job, or marriage, adolescent multiples need to have permission to make their own choices.

A single-born teenager choosing a college does more than ponder what she wants to study, what she can afford, and what kind of school she'd like. She's also considering how close to, or far away from, her family she'd like to be. This is a delicate decision for a young adult who is not entirely independent from her parents.

Multiples make these same decisions, too, but also must consider whether to stay physically close to their co-multiples or to branch out on their own.

Many twins do branch out at this point. Usually it's because their different interests pull them in different academic directions. It's important for twins to be aware that the decision to go to separate schools can be appropriate, but it's not necessary. That decision should be made because that's what they really want, not because it's expected. My daughters, who attended the same college during their undergraduate years, said they met twins there who had chosen separate schools because they "thought they were supposed to."

The most important thing is for twins in their later high-school years to communicate their feelings. It's best if your multiples can be honest about their college or job decisions and discuss them openly with each other and with you.

"I think we avoided the issue," a college-age dizygotic twin told me. "He said he'd do music, and I said I'd do business. We assumed that we'd go to different schools no matter what our majors would be. We didn't talk about it, so we never knew why. I would have liked Jim to come to the same school as me." And he added, with his voice trailing off, "It would have been different, you know."

I spoke with a young woman who attended a different college from her monozygotic twin and feels that, in a sense, the experience has made them closer. The girls grew up in Hawaii, and both went to different schools in Los Angeles.

"It was all unspoken," she recalls. "We wanted to be kind of close together. We never said we'd go to different schools; we just applied to different schools." The two young women have pursued different careers, one in medicine, one in law, and their studies have separated them. Being apart did make them enjoy being together. "We appreciated our friendship more. Each visit was a special occasion," she says.

It's sure to be a bittersweet moment for you as parents when your adolescent children take wing and fly from the nest. And yet if your multiples have a strong and healthy relationship with each other, you can have the satisfaction of knowing that their closeness and support will nurture them throughout their lives.

CHAPTER FOURTEEN

REFLECTIONS ON TWINSHIP

ADULT TWINS SPEAK THEIR MINDS

"*Our twins, a son and daughter, are now twenty years old. They were a pleasure to raise. How will their relationship change in adulthood? What should we expect of them in adulthood? They are fairly close, and include each other in almost all aspects of their lives. Our daughter is leaving for the summer and has symptoms of separation anxiety.*"

This letter to Twin Services illustrates a concern of parents of adult twins. What is adulthood like for twins and multiples? What issues do they face? Can parents help?

Since birth and before, the twin relationship has evolved and grown. Throughout childhood, twins cycle between closeness and distance, between cherishing their sameness and asserting their differences.

Adulthood does not bring this process to an end. Even though most twins build full lives as individuals, their attachment to their twin exerts a pull that is stronger during different phases of life.

It is well known among researchers that a call for twin subjects usually generates more responses from female twins than from male twins. Perhaps it is because females as a group are more likely to reap the benefits of twinship. The close bond twinship offers is compatible with our expectation that girls and women are interactive and social. That closeness presents a somewhat awkward framework for the development of the rugged independence we traditionally value in boys and men.

It isn't surprising, then, to discover that the degree of closeness between adult multiples is greatest between monozygotic sisters, followed by monozygotic brothers, dizygotic sisters, dizygotic brothers, and finally boy-girl twins.

In this chapter we'll examine the perspectives that adult twins have gained on their relationship as they look back toward childhood and ahead toward old age.

THE TRANSITION ZONE: EARLY ADULTHOOD

As we discussed in the last chapter, the end of adolescence brings with it the sometimes difficult and delicate process of moving out into the world as individuals while still maintaining the twin relationship.

Kay Cassill, an author, a twin, and founder of the Twins Foundation, says that the need to separate may not come at the same time for both. "It usually happens for one before the other. The pressure is on to find one's own way forward and not hurt the other—this happens to all types of twins. One man told me, 'Oh, my sister decided to get married, and suddenly I'm left out.'

"A singleton has plenty of pressures, but twins have this additional one—while they're trying to leave the family, they also have to find a new way to fit their twin into the picture. They're forming a new alignment."

CAREER CHOICES

As they adjust to their evolving relationship, young adult twins must also accomplish other tasks, including choosing a career. Should it be the same career, or different careers? If both love theater, can both be actors, or does one get dibs? Decisions about careers are more complex in the twin setting, in part because they so clearly set young adults on paths that will either diverge or remain parallel.

A young lawyer who is a monozygotic twin reflects on how she and her sister, a pediatrician, sorted out their separation and career choices. They attended different colleges but took similar courses. Later her sister became interested in medicine, while Pamela leaned away from it.

"We both wanted to go to grad school, and were both taking the tests and applying at the same time, but for different professions. I think that if we'd gone into the same field, we would have been competitive and it would have made us sad and less close. I think I would have felt so competitive inside—and then I would have felt guilty about it.

"I think that when twins go into different fields and seem to have their own lives, it's interesting. I'm interested in her field and her life, and she is in mine. We're never bored at all."

Kay Cassill writes about a particular difficulty of twins who pursue the same career: getting confused with one another, either because of the similarity of their names or because of their similar appearance. She describes actresses who learned to disguise their resemblance so they would be viewed and hired as individuals, and a psychiatrist who feared that his patients would meet his monozygotic twin brother and inadvertently reveal their problems to him.

Career and job decisions also involve decisions about where to live. As with single young adults, the first job may offer the first experience of living alone, away from home. For twins, that separation from one another can be painful. A woman in her forties recalls the abandonment she felt the first time her dizygotic twin left home. "She went off to work on a dude ranch one year. It was weird. We didn't get along that well, didn't hang around together that much. But I cried, I missed her so much."

DATING AND MARRIAGE

Adult twins often look back with amusement at the particular dimensions of twin romance. One pair of dizygotic twin girls were dissimilar in appearance but had identical voices. They recall that when one was chatting with her boyfriend on the telephone and wanted to take a break, she'd put her sister on to hold up the conversation until she returned.

A young adult twin recalls that in college, young men would sometimes show an interest in dating both twins.

But the advent of serious romantic attachments, whether in high school or college, brings another realm in which twins must struggle with separation. This arena can be complicated by anxiety and jealousy, as the which-friend-is-whose question becomes "Which boyfriend/girlfriend is whose?"

Yet in most cases twins manage to sort this out. One man in his fifties, a monozygotic twin, married a dizygotic twin woman. He describes their first date—he and a friend went on a double date with the two sisters, who resembled one another strongly.

"It was a blind date," he recalls. "I was paired up with her sister. In the middle of the date, I switched to be with my wife-to-be, and my buddy didn't even know it until I told him the next day. He said, 'Why would you switch? They're just the same.' I said, 'Oh, no, they're not!' "

Monozygotic twins do have many attributes in common, of course, but by the time they are adults establishing relationships, they usually have distinct preferences.

"We do have different tastes in women," said one monozygotic twin. "I prefer a quiet, classy type—I've been with my girl seven years. My brother goes for flashier types and has already been married and divorced."

Marriage represents a particularly sharp separation for multiples. Unlike leaving for college or moving to another town, marriage marks the beginning of a new, intensely intimate relationship—one that inevitably excludes the other twin.

And this experience can raise painful questions, says Cassill. "Does the spouse accept the twin? Does the twin who is left behind *feel* left behind? Sometimes they all remain great friends. But there are others who say, 'My twin and I were great friends, but now he won't let her see me.'" It can be quite painful. One woman remembers that on her wedding day, as she was putting on her wedding gown, her twin sat on the floor beside her, sobbing.

The sense of loss can be augmented by the inevitable comparisons that twins have been subject to all along. One twin in her early twenties whose sister had married found it annoying that acquaintances acted so solicitous of her. People would ask her how she felt about her twin being married and sounded relieved when they learned she had a boyfriend.

CLOSING THE DISTANCE

It's not uncommon for twins to diverge and then reconnect in their academic lives, their career choices, and their places of residence. Of course, this is not just an aspect of twinship; changing careers or majors, transferring to other institutions, and moving back to the hometown are everyday occurrences.

With multiples, however, it's part of the dance. They may start out in the same college, then diverge, then find out they're pursuing the same profession. Other siblings might do the same, but it arouses less interest.

A twenty-nine-year-old monozygotic twin said that when she first moved to a distant city, she missed her sister. Eventually she forged her own identity and friendships in the new place, and then her sister moved to the same city.

"I had mixed feelings about it," she said. "She knew I felt infringed upon. For example, I had a good friend named Jim. If Jim called Maureen for lunch, I felt like, 'Oh, my friend is being stolen away.' Sometimes the twin syndrome rears its ugly head. And I think, 'I'm acting like a child again.'"

I spoke recently with a twenty-eight-year-old man who

describes his relationship with his dizygotic twin this way: "Yes, we're close. But we're real competitive. So much so that it's sometimes mean. We're like the best of friends and the worst of enemies at times. Since puberty, once we hit the teens, we each took our own way—wanting to be dominant."

He added, "We have the funniest of times, and we *are* very close. But we have gotten into scuffles before, when we haven't talked in months."

It's important to note that this cycling back and forth between feeling close and feeling separate, while intense in twins, is part of life. As Amram Scheinfeld writes in his book *Twins and Supertwins*, the conflict between the desire for closeness and the desire for separation is not unique to twins. We all experience that conflict with parents, friends, and in marriage.

"The mature person can adjust to both pulls, toward independence and toward attachment, in any situation," he writes. "And the twin who has been helped to achieve maturity will be happily and wholesomely adjusted not only to his or her twin, but to all other people as well."

DEFINING TWINSHIP FOR THE WORLD

In an earlier chapter, we talked about how you, as parents, may find yourselves having to educate the world about twinship and twin issues. Now your children, as adults, find themselves doing this on their own. They decide how to describe themselves, and their relationship, to others. It's a process that becomes second nature over time.

"People are trying to fit us into the singleton niche, and sometimes we'd like to fit but we can't," Cassill told me. "That's where the sense of humor comes in—most of the twins I know have one!"

When twins get together, they do attract attention. And that attention is something they must live with. If they've been apart for a while, they sometimes forget what it's like until they appear in public together. My daughters, who are both archeologists working in different states, recently attended a professional conference together. As they entered the hotel one morning, Kelda went through the revolving door and Krista went through the side door. As they passed through the lobby, a stranger who had watched them commented to his companion, "They must not be too dependent. They went through different doors."

"I'd forgotten how it was all the time—constantly being evaluated and judged," Krista told me. "Single-born people assume that when twins do similar things, they must have an 'unhealthy' dependency. And they assume that if twins do different things, they must be 'healthy.' It's a very strange standard—they don't apply it to themselves.

"People always gave us a hard time for having the same major. I would point out that both of my older sisters, who are not twins, majored in biology—did anyone give *them* a hard time?

"At the same time, people romanticize twinship. They talk about it as if it were some idyllic state. I tell them that it's nice to have a twin and that there are advantages, but it doesn't guarantee a wonderful life."

FINDING BALANCE: THE MIDDLE YEARS

After the transitional years of early adulthood comes a period of consolidation. Although not everyone "grows up" at the same time, most people settle down in their thirties, after what might have been an unsettled period during college and the early years of career and relationships. Studies have shown that twins and multiples find balance during these years as well and suffer no greater difficulties in life than their single counterparts.

Most adult twins have a positive view of twinship and remain close to some extent after marriage. Once they have negotiated a degree of separation and have established careers and partnerships on their own, twins often take great pleasure in coming back together in a more mature way.

Most studies show little or no difference between the marital histories of twins and single-born adults. And multiples' overall mental health is no different from that of other adults—there's no difference in the incidence of psychological problems or suicide.

In a study of adult twins and singletons, psychotherapist Eileen Pearlman found nothing to substantiate the often-reported notions that twins have more difficulty than the single-born in developing self-esteem, in establishing and maintaining relationships with others, or that twins are less likely to marry.

All the participants in the study, both twins and single-born, had similar marital histories. Most were in a first marriage. Those who were single, both twins and the single-born, were living with at least one person. There were no significant differences in the degree of differentiation and self-esteem between the twins and the singletons.

Pearlman points out that the relationship between adult twins changes when one reaches a new developmental level before the other. If one marries and the other is single, one has children and the other cannot, or one achieves more career success, these differences can put a strain on the relationship. Sometimes these difficult stages can pull twins together, but sometimes they push them apart.

RAISING FAMILIES

Twins often look forward to having children at about the same time and raising the cousins as close friends and companions. "My sister and I wanted to have babies at the same time," says a monozygotic twin. "We got pregnant, and at three months I was much bigger. It turned out I was having twins, and she had one baby. The three kids were born three and a half weeks apart. It's a lot of fun!"

"I got married first," said another adult twin, "and she had children first. She had a boy, and then I did. She had a girl, and then I did. She called me up in the hospital and said, 'Susan, can't you do anything original?'

"I really wanted twins, but when my first one was born, I thought, 'I'm so much happier *being* a twin than I would be being a parent of twins.' Our stepmother was an angel—she had to put up with so much from us."

The pleasures of the adult twin relationship extend to the children of twins. If the adult twins live close together or visit frequently, the cousins will be close as well. The children of twins have more in common than most cousins, because of their shared genetic background. So adult twins often take a particular pleasure in their nieces and nephews. And childless twins often take particular delight in the children of their twins.

THE TWIN BOND IN MIDDLE ADULTHOOD

Even when adult twins have established separate lives—marriage, family, career—the twin relationship continues.

A forty-eight-year-old woman says of her dizygotic twin, "She drives me crazy, but there's this bond. It's so different from anything I have with anyone else. I'll hesitate when I'm talking, and she instantly jumps in and knows what I'm trying to say. There's definitely some kind of wavelength thing. She lived without a phone once, so I couldn't call her, and I'd be worried about her. Then she'd call up and say, 'All *right*, already! I'm calling!' as if she knew."

Another twin says, "We call each other once a day, often at the same time, so the line will be busy because we're both calling."

Because monozygotic twins resemble each other so strongly, each is a mirror for the other—and their own flaws can be seen plainly in the other as well. There's no hiding from them. It can be hard when one twin is in no mood to see his or her flaws magnified in the other—especially as they age. However, a "twin mirror" can also be a plus—after all, you can see how a new haircut will look on you just by checking it out on your twin. As one man said jokingly to Cassill, "We can check to see if our ties are straight before we go out."

Some twins, however, see past the physical similarities. "I don't look physically at my twin," one woman told researcher Jean Kozlak. "When you know someone so well, it's hard to look at them just physically. You don't look at the surface. When I look at my twin, I see someone so completely different from me that our physical similarity just doesn't register."

THE LONG VIEW

The twin relationship is for life. If the relationship is respected and the twins have the chance to renew and update it on their own terms, it can be a lifelong resource that few others are lucky enough to have.

I spoke with one eighty-year-old man who has been married for fifty years. He and his wife are both monozygotic twins. Her married twin sister lives on the same block, and the families have been friends for years.

He reflected on his childhood with pleasure. "I think growing up a twin is a great thing," he told me, "because the twins always have someone the exact developmental age, so they always have a companion, and that's a marvelous thing to have—making up stories, playing mumblety-peg, playing on the swings, or going for a hike in the hills."

A monozygotic twin woman in her sixties says, "When we get together, it's a shock to me. It's like looking in the mirror when she gets off the plane—it's me. We dress similarly because we like the same styles. I see her talking with her hands and think, 'Oh, I'm talking with my hands too much, or I am talking too fast'—that kind of thing."

I know a monozygotic twin woman now in her eighties who remembers how she suffered as a young woman because she had been persuaded that she and her twin should choose different careers. The woman's sister had entered a convent directly out of high school. This woman longed to do the same but felt she couldn't because that choice had been "taken" by her sister. She finished her college and graduate studies before she too became a nun.

As multiples age, they begin to worry about the ultimate abandonment of death.

"As you get older, you begin to fear the loss of your twin more and more," said Cassill. "Even if you aren't living near each other, you can't get rid of that feeling of 'What am I going to do when I lose him or her?' When you do lose your twin, it's very difficult. There are no answers for it."

There is perhaps some comfort, however, in the realization that twins are likely to have one another throughout most of their lives. Monozygotic twins usually have very similar life-spans if they die of natural causes. Even dizygotic twins are more likely to have each other in old age than siblings who are not the same age.

As one mother of twins says, "My grandmother had a twin brother. They were always very close. When they had both lost their partners, they would travel together. They died within a month of each other at ninety-six. I always thought that relationship was so special. They led very independent lives, but in the end, when they had lost their spouses and most of their friends, they had each other."

CHAPTER FIFTEEN

COPING WITH CRISIS

Twins are, indeed, a kind of miracle. The special circumstances of their creation, the excitement and thrill of their arrival, and the heroic efforts needed to get them through the early years can make parents feel both blessed and tested at the same time.

And yet twins are born into all kinds of families. Some are strong, resilient, prosperous, fortunate. Other families are less strong, have fewer resources, or simply experience a challenging crisis, such as marital conflict, divorce, or the serious illness or death of a twin. There are also problems related to the twins themselves.

In this chapter we'll examine some of the challenges that make raising twins more difficult, the various strains multiple birth can place on the family, and how the dynamics of the multiple family change in time of crisis. And we'll examine what parents can do to make the best of a difficult situation.

FINANCIAL CRISES

The arrival of multiples can't help but have a dramatic impact on the family budget. More babies mean more bills—bills from the hospital and expenses for diapers, formula, household help, clothing, medical care, and child care.

Yet the increased financial burden that multiples bring often comes at a time when family income declines. Mothers have often had to take extended leave from work; they may be unable to return as soon as they had hoped. The greater cost of child care for two or more babies may make employment uneconomical.

For families who are already on the edge economically, the arrival of multiples can be devastating indeed. Whether the result is some serious belt tightening or a true financial crisis in the family, the adults and even the older siblings will certainly connect the arrival of the babies with the shortage. In such times it will be important for everyone's mental health and welfare to avoid blaming or in any way scapegoating the babies, who after all are innocent parties.

There are two elements to dealing with this kind of family crisis. There is the practical element—the financial crunch you will have to cope with. But there's an emotional element as well. This crisis is about new babies, about new members of the family. You will have to give consideration to the feelings and emotional well-being of every member of the family.

How to Cope Emotionally

The most important issue here is the well-being of the family, the adult relationship, and the babies. The family needs to stay together, support one another through the hard times, and be resources for one another—not drift into blame, rancor, exhaustion, or abandonment.

Talk openly with your partner about the situation itself and your feelings about it. It's natural to feel some bitterness and resentment at the circumstances that have brought you to these difficulties. That's especially true if you weren't both equally enthusiastic about the multiple birth. Resentment, of course, can boomerang into feelings of guilt that may or may not be acknowledged.

Get outside help if necessary. If the normal concerns you have become extreme—if you feel you are experiencing depression, extreme anger, or disabling anxiety—seek help. Don't let financial concerns keep you from taking care of your emotional needs; if your health insurance doesn't cover such services, seek assistance through charitable agencies or a public mental health center.

Talk in age-appropriate ways to older siblings. Acknowledge your distress, and let the children know you are coping with it. When belt tightening is a family project, children are less likely to feel threatened or resentful. "Mom is going to stop working so she can stay with the babies," you might tell your older children. "It means we'll have less money, so we'll have to put our heads together and find ways to be thrifty."

Remember that financial reversals can be overcome with time. As difficult as it may be to manage on less, you can get through the hard times if you stick together.

How to Cope Financially

This is the time to ask for help from family, if that's feasible. You may have a relative who can subsidize your family, even in a small way, until the babies are older and you get back on your feet. Also, friends and family can pitch in with donations of groceries, formula, diapers, or equipment. One family I know was helped when the grandfather was able to obtain baby products at a discount where he worked.

With your increased family size and difficult work situation, you may be eligible for county or state assistance. The federal WIC (Women, Infants, and Children) program provides food and formula vouchers for pregnant women and new mothers. You may also qualify for subsidized child care or housing.

A good place to begin if you are unfamiliar with services in your area is the social services department at the hospital where the babies were born. If you have just had multiples and you are in a financial crisis, this is not the time to be too proud to accept help.

Some families may consider relocating to a region of the country where living costs are lower. Beyond that, basic budgeting, cost cutting, and careful shopping will be essential. Garage sales, used-clothing stores, and thrift shops are great sources of perfectly good clothing and household items. Clip coupons, buy in bulk, and consider joining a membership warehouse where you can buy food and household supplies at considerable discounts. Always ask if twin or multiple discounts are available at department or baby stores. Also, pediatricians and nursery schools sometimes offer discounted fees for multiples. It never hurts to ask.

Be sure to network with multiple-birth organizations for information on discount purchasing. Often these organizations have flea markets and secondhand sales, and run classified ads in their newsletters. These are good sources for used strollers and other equipment.

Finally, weigh carefully the costs and benefits of employment. The advantages of two working parents can evaporate quickly when the costs of child care for twins, triplets, or more are factored in.

For example, suppose that your take-home pay, after federal and state taxes are deducted, comes to $13,000. If child care for both your twins at a center costs $250 per week, your yearly cost of child care alone is $13,000, and you gain nothing financially by working. You would actually lose, since you would also need to pay for the cost of transportation, meals eaten at work, and clothing.

In this situation, it would make more sense financially to stay home while the twins are little. You could reassess your costs after a few years, because infant care is more costly than toddler or preschool care, and those costs will go down over time.

If, however, you bring home $25,000 after taxes, and you can arrange in-home care for your twins at $300 per week, your child care costs are $15,600 per year. The amount you clear is not much, but it may be financially justifiable, especially when you consider the value of health insurance and other benefits you might receive at work.

This decision is not strictly economic, of course. If the numbers say you should work but you dread leaving your babies and find your job physically and emotionally draining, the economic benefits might not pay off in the long run. Or if keeping your job means you must spend your earnings on child care, it may still be worth it if that's what keeps you happiest. Parents have often told me that they go back to work to get a rest—full-time twin care can be so exhausting that employment is the only break they get. To the extent that you can afford it, make the decision that will keep you and your family happiest.

SINGLE PARENTHOOD

As we have shown throughout this book, bringing up multiples is not a one-person job. Whether married or not, parents need all the help they can get. But surely the challenges of keeping all those mouths fed, bottoms wiped, and spirits nourished is even more daunting when a parent is coping alone.

Whether by choice or because of divorce or widowhood, many single parents are raising multiples by themselves. Some are teenagers. Others must manage on their own if jobs or military service keep one parent away for long periods.

At Twin Services, we asked several single mothers about how they managed to feed, clothe, love, and support their multiples alone.

One woman we talked with became a single mother when her husband, unable to accept the idea of impending triplets, abandoned her during her pregnancy. Another mother was single, with teenagers at home, when she became pregnant.

They reported many of the same concerns that all parents of multiples raise—how to get the babies to sleep through the night, how to find enough time for both or all the babies, how to keep toddlers safe. But their major concerns were threefold.

• *Fatigue.* Again, this is a theme that is familiar to all parents of multiples, especially in the first year. But when a parent has no partner, the problem is understandably worse. And with fatigue comes illness—a calamity in a multiple family with only one parent. What happens to the babies when Mom has the flu?

• *Financial challenges.* The factors mentioned above are even more significant for single parents. When one parent has to be both primary caregiver and the sole breadwinner, again the challenge is multiplied.

• *Isolation.* Single parents of multiples have great difficulty maintaining contact with the outside world, especially if they are staying at home with the babies. Their social life as single people is somewhat constricted as well. And when singles can't get out and interact socially, it's harder to connect with others and build friendships and romances—and so the isolation can be self-sustaining.

In addition, the lone adult must handle all the emotional stresses of parenting, with no in-house partner to share the struggle. This is especially difficult in the early years, when the babies are too little to provide true companionship and conversation.

How did these mothers cope? They recognized that the health and survival of their families depended on how well they were able to mobilize a support system and ask for (and accept) help. As we've said throughout this book, it's just about impossible to raise multiples without outside help. This goes double, or triple, for single parents.

If you are raising multiples alone, you need to do whatever you can to get enough rest and fend off illness. Sleep deprivation is a real risk for parents of multiples, especially in the early months. It's a particular risk for single mothers. When you don't get at least some decent sleep, you become more susceptible to illness, less alert, and less effective as a parent. And you develop a short fuse and are more likely to explode at your children or discipline them harshly.

Place a priority on sleep and rest. When the babies sleep, you sleep—don't clean the house or do other "constructive" tasks. Reach out to friends and your support system to watch the babies while you rest. Routine illness is one thing—mothers have soldiered on through colds and flu since the beginning of time. But serious illness—mental or physical—is something you need to avoid if possible, or get immediate help for if it occurs. Your babies need you at home, not in the hospital.

Try to reduce the sense of isolation by calling upon friends and helpers to come and visit you, or watch the babies so you can get out once in a while. Sometimes the key element is something as simple as a twin stroller, or a stroller plus a baby backpack, so that you have the means to get yourself and the babies out of the house.

You might ask a friend or helper to watch the children while you soak in the tub. You can trade massages with a friend, or do one another's hair, so you feel you're giving as well as receiving. You can invite another parent and children to your home for a barbecue or just watch a rented movie together. You can bring a friend along when you take a trip to the playground or the park with the kids.

The telephone and e-mail are also wonderful resources for fighting isolation. You can search the Internet—at the library, if you don't own a home computer—for other parents in the same situation. Search under "twin" on the Internet; call the National Organization of Mothers of Twins Clubs and ask for a connection to someone in similar circumstances.

In addition to your support system, it may be necessary

to seek out organizations that help parents stay functional. Depending on where you live, that may include community and civic organizations, local government programs, or religious service organizations. Some provide crisis support, crisis nursery services, counseling, and support through telephone hotlines. The telephone book is the best place to start, in the yellow pages under community, family, or human resources. Teen mothers may find additional help from their school districts or county youth programs.

ABOVE ALL, LEARN TO BE COMFORTABLE ASKING FOR HELP

Recently I spoke with a single mother who was six and a half months pregnant with triplets. She has an eight-year-old who is very excited about the babies. The babies are growing well, but she is worried about how she'll be able to get out and assemble all the baby clothing and equipment she'll need—and how she'll pay for the thirty diapers a day she calculates she will need. She's also worried about how the family will fit into her one-bedroom apartment.

When I asked her whether she was working on developing a support system of friends and relatives, she said, "It's hard for me to think about asking for help. I'm independent already. This is a big turnaround for me."

I told her that most of us are reluctant to ask for help, especially when we've been self-reliant for a long time. I urged her to make arrangements right away, before the babies arrive, for friends to help out during the first weeks.

She began to warm to the idea when I suggested that if she were the friend of someone in her situation, she would be delighted to help—especially if she knew what kind of help was needed.

It also helped her to realize that she can ask for specific favors for a short period of time, see what works, and renegotiate as needed. She might, for example, ask her sister to come on Monday and Wednesday after work, bring a take-out dinner, and go on baby duty while she naps for three or four hours.

She decided to contact her church to see what volunteer help might be available. She'll look for a teenager in the neighborhood whom she might hire to come in for a few hours after school.

I remember taking a call from a mother of toddler triplets in Canada. Her husband's job as a helicopter bush pilot took him away for ten days at a time, leaving her to cope alone. It was a fierce winter, and she couldn't get outside with the children.

Every day she looked forward to afternoon nap time, when the babies and she would sleep. On the day she called me, she had gone to sleep—and the triplets had not. Quietly they had peeled the wallpaper off one wall of their room, let the feathers out of their pillows, and shaken talcum powder all over the mess.

When she opened their door, the breeze blew the feathers and the powder into the air like a snowstorm. When she saw the chaos, she was afraid she would lose her mind. She closed the door and called Twin Services. As we talked, she began to relax and soon was anticipating the day—probably several years ahead—when she would think back to the scene and laugh.

Most of the crises that parents of multiples face are like this woman's—they are not life-threatening, and they don't involve serious injury to the children. They are just endlessly frustrating and exhausting. And yet we get through them.

A LITTLE VALIDATION GOES A LONG WAY

Twin Services sponsored a respite program for multiple-birth families in crisis for several years. Many of these families were headed by single parents, and I was impressed over and over again at their ability to muster their inner resources and courage to provide a loving home for their children in the face of great adversity.

The respite funds Twin Services provided were minimal, but the parents magnified the impact of the small grants by the energy and creativity with which they applied the funds to improve their situations. Ordinarily a respite grant was for a maximum of $200 allocated over a period of three months to pay for household help or child care.

Our files are filled with letters from single parents whose small respite grants enabled them to cope. Although the program is no longer funded, its lessons still apply: Single parents need timely access to resources, but they also need validation—the sense that their efforts are recognized and supported.

Ultimately, single parents can raise multiples, and can do so successfully. In some cases they report that their family life is more satisfying than it would have been had they had to share their strained emotional resources with another adult.

DIVORCE

It's evident from the discussion above that raising twins is an easier task when two committed parents are part of the family. Yet parents of multiples do separate and divorce, and this presents not only logistical difficulties for the parents but also emotional issues that must be addressed for both parents and children.

Although often the separation is the result of matters that have nothing to do with the twins, the arrival—or anticipated arrival—of multiples can put an incredible strain on a marriage that is already in difficulty.

On more than one occasion, the news that twins were on the way has been so upsetting that it has broken up families, especially when one of the parents-to-be did not want children, or more children.

Sometimes separation is precipitated by family violence, or by extreme family stress that is brought on by the difficulties of caring for premature twins. The endless crying, the unbroken cycle of care, lack of sleep, and lack of time for the adults to devote to one another can be an insurmountable problem for a marriage. The same situation sometimes occurs when the multiples have disabilities that require intensive care.

Occasionally the loss of one or more babies throws the couple into anguish, and they are unable to communicate or console one another.

During one memorable week, I received calls from two fathers whose overwhelmed wives had walked out on them and their toddler twins. Although we couldn't do much about their immediate family crises, we were able to link them up for mutual support as phone buddies.

In cases of divorce or separation:

- Discuss with the children what is happening, in age-appropriate ways. Very young children don't need to know the details of adult emotional difficulties, but they do need to know that there is a problem, that you are working on it, and that you will continue to care for them. Make it very clear to the children that they had nothing to do with the divorce. This is standard advice in divorce situations, because children may worry that they caused the break up. But in multiple families, children who are old enough may know that their arrival brought stress and strain to the family. They are particularly at risk of feeling responsible.
- Reach out to other adults to help maintain support and continuity for your children: grandparents, godparents, aunts, uncles, friends, teachers—anyone whom the children trust and can lean on somewhat during the difficult times.
- Seek family counseling that is sensitive to the twin dynamic and can help the children express their fears

and gain reassurance that not all couples are doomed to a rupture. Twins sense that their own relationship is that of a couple and that in some ways it parallels yours with your partner. They may worry that if your couplehood ends, theirs might as well. We've talked throughout this book about respecting the twins' relationship, so it's important to be sensitive in your discussions and in your decisions about custody and visitation.

THE ISSUE OF CUSTODY IN MULTIPLE FAMILIES

Who gets the kids? This is an essential issue when marriages end, and it's particularly difficult when parents do not agree on what is best for the children. In the past, the custody of twins was sometimes split between the divorcing spouses under the assumption that twins could be divided like the family silver, keeping everyone happy.

But in most cases it is best for twins to be kept together if possible. Fortunately, our records indicate that this is the most common practice.

One family I know went through a painful divorce when their monozygotic girls were about eight years old. The parents thought very carefully about the impact on the girls and worked out a custody arrangement whereby each parent had one girl for three days, and then traded.

At first both parents talked about how good it was to have special time alone with each of the girls. But the arrangement wore thin after a while. The logistics of trading houses every three days were hard on everybody, but especially on the girls. They were hardly ever together, and they began to miss each other very much. Gradually the family fine-tuned the arrangement until both girls went together from parent to parent and stayed for longer intervals. This gave the children a greater sense of security, and the parents were able to have some time alone to adjust to their single status.

The best course is to talk to the children (again, in age-appropriate ways), to reassure them, and to work together to develop flexible custody arrangements that suit the children's needs and can be adjusted as those needs change.

When twins are together in custody arrangements, it gives them a chance to use their own relationship as solace. That relationship can actually provide some degree of buffering against the pain of divorce.

I recall an extreme case of twins "parenting" each other when the upheaval of divorce caused the children to be abandoned entirely. According to an article in the *San Francisco Examiner*, thirteen-year-old monozygotic twins were left in San Bernardino, California, by their father when he returned to live in Mexico. Their parents had divorced when the boys were nine, and their mother had returned to Mexico then.

The boys managed to earn enough from part-time jobs to maintain their trailer home and graduate from high school without being discovered by authorities. They accomplished this by parenting each other. They said the hardest times were holidays and other big events such as graduation, when they had no parent to appreciate or support them.

"Sometimes we have little arguments," one of the boys said. "You can call it like best friends. We stick up for each other. We like to see both of us succeed at the same time."

TWIN LOSS

Nothing is more heartbreaking than the loss of a child. Whether the loss takes place early in pregnancy, at birth, or when the child is older, it is perhaps life's most painful blow. In multiple pregnancy, in which premature birth is so commonplace, there is a higher risk of loss of one or more of the babies. It may involve miscarriage, selective reduction of one fetus or more, the loss of a fetus during pregnancy and the survival of others, or the loss of all the babies. One or more babies may die in the hospital, or later of sudden infant death syndrome.

Parents who have experienced loss in these situations remind us over and over again that grief for a lost child is powerful and intensely individual—no one can tell you how much grief you should feel, that you should "be grateful you have one healthy baby," or how long your grief process should take.

Multiple pregnancies inevitably lead to situations where grief and guilt are tangled together more closely than in single pregnancies. A single pregnancy may be terminated for medical reasons or may result in miscarriage. But multiple pregnancy may mean that the parent must decide how many embryos to spare. One or more babies may be healthy; another may suffer a lifelong disability.

Selective reduction raises difficult issues for parents. Usually it is suggested in order to save one or more embryos when the number of multiples is high, usually triplets or more. Often this difficult dilemma arises as a result of infertility treatment, in which multiple babies are conceived or implanted after in vitro fertilization. The Center for Loss in Multiple Birth (CLIMB) offers information and a network of bereaved parents for mutual support (see Resources).

I recently received a telephone call from an anxious expectant father asking about the relative health risks of twins and triplets. I learned that he and his wife had lost a pregnancy before, and had conceived again via in vitro fertilization.

Three fertilized eggs were implanted, and the father told me he'd had to put up a fight with the doctor and his wife to keep the number of implants to three. He is trying to learn everything he can to make an informed decision about reduction, should that be recommended. "I know they can do wonders for small babies these days, but I'm worried that if it's triplets, we may end up with three sick babies."

Sometimes parents keep this painful decision-making process secret from their extended family. This isolates them emotionally and may compound their difficulties. It is really a shame that sophisticated medical technology leads parents to this point, then sometimes leaves them stranded, forced to make these decisions without appropriate emotional support.

Twin loss is also often complicated by the fact that there may be a surviving baby or babies in the midst of the grief—a baby or babies who deserve to be celebrated. I cannot think of a situation more emotionally challenging than when parents are called upon to mourn the loss of one or more babies while caring for and celebrating the life of the survivors.

I learned much about this poignant situation from a couple who had lost one of their twins at birth. The father rallied the family's grief in support of the surviving baby. He gave the baby extra soothing, and encouraged the older children to hold him often, telling them, "He's missing his twin."

The mother told me that she used the time when the older children were in school to mourn her lost baby, drying her eyes when she heard the school bus bringing them home in the afternoon.

LOSS OF A TWIN DURING CHILDHOOD OR ADOLESCENCE

Later in childhood, the loss of a twin is heart-wrenching for the whole family. For the surviving twin, however, there is the additional loss of a special partner. The survivor may have unresolved resentment toward the dead child, and the accompanying guilt. And along with the sorrow come memories of good times and bad.

I recently heard of twin girls who, at the age of twelve, were crossing the street hand in hand when one was killed by a car. Today, two years later, the family and surviving twin are still looking for counseling and support for this devastating situation.

Although it can be difficult to find such sensitive counselors, I strongly recommend doing whatever it takes to find help for the whole family. We have learned much in the last twenty years about the nature of the grief process. You and your surviving children will benefit greatly from learning about the process and the ways other families continue to remember and celebrate the life of their lost child.

In his memoir *Angela's Ashes*, Frank McCourt describes the deaths of his twin brothers at the age of three. The first, Oliver, died of starvation, and his twin, Eugene, died six months later, after watching by the window in vain for Oliver's return. Although this family's suffering was unusual for its extreme poverty, their story illustrates the powerful connection experienced by twins—which must be addressed when there is a loss.

Most twins who lose a co-twin survive, of course, but they experience great sorrow and run the risk of lifelong emotional pain if their needs are not addressed.

A study of surviving twins found that the intensity of grief for the loss of a twin was higher in monozygotic pairs than in dizygotic pairs, and was higher than for the loss of the mother, father, or other close relative.

The challenge for parents is twofold: working through their own grief, and at the same time helping the surviving baby or child. It is particularly poignant when, in the case of monozygotic twins, the lost child is forever remembered in the face of the living child.

During all this, parents must weather well-intentioned but inept condolences. Even the hospital staff may dismiss the lost child and the parents' need to talk about their loss.

DEALING WITH GRIEF

Jean Kollantai, founder and director of the Center for Loss in Multiple Birth, has found a way to give parents great comfort by networking families with similar losses. CLIMB's newsletter offers parents the chance to tell their stories and celebrate their lost infants.

She says, "The whole point is to heal from and cope with a very difficult loss. You've had a baby who died. Find the meaning that it has for you. Look for support in different places. It may be that suddenly your good friends aren't your good friends anymore—they just don't understand what you're going through. Find people and a place where you can talk and experience what the meaning is for you. Over time, you will be able to cope and heal, and be able to look at your surviving child without imposing your feelings on him."

In coming to terms with your own sorrow, consider these suggestions:

- Allow yourself to acknowledge the sorrow you feel and to grieve for however long it takes.
- If the death occurs when the infants are newborns, name the baby or babies. Make every effort to see and hold the babies after death. Ask for (demand, if necessary) all the medical information about the death.
- Learn about the process of grieving. Try to understand that people do not grieve in the same way or at the same pace. For some, a period of withdrawal and contemplation is necessary; for others, talk is the most comforting activity. For some, returning to the routines of family and daily life is the best way of coping; for others, a return to normality is impossible for quite some time.
- Recognize and accept that you and your partner may handle sorrow differently. Sometimes one parent will feel that the other doesn't understand, or one may feel unfairly criticized when he or she is already grieving in his or her own way. It is important not to let these differences deteriorate into a rift between the couple.
- Resist the pressures of well-intentioned relatives and friends who urge you to get on with your life before you feel capable of moving on. Also, be aware that they may not know what to say, and may say nothing. This can leave you in an island of silence about the baby and your

loss. It helps everyone if you can understand that this comes from their concern about your sorrow, and most will respond kindly if you can tell them what you need in terms of support.

HELPING THE SURVIVOR

Whether your surviving child is an infant or an older child, he or she will suffer from the loss. In your own grief, you will be called upon to ease the pain of another to the extent you can.

- If your child lost a twin in infancy, his need for physical closeness and comforting will be even greater than it is for other infants because he has lost the physical presence of this twin. As he grows, do let him know about his history. Most children appreciate this knowledge.
- At any age, make it clear that, sorrowful as you are, you still view the surviving child as wonderful in his or her own right—not as part of a "broken" set.
- If the loss occurs when the children are older, it's important to help the surviving child remember the lost child. Keep photos and mementos of the lost child, and talk about your memories.
- Resist your own temptation to overprotect your surviving child. Childhood death is no more likely for twins than single children. The exception is SIDS, which may be a risk factor for a child whose twin succumbed to that condition (we discuss precautions in Chapter Six). It's common for one or both parents to hover over the survivor, afraid to let the child out of their sight. Or sometimes one parent may reject the survivor as too vivid a reminder of pain.
- Be aware that your feelings of overprotectiveness are normal and will ease in time. As your surviving children grow more robust, your anxiety will ease.
- Prepare yourself and your children for questions about

the lost child. There are a lot of children who, to all appearances, are twins or triplets, but who are actually the survivors of triplet, quadruplet, or quintuplet births. They are constantly reminded of that when asked, "Are you twins?" They will benefit from being prepared and knowing how they want to answer such questions. It is unlikely that they, or anyone, would be comfortable bringing up the most heartbreaking details in casual encounters. But they may want to mention their lost siblings to close friends.

- Try not to impose your own grief process on your surviving child. Balance your own feelings with your child's needs. Children benefit from knowing about their lost multiple, but they should not feel the responsibility to memorialize the dead child.

LOOKING AHEAD TOWARD HEALING

The hurt of losing a child never goes away entirely, but the grieving process—if allowed to do its work—changes the pain into something different. Gradually the sharp edge softens. Anguish evolves into poignant memories that become part of life's tapestry of joy and sorrow.

As Kollantai puts it, "When your surviving child is celebrating his third or fourth birthday, you will be sad, but you will have gotten used to it and you will have ways to deal with it. It's not that it's over. You know your feelings are normal and you're doing the best you can. You will have adapted to the complicated grieving process."

Parents report that there are ways to remember their loss with tenderness, and ways that allow the surviving children to move on with their lives as well.

One mother, writing in a multiple-birth newsletter, tells how her family remembered a twin daughter who died of SIDS. "On her third anniversary a friend bought a new book in French about two little girls and then donated the book to our local library in my daughter's memory. It was a beautiful gift, and I in turn have done the same for another friend. My older sister . . . makes a donation every year to the SIDS Foundation and calls me. Those are probably the things that touch me the most. People who never met her and yet show me they remember her and also help in keeping her memory alive."

Another mother reflects, "I am glad to be five years down the road, as I remember the pain of the first year and trying to have a subsequent baby. But I am sad as well, as I think of what my life could have been like. My life is busy. I have an active preschooler and a new baby due the first of the year, but I wonder what it would be like to have the challenge of raising triplets."

DISABLED TWINS

The risk of disability is, as we've said, significantly higher—twice as high, in fact—for multiples than for single babies. This risk is due in part to the frequency of prematurity, but also sometimes due to the stresses of sharing a prenatal environment.

Again, the pain parents suffer when a child is disabled is complicated by the twin relationship: All or both babies may have the same disability, different degrees of the same disability, or different disabilities. Or one twin may be healthy and the other disabled.

No matter what the situation, parents have the challenge of dealing with their own sadness and guilt and at the same time doing what is best for their children, whose needs may be quite varied.

Although many disabilities are evident at birth, some may not appear until later in childhood. Whenever the diagnosis occurs, the knowledge that one's babies may have lifelong difficulties can be devastating.

There is much information available about specific disabilities and the challenges of raising children who have those disabilities. Parents need to find resources and sources of support, and make long-term plans for their children. A good source of information and guidance is the national organization for the particular disability your child has, along with multiple-birth clubs, which may be able to direct you to information and other parents in similar circumstances.

Here are some points to consider:

- Parents of disabled babies may suffer from isolation if others avoid them or avoid acknowledging the situation.
- Diagnosis of problems may occur right at birth or later in babies that seem to be normal. It's important for parents to follow up any intuitive feelings that something isn't right by asking their children's pediatrician.
- Again, overprotection is a natural response that parents need to be aware of and limit.
- Even when the baby survives, parents need to grieve the loss of the "perfect" child.
- The disabled child needs information about the disability and encouragement to live to the best of his or her abilities.

HELPING THE HEALTHY TWIN

I remember hearing from a mother of three-year-old twins, a healthy girl and a boy with serious disabilities. Beginning at the age of five months, and continuing for two years, the boy had repeated stays in the hospital, which proved upsetting to the healthy twin. She would cry more and have uncharacteristic tantrums during the periods of her brother's hospitalization.

The children's grandmother pointed out how difficult the separation was for the little girl. Heeding her point, the parents began turning their attention to her needs. "At the first sign of upset, we would talk about her brother's belongings, toys, bed; we'd say that we loved him and would soon be bringing him home. In every single instance, this calmed her down."

The healthy twin needs continuing reassurance that evolves as she matures. She may need to know that she is not responsible for the disabled twin's problems, that the disability is not "catching," and that the family will continue to care for and nurture both children no matter what.

Here are some suggestions from social worker Rachel Biale:

- Recognize the cyclical nature of the adjustment your family must make whenever your well child reaches a new stage of physical maturity—such as walking, for example.
- Help your disabled child understand the nature of the disability. Help her grieve and come to terms with her limitations, just as you do.
- Find a balance between encouraging your child to work to capacity, on one hand, and recognizing his or her limitations, on the other. If the limitations are minimized or ignored, both children may view the disability as some kind of punishment.
- Encourage your well child to be compassionate and kind, but remind him that kindness doesn't mean he should reduce his expectations for his own achievements to the ability of the disabled sibling.
- Recognize the potential for mutual support when both are disabled.

One psychotherapist suggests that in families with one healthy twin and one disabled twin, sometimes the healthy twin has less contact with the mother and consequently bonds more closely with the disabled twin. The mother in these cases may reinforce this by expecting the healthy twin to look out for the other. This therapist strongly recommends that parents who have a disabled child allow themselves to mourn for the perfect child this child might have been, and work to reduce the pressure on the healthy child to be the other child's caretaker.

So often, even in the most difficult circumstances, families cope with adversity in ways that allow their children to thrive. I remember visiting a family in which one of the monozygotic twin boys was healthy and the other seriously disabled. I sat in the living room with the three-year-olds and their mother while the two boys were playing happily, the healthy boy chugging his truck over his brother. The disabled boy had just returned from the hospital after surgery, but although their mother was watchful, she was not sad or overprotective. She was comfortable with who her sons were, disabled or not.

And as the boys rolled happily around on the floor like little bear cubs, they too were comfortable with themselves and with one another.

CELEBRATING TWINSHIP

From conception onward, the care of twins and higher-order multiples will challenge your material and inner resources and require your creative response to their unique needs. I hope this book will help you cope well with your own experiences of the stresses and joys that come with having twins.

The information in this book is meant to serve as a guide, not a directive. You and your family are not living life as statistics, but as real people. I hope you've been able to learn something you can apply to your own circumstances and your own children. This is the art of parenting twins.

Whether you are new parents learning the ropes of the neonatal intensive care unit and taking care of your newborn premature babies, a single parent reaching out for resources, an intrigued observer of your six-year-olds' make-believe play, or a referee for squabbling thirteen-year-olds, you belong to a hardy band. We parents of multiples have many blessings. We must also make our way through much uncharted territory during pregnancy, childhood, and the teen years.

It is no simple matter to undergo infertility treatment in hopes of conceiving one healthy baby and to find your arms full of premature babies instead; to have a full-term pregnancy and give birth to healthy multiples in the care of a medical system that seems to favor technical intervention and emergency treatment over preventive care; to breastfeed multiples when even nurses and doctors tell you not to bother; to house and feed the numbers without losing your sanity and your jobs; to give each child what he or she needs, when he or she needs it; to support the twins' relationship in age-appropriate ways; or to match their classroom placement with their individual needs.

But it can be done. It *is* being done by the 52,000 families who give birth to multiples each year in the United States. Sometimes it's done with difficulty, but often with humor and joy and the hope that their twins' lives will be forever enriched by their special friendship.

As one mother of two sets of twins puts it, "They're not just twins—they're more than twins. They have incredible individual souls and can do anything they want."

And a mother of boy-girl six-year-olds says: "I desperately want them to maintain some part of their relationship, not so that it cripples them from going on with their lives, but they have such a special bond, special relationship. What I hope is that they can keep that their whole lives."

Adds a father of sixteen-year-olds: "I secretly hope that they choose the same college."

My hope is that someday parents of twins will have as much information as all other parents about how to nourish their children's healthy physical and psychological development. I foresee that someday the single-born population and those who call themselves "twin researchers" will come to understand how much we have to learn about ourselves from the lives of twins. Twins experience a duality that the rest of us do not; their relationship is a dance, and they are partners in it from cradle to grave. Most of us come to the dance of relationship and intimacy after two or more decades of solo living. Might we all not profit from the experience of twins, whose birth together plants them in a couple relationship from the beginning?

I hope that you too will do what you can to advance understanding and awareness of the issues that affect multiples and their families. I hope you will promote community resources and opportunities for multiples. Many parents volunteer time and resources to local support groups or clubs for parents, write newsletters, or collect clothing and equipment for flea market sales.

I invite you to participate in the Council of Multiple Birth Organizations, of which I am the past chair. It is a committee of the International Society for Twin Studies, which promotes the health and welfare of multiples throughout the world. In 1995 we published a Declaration of Rights and Statement of Needs of Twins and Higher-Order Multiples, which has been ratified by multiple-birth organizations and scientists on five continents (see Appendix for the text of the Declaration and multiple-birth-specific resources).

Above all, as you go through your busy days and nights as parents of twins, I hope you will remember to delight in your children and the blessings that they bring to you and to one another.

I spoke with one mother whose words put it all in perspective for me. The mother of eighteen-year-old twins, she draws on her Chinese heritage as she muses about the relationship between her son and daughter:

"I hope that they experience the great creativity and pleasure that comes with knowing how the other gender works—they've had it up close and personal. And other people have to work so much harder to get past gender in this society. The Chinese have this symbol of good which incorporates the male and female together, and our family has always seen their twinship in that light—as good fortune."

RESOURCES

MULTIPLE-BIRTH-SPECIFIC RESOURCES

U.S. ORGANIZATIONS

NONPROFIT ORGANIZATIONS PROVIDING GENERAL PARENTING SUPPORT

The Center for Study of Multiple Birth. Information, publications, and referrals for parents and professionals, especially regarding pregnancy management.
333 E. Superior St., Suite 464
Chicago, IL 60611
Tel. 312-266-9093

National Organization of Mothers of Twins Clubs, Inc.
Nationwide network of parent clubs and parenting resources.
P.O. Box 23188
Albuquerque, NM 87192-1188
Tel. 800-243-2276
Web site: http://www.nomotc.org/

The Twins Foundation. Multimedia resource center,
publications, research, and National Twin Registry serving twins,
their families, the media, and medical and social scientists.
P.O. Box 6043
Providence, RI 02940-6043
Tel. 401-729-1000
E-mail: twins@twinsfoundation.com
Web site: http://www.twinsfoundation.com

Twin Services Inc.® On-line articles for parents about twin
development and care. Publications, consultations, and training
about multiple pregnancy, infancy, and childhood for parents
clubs, health and family service professionals, and educators.
P.O. Box 10066
Berkeley, CA 94709
Tel. 510-524-0863
E-mail: twinservices@juno.com
Web site: http://www.twinsfoundation.com

Special Topics

Center for Loss in Multiple Birth, Inc. (CLIMB)
P.O. Box 1064
Palmer, AK 99645
Tel. 907-746-6123
E-mail: climb@pobox.alaska.net

International Twins Association. Annual fellowship meeting for twins.
ITA c/o Lynn Long or Lori Stewart
6898 Channel Rd. NE
Minneapolis, MN 55432

Twin Hope, Inc. Information about twin-related diseases.
2592 W. 14th St.
Cleveland, OH 44113
Tel. 216-228-8887
Web site: http://www.twinhope@mail.ohio.net

The Twin to Twin Transfusion Syndrome Foundation, Inc.
411 Longbeach Parkwy.
Bay Village, OH 44140
Tel. 216-899-8887
E-mail: TTTSFound@aol.com
Web site: http://www.tttsfoundation.org

Twinless Twins International
11220 St. Joe Road
Fort Wayne, IN 46835
Tel. 219-627-5414
Web site: http://www.fwi.com.twinless

TwinSight. Counseling and consultations for multiples of all ages.
Tel. 310-458-1373
E-mail: twinsight@aol.com

TRIPLETS OR MORE

Mothers of Supertwins
P.O. Box 951
Brentwood, NY 11717
Tel. 516-434-MOST
Web site: http://www.MOSTonline.org

The Triplet Connection
P.O. Box 99571
Stockton, CA 95209
Tel. 209-474-0885
E-mail: triplets@inreach.com
Web site: http://www.tripletconnection.org

INTERNATIONAL ORGANIZATIONS

Council of Multiple Birth Organizations (COMBO). A working
group of the International Society for Twin Studies.

c/o Secretary General, Jaakko Kaprio, M.D.
Department of Public Health
P.O. Box 41
(Mannerheimintie 172) FIN-00014
University of Helsinki
Tel. +358-9-191-27-59
E-mail: Jaakko.Kaprio@helsinki.fi
Web site: http://www.kate.pc.helsinki.fi/twin/ists.html

Australian Multiple Birth Association, Inc. Network of parent
clubs.
c/o The National Secretary
P.O. Box 105
Coogee, N.S.W. 2034 Australia
Tel. 049-46-8030

Multiple Births Foundation (MBF). Services for parents and
professionals.
Queen Charlotte's and Chelsea Hospital
Goldhawk Road
London W6 U.K.
Tel. 0181-383-3519
E-mail: mbf@rpms.ac.uk

New Zealand Multiple Birth Association (NZMBA). Network of
parent clubs.
P.O. Box 1258
Wellington, New Zealand
E-mail: lizblake@xtra.co.nz

Parents of Multiple Births Association of Canada (POMBA).
Network of parent clubs.
P.O. Box 234
Gormley, Ontario, Canada L0H 1G0
E-mail: office@pomba.org
Web site: http://www.pomba.org

Twins and Multiple Births Associations (TAMBA). Network of
parent clubs.
Harnott House
309 Chester Rd.
Little Sutton
South Wirral L66 1QQ U.K.
Tel. 0870-121-4000

BOOKS

Kathryn McLaughlin Abbe and Frances McLaughlin Gill, *Twins on Twins* [photographs], Crown, 1980.

Ricardo Ainslie, *The Psychology of Twinship*, rev. ed., Jason Aronson, Inc., 1997.

Linda Albi, Deborah Johnson, Debra Catlins, Donna Florien Duerloo, and Sheryll Greatwood, *Mothering Twins*, Simon and Schuster, 1993.

Elizabeth M. Bryan, *Twins, Triplets and More: Their Nature, Development and Care*, rev. ed., St. Martin's Press, 1999.

Kay Cassil, *Twins: Nature's Amazing Mystery*, Atheneum, 1982.

Herbert Collier, Ph.D., *The Psychology of Twins*, rev. ed., Twins Magazine Publications, 1996.

David Fields, Ruth Sandweiss, Rachel Sandweiss, *Twins*, Running Press, 1998.

Elizabeth Friedrich and Cherry Rowland, *The Parents' Guide to Raising Twins*, St. Martin's Press, 1990.

Debbie Gantz, Lia Gantz, Alex Tresmowski, and Bill Ballenberg, *The Book of Twins: A Celebration in Words and Pictures*, Delacorte Press, 1998.

Karen K. Gromada, R.N., *Mothering Multiples*, La Leche League International, Inc., 9616 Minneapolis Ave., Franklin Park, IL 60131, 1985.

Judy Hagedorn and Janet Kizziar, *Gemini: The Psychology and Phenomena of Twins*, Droke/Hallux, 1983.

Elizabeth Noble, *Having Twins*, Houghton Mifflin, 1991.

Pamela Novotny, *The Joy of Twins: Having, Raising and Loving Babies Who Arrive in Groups*, Crown, 1994.

Betty Rothbart, M.S.W., *Multiple Blessings: From Pregnancy Through Childhood, a Guide for Parents of Twins, Triplets or More*, Hearst Books, 1994.

Audrey Sandbank, *Twins & the Family*, Twins and Multiple Births Association (TAMBA), 1988.

Amram Scheinfeld, *Twins and Supertwins*, Penguin Books, 1974.

Nancy L. Segal, *Entwined Lives: Twins and What They Tell Us About Human Behavior*, Dutton, 1999.

PERIODICALS

TWINS Magazine [bimonthly]
5350 S. Roslyn St., Suite 400
Englewood, CO 80111-2125
Tel. 888-55-TWINS
E-mail: TWINS.editor@businessword.com
Web site: http://www.twinsmagazine.com

AMBA News [bimonthly]
Australian Multiple Birth Association (AMBA)
A.M.B.A. Inc.
P.O. Box 105
Coogee NSW 2034
Australia

Double Feature [quarterly]
Parents of Multiple Births Association (POMBA)
P.O. Box 234
Gormley, Ontario, Canada L0H 1G0
E-mail: office@pomba.org
Web site: http://www.pomba.org

MOST (Mothers of Supertwins) [quarterly]
P.O. Box 951
Brentwood, NY 11717-0627
Tel. 516-859-1110
E-mail: Mostmom@Pipeline.com

Multiple Births Foundation Newsletter [quarterly]
Multiple Births Foundation
Queen Charlotte's and Chelsea Hospital
Goldhawk Road
London, England W6 U.K.
Tel. 0181-383-3519
E-mail: mbf@rpms.ac.uk

Notebook [bimonthly]
National Organization of Mothers of Twins Clubs (NOMOTC)
P.O. Box 23188
Albuquerque, NM 87192-1188
Tel. 800-243-2276
E-mail: NOMOTC@aol.com

NZMBA Newsletter (New Zealand Multiple Birth Association)
[quarterly]
New Zealand Multiple Birth Association
P.O. Box 1258
Wellington, New Zealand

Our Newsletter: A Multiple Birth Loss Support Network
[quarterly, plus special issues]
Center for Loss in Multiple Birth (CLIMB)
P.O. Box 1064
Palmer, AK 99645
Tel. 401-729-1000
E-mail: climb@pobox.alaska.net

The Triplet Connection [quarterly]
P.O. Box 99571
Stockton, CA 95209
Tel. 209-474-0885
E-mail: tc@tripletconnection.org

The Twins Letter [biannually]
The Twins Foundation
P.O. Box 6043
Providence, RI 02940-6043
Tel. 401-229-1000

Twins, Triplets and More Magazine [quarterly]
Twins and Multiple Births Association (TAMBA)
Harnott House
309 Chester Rd.
Little Sutton
South Wirral L66 1QQ U.K.
Tel. 0870-121-4000

GENERAL RESOURCES FOR CHILD REARING

ORGANIZATIONS

Sidelines: An Organization for Women Experiencing
Complicated Pregnancies
Tel. 949-497-2265
Web site: http://home.earthlink.net/~sidelines/

La Leche League International
Most local chapters are listed in the white pages
Web site: http://www.lalecheleague.org

Post-Partum Depression: Depression after Delivery, Inc.
Box 278
Belle Mead, NJ 08502
Tel. 800-944-4PPD
Support for mothers with postpartum depression; services include
education, information, and telephone support, provided by
volunteers and by referral

The Preemie Store
Premature-baby-size clothing
Tel. 800-O-SO-TINY or 800-676-8469

BOOKS

Joanne Cuthbertson and Susie Schevill, *Helping Your Child Sleep Through the Night*, Doubleday, 1985.

Adele Faber and Elaine Mazlish, *Siblings Without Rivalry*, Avon, 1988.

Elmer Grossman, M.D., *Pediatrics for Parents: A Thoughtful Guide for Today's Families*, Celestial Arts, 1996.

Helen Harrison, *The Premature Baby Book*, St. Martin's Press, 1983.

Sandy Jones, *Crying Baby, Sleepless Nights*, Warner Books, 1983.

Sheila Kitzinger, *The Year After Childbirth*, Scribner, 1994.

Marshall H. Klaus, M.D., John H. Kennell, M.D., and Phyllis H. Klaus, CSW, MFCC, *Bonding, Building the Foundations of Secure Attachment and Independence*, Addison-Wesley, 1995.

Barbara Luke and Tamara Eberlein, *When You're Expecting Twins, Triplets, or Quads*, HarperCollins, 1999.

Frank Manginello, *Your Premature Baby*, rev. ed., John Wiley & Sons, 1998.

Mary Metzger and Cinthya Whittaker, *The Child-Proofing Checklist: A Parent's Guide to Accident Prevention from Birth to Age Five*, Doubleday, 1988.

Janet Poland, *Getting to Know Your One-Year-Old*, St. Martin's Press, 1995.

Janet Poland, *Making Friends with Your Three-Year-Old*, St. Martin's Press, 1995.

Janet Poland, *Surviving Your Two-Year-Old*, St. Martin's Press, 1995.

Marcia Routburg, *On Becoming a Special Parent: A Mini-Support Group in a Book*, Parent/Professional Press, P.O. Box 5930, Chicago, IL 60645, 1986.

Benjamin Spock, M.D., *Dr. Spock's Baby and Child Care*, rev. ed., Pocket Books, 1998.

Charlotte Thompson, M.D., *Raising a Handicapped Child*, Ballantine, 1986.

Amy E. Tracy and Dianne Marony, *Your Premature Baby and Child*, Berkley, 1999.

ADDITIONAL ONLINE RESOURCES

Begin your search with the Web sites of the multiple-birth organizations listed above. Some other multiple-birth sites:
http://www.owc.net/~twins/resource.htm
http://www.multiplesguide@miningco.com
http://www.vic.com/news/groups/alt.parenting.html
http://pages.prodigy.net/twingles/twins.htm
http://www.hq.net/twin/twinkids/serv.html
http://www.twinspace.com
http://www.katsden.com/webster/twins.html
http://www.nofotc.org (National Online Fathers of Twins Club)

For on-line chats and messageboards, try the following:
http://www.parentsplace.com/family/multiples
http://www.parentsoup.com/html/ (go to Parents of Multiples)
http://www.momsonline.com/chat/home.asp

BABY PRODUCTS DISCOUNTS AND COUPONS FOR MULTIPLE-BIRTH FAMILIES

The following companies may provide complimentary products or discount coupons:

Associated Hygienic Products
770-497-9800
Offer: Coupons.

Beechnut Baby Food
800-523-6633
Offer: New parent packet.

Buster Brown Shoes
Offer: Check with your local store for policies. Some provide discounts for twins.

Carnation Formula
800-782-7766
Offer: "Special Delivery Club" sends literature, coupons for free formula, and dollars-off coupons. Membership is valid for one year. You can call as needed for additional coupons.

Dundee Mills, Inc.
Attn: Georgann Malesci
104 W. 40th St., 8th Floor
New York, NY 10018
212-556-6300
Offer: Free samples. Requires proof of birth.

Earth's Best Baby Foods
800-442-4221
Offer: Coupons.

Evenflo Products
Multiple Births
1801 Commerce Drive
Piqua, OH 45356
800-356-2229
Offer: Coupons. Return card and proof of birth for free samples.

The 1st Years
Parent Service Center
Multiple Birth Program
1 Kiddie Drive
Avon, MA 02322
800-533-6708
Offer: Free samples. Requires proof of birth.

Fisher Price
800-432-5437
Offer: Family registry to receive coupons and catalogs.

Gerber Baby Food
800-4-GERBER
Offer: Coupons, newsletter, mailings for every stage of food.

Johnson & Johnson Baby Products
800-526-3967
Offer: Coupons and baby-care literature

Kimberly Clark (Huggies or Pull-ups)
P.O. Box 2020
Dept. QMB
Neenah, WI 54957-2020
800-544-1847
Offer: Write for coupons; proof of birth required. Also, proof-of-purchase rewards program and mailing list.

McNeil Consumer Products Group (Tylenol, etc)
800-962-5357
Offer: Coupons for over-the-counter pharmaceuticals.

Mead Johnson (Enfamil, etc.)
812-429-5000
Offer: Coupons and Enfamil Family Beginnings Program. Proof-of-purchase rewards program. For a free case of formula for each child, have your pediatrician contact the company.

Midas Muffler Shops
800-621-0144
Offer: Discounts on new infant car seats for babies up to forty pounds ($42 each). You can return the seats to Midas and receive credit for services at most Midas shops. Call your local shop to make sure it participates.

Playtex Products, Inc.
Consumer Affairs Department
P.O. Box 728
Paramus, NJ 07652
800-222-0453
Offer: Starter nurser gift pack (bottles, pacifiers). Requires proof
of birth.

Proctor and Gamble (Pampers, Luvs)
800-285-6064
Offer: For twins, a mailing list for diaper coupons. For triplets or
more, coupon for one-time diaper sample.

Sassy, Inc.
Attn: Multiples Coordinator
1534 College SE
Grand Rapids, MI 49507
616-243-0767
Offer: Buy one, get one free training cup or utensils. Requires
proof of birth.

Summer Infant Products, Inc.
Customer Service
33 Meeting St.
Cumberland, RI 02864
800-926-8627
Offer: Multiples discount on catalog items. Requires proof of
birth.

Ross Labs (Similac, etc.)
800-367-6852
Offer: Welcome Addition Club will supply one starter set of
formula for each child, coupons, and newsletter, plus free teddy
bears if you answer the survey they send. Request two bears on
the return card.

Sandoz Pharmaceutical (Triaminic)
800-453-5330
Offer: Packet of free samples.

William Carter Co.
1124 Carver Rd.
Griffin, GA 30223
770-228-0930
Offer: Multiple program for triplets or more. Will send two baby
suits, two side-snap shirts, and one sleeper with feet per baby.
Requires proof of birth.

DECLARATION OF RIGHTS AND STATEMENT OF NEEDS OF TWINS AND HIGHER-ORDER MULTIPLES

Introduction: The mission of the Council of Multiple Birth Organizations (COMBO) of the International Society for Twin Studies is to promote awareness of the special needs of multiple birth infants, children, and adults. The multinational membership of COMBO has developed this Declaration of Rights and Statement of Needs of Twins and Higher-Order Multiples as benchmarks by which to evaluate and stimulate the development of resources to meet their special needs.

DECLARATION OF RIGHTS

WHEREAS myths and superstitions about the origins of multiples have resulted in the culturally sanctioned banishment and/or infanticide of multiples in some countries:

I. **Multiples and their families have a right to full protection, under the law, and freedom from discrimination of any kind.**

WHEREAS the conception and care of multiples increase the health and psychosocial risks of their families, and whereas genetic factors, fertility drugs, and in vitro fertilization techniques are known to promote multifetal pregnancies:

II. **Couples planning their families and/or seeking infertility treatment have a right to information and education about factors which influence the conception of multiples, the associated pregnancy risks and treatments, and facts regarding parenting multiples.**

WHEREAS *the zygosity of same-sex multiples cannot be reliably determined by their appearances; and whereas 1) the heritability of dizygotic (two-egg) twinning increases the rate of conception of multiples; 2) the similar biology and inheritance of monozygotic (one-egg) multiples profoundly affect similarities in their development; 3) monozygotic multiples are blood and organ donors of choice for their co-multiples; and 4) the availability of the placenta and optimal conditions for determining zygosity are present at birth:*

III. A) Parents have a right to expect accurate recording of placentation and the diagnosis of the zygosity of same-sex multiples at birth.

    B) Older, same-sex multiples of undetermined zygosity have a right to testing to ascertain their zygosity.

WHEREAS *during World War II twins were incarcerated in Nazi concentration camps and submitted by force to experiments which caused disease or death:*

IV. Any research incorporating multiples must be subordinated to the informed consent of the multiples and/or their parents and must comply with international codes of ethics governing human experimentation.

WHEREAS *inadequate documentation, ignorance, and misconceptions regarding multiples and multiple birth increase the risk of misdiagnosis and/or inappropriate treatment of multiples:*

V. A) Multiple births and deaths must be accurately recorded.

    B) Parents and multiples have a right to care by professionals who are knowledgeable regarding the management of multiple gestation and/or the lifelong special needs of multiples.

WHEREAS *the bond between co-multiples is a vital aspect of their normal development:*

VI. Co-multiples have the right to be placed together in foster care, adoptive families, and custody agreements.

STATEMENT OF NEEDS

Summary: Twins and higher-order multiples have unique: conception, gestation, and birth processes; health risks; impacts on the family system; developmental environments; and individuation processes. Therefore, in order to insure their optimal development, multiples and their families need access to health care, social services, and education which respect and address their differences from single-born children.

WHEREAS twins and higher-order multiple births are at high risk of low birth weight (<2500 grams), and very low birth weight (< 1500 grams), disability, and infant death:

I. **Women who are expecting multiples have a need for:**

A) **education regarding the prevention and symptoms of pre-term labor,**

B) **prenatal resources and care designed to avert the pre-term birth of multiples, including:**

1. **diagnosis of a multiple pregnancy, ideally by the fifth month, which is communicated tactfully, with respect for the privacy of the parents;**
2. **nutrition counseling and dietary resources to support a weight gain of 18–27 kilos (40–60 pounds);**
3. **obstetrical care which follows protocols of best practice for multiple birth;**

and when the health of the mother or family circumstances warrant:
4. **extended work leave;**
5. **bed rest support; and**
6. **child care for siblings.**

WHEREAS breastfeeding provides optimal nutrition and nurture for pre-term and full-term multiples; and whereas the process of breastfeeding and/or bottle feeding of multiples is complex and demanding:

II. **Families expecting and rearing multiples need the following:**

    A) **education regarding the nutritional, psychological, and financial benefits of breastfeeding for preterm and full-term infants;**

    B) **encouragement and coaching in breastfeeding techniques;**

    C) **education and coached practice in simultaneous bottle feeding of co-multiples; and,**

    D) **adequate resources, support systems, and family work leave to facilitate the breastfeeding and/or bottle feeding process.**

WHEREAS 60% of multiples are born before 37 weeks gestation and/or at low birth weight and experience a high rate of hospitalization which endangers the bonding process and breastfeeding; and whereas newborn multiples are comforted by their fetal position together:

III. **Families with medically fragile multiples need specialized education and assistance to promote and encourage bonding and breastfeeding. Hospital placement of medically fragile multiples and hospital protocols should facilitate family access, including co-multiples' access to each other.**

WHEREAS multiple birth infants suffer elevated rates of birth defects and infant death:

IV. **Families experiencing the disability and/or death of co-multiples need:**

    A) **care and counseling by professionals who are**

sensitive to the dynamics of grief associated with disability and/or death in co-multiples; and

B) policies which facilitate appropriate mourning of a deceased multiple or multiples.

WHEREAS *the unassisted care of newborn, infant, and toddler multiples elevates their families' risk of illness, substance abuse, child abuse, spouse abuse, and divorce:*

V. Families caring for multiples need timely access to adequate services and resources in order to:

A) insure access to necessary quantities of infant and child clothing and equipment;

B) enable adequate parental rest and sleep;

C) facilitate healthy nutrition;

D) facilitate the care of siblings;

E) facilitate child safety;

F) facilitate transportation; and

G) facilitate pediatric care.

WHEREAS *families with multiples have the unique challenge of promoting the healthy individuation process of each co-multiple and of encouraging and supporting a healthy relationship between the co-multiples; and, whereas the circumstance of multiple birth affects developmental patterns:*

VI. Families expecting and rearing multiples need:

A) access to information and guidance in optimal parenting practices regarding the unique developmental aspects of multiple-birth children, including the processes of: socialization, individuation, and language acquisition; and

B) access to appropriate testing, evaluation, and schooling for co-multiples with developmental delays and/or behavior problems.

WHEREAS *twins and higher-order multiples are the subjects of myths and legends and media exploitation which depict multiples as depersonalized stereotypes:*

VII. **Public education, with emphasis upon the training of professional health and family service providers, and educators, is needed to dispel mythology and disseminate the facts of multiple birth and the developmental processes in twins and higher-order multiples.**

WHEREAS *twins and higher-order multiples suffer discrimination from public ignorance about their biological makeup and inflexible policies which fail to accommodate their special needs:*

VIII. **Twins and higher-order multiples need:**

A) **information and education about the biology of twinning; and**

B) **health care, education, counseling, and flexible public policies which address their unique developmental norms, individuation processes, and relationship. For example by permitting and/or fostering:**

1. **the treatment of medically fragile co-multiples in the same hospital;**
2. **the neonatal placement together of co-multiples in isolettes and cribs to extend the benefits of their fetal position together;**
3. **medical, developmental, and educational assessment and treatment which is respectful of the relationship between co-multiples;**
4. **the annual review of the classroom placement of co-multiples, and facilitation of their co-placement or separate placement according to the particular needs of each set of co-multiples;**
5. **the simultaneous participation of co-multiples on sports teams and other group activities;**

6. specialized grief counseling for multiples at the death of a co-multiple;
7. counseling services addressing the special needs of adult multiples.

WHEREAS *the participation by multiple birth infants, children, and adults as research subjects has made important contributions to scientific understanding of the heritability of disease, personality variables, and the relative influence of nature and nurture on human development; and, whereas relatively little is known about optimal management of plural pregnancy and the unique developmental patterns of multiples:*

IX. Scientists must be encouraged to investigate:

A) the optimal management of plural pregnancies;
B) norms for developmental processes which are affected by multiple birth such as: individuation, socialization, and language acquisition;
C) benchmarks for healthy psychological development, and relevant therapeutic interventions for multiples of all ages and at the death of a co-multiple.

Adopted by the Council of Multiple Birth Organizations and endorsed by the Board of Directors of the International Society for Twin Studies at the Eighth International Twin Congress, Richmond, Virginia. May 1995.

Patricia Malmstrom, Chair
Council of Multiple
Birth Organizations

Lindon Eaves, President
International Society
for Twin Studies

REFERENCES

CHAPTER 1

Boklage, C. E. (1989). The embryology of human twinning: "It is well known that . . ." *Acta Genet. Med. Gemellol.*, 38, 118.

Boklage, C. E. (1995). The frequency and survival probability of natural twin conceptions. In L. Keith, E. Papiernik, D. Keith, & B. Luke (Eds.), *Multiple Pregnancy*, 41–50. Pearl River, New York: Parthenon Publishing Group, Inc.

Bomsel-Helmreich, O., & AlMufti, W. (1995). The mechanism of monozygosity and double ovulation. In L. Keith, E. Papiernik, D. Keith, & B. Luke (Eds.), *Multiple Pregnancy*, 25–40. Pearl River, New York: Parthenon Publishing Group.

Cassill, K. (1982). *Twins: Nature's amazing mystery*. New York: Atheneum.

Luke, B. (1994). The changing pattern of multiple births in the U.S., Characteristics, 1973 and 1990. *Obstetrics and Gynecology* 84 (1), 101–106.

Machin, G. (1997, spring). The alphabet soup of twin biology. *Twin Services Reporter* 13, 1, 3.

Malmstrom, P. M., Faherty, T., & Wagner, P. (1988). Essential nonmedical perinatal services for multiple birth families. *Acta Genet. Med. Gemellol.* 37, 193–198.

Report of Final Nativity Statistics, 1996. Vol. 46, No. 11 supplement. Hyattsville, Maryland: National Center for Health Statistics, 1998.

Taffel, S. M. (1995). Demographic trends in twin births: USA. In L. Keith, E. Papiernik, D. Keith, & B. Luke (Eds.), *Multiple Pregnancy*, 133–143. Pearl River, New York: Parthenon Publishing Group, Inc.

CHAPTER 2

Hay, D. A. (1990). What information should the multiple birth family receive before, during and after the birth? *Acta Genet. Med. Gemmellol. 39*, 259–269.

Malmstrom, P. M., Faherty, T., & Wagner, P. (1988). Essential nonmedical perinatal services for multiple birth families. *Acta Genet. Med. Gemellol. 37*, 193–198.

Malmstrom, P. M. & Biale, R. (1990). An agenda for meeting the needs of multiple birth families. *Acta Genet. Med. Gemellol. 39*, 507–514.

Robin, M., Bydlowski, M., Cahen, F., & Josse, D. (1991). Maternal reactions to the birth of triplets. *Acta. Genet. Med. Gemellol. 40*, 41–51.

Robin, M., Josse, D., & Tourrette, C. (1991). Forms of family reorganization following the birth of twins. *Acta. Genet. Med. Gemellol. 40*, 53–61.

CHAPTER 3

Bulfinch, T. (1947). *Bulfinch's Mythology*. New York: Thomas Y. Crowell Company.

Draper, E. D., & Baron, V. (Eds.) (1994). Twins. *Parabola, The Magazine of Myth and Tradition, 19, 2*. 86–87.

Goshen-Gottstein, E. R. (1980). The mothering of twins, triplets and quadruplets. *Psychiatry, 43*, 189–203.

Groothius, J. R., Altmeier, W. A., Robarge, J. P., O'Connors, S., Sandler, H., Vietze, P., and Lustig, J. (1982). Increased child abuse in families with twins. *Pediatrics*, 70, 769.

Machin, G. (1997, March). Some selected clinical topics in twins and twinning. Paper presented at the Neonatal Horizons Conference of the Northern California Region of Kaiser Permanente.

Malmstrom, P. M., & Malmstrom, E. J. (1988). Maternal Recognition of Twin Pregnancy. *Acta. Genet. Med. Gemellol. 37,* 187–192.

Malmstrom, P. M. (1993). Twin myths. *Twin Services' Resource Series 500: #501.* Berkeley, California: Twin Services, Inc.

Nelson, H., & Martin, C. (1985). Increased Child Abuse in Twins. A report from the Department of Psychiatry. University of Kentucky Medical Center, Lexington, Kentucky.

Pearlman, E. M. (1990). Separation-individuation, self-concept, and object relations in fraternal twins, identical twins, and singletons. *The Journal of Psychology, 124,* 2, 619–628.

Pearlman, E., & Segal, N. (1993, November). Twin myths. In E. Pearlman (chair), "Demystifying the twin experience," symposium conducted for the Extension Division of the University of California at Los Angeles.

Robarge, J. P., Reynolds, Z. B., & Groothius, J. R. (1982). *Research in Nursing and Health,* 5, 199–203.

Wilson, K. M. (1997). Attitudes towards twins from an ecological perspective. Unpublished manuscript, Idaho State University at Pocatello.

CHAPTER 4

Brown, J. E., & Schloesser, P. T. (1990). Prepregnancy weight status, prenatal weight gain, and the outcome of term twin gestations. *Am. J. Obstet. Gynecol. 162,* 182–6.

Dimperio, D. L. (1994, fall). Nutritional management of multiple pregnancy. *The Perinatal Nutrition Report 1,* 1, 6–7.

Dubois, S., Dougherty, C., Duquette, M-P., Haney, J. A., &

REFERENCES

Mountquin, J-M. (1991). Twin pregnancy: the impact of the Higgins Nutrition Intervention Program on maternal and neonatal outcomes. *Am. J. Clin. Nutr.* 53, 139–140.

Ferris, J. (1995). Preventing adverse outcomes of twin gestation. Unpublished manuscript, University of California, Berkeley.

Hobel, C. J., & Day, C. (1993). Preventing preterm birth: Preventing and recognizing preterm labor. Citrus Heights, California: Perinatal Health, Inc.

Lam, F., & Gill, P. J. (1995). Ambulatory tocolysis. In L. Keith, E. Papiernik, D. Keith, & B. Luke (Eds.) *Multiple Pregnancy*, 471–490. Pearl River New York: Parthenon Publishing Group, Inc.

Luke, B. (1995). Maternal characteristics and prenatal nutrition. In L. Keith, E. Papiernik, D. Keith, & B. Luke (Eds.) *Multiple Pregnancy*, 299–308. Pearl River, New York: Parthenon Publishing Group, Inc.

Machin, G. (1995). The twin-twin transfusion syndrome: Vascular anatomy of monochorionic placentas and their clinical outcome. In L. Keith, E. Papiernik, D. Keith, & B. Luke (Eds.), *Multiple Pregnancy*, 367–394. Pearl River, New York: Parthenon Publishing Group, Inc.

Machin, G. (1997, March). Some selected clinical topics in twins and twinning. Paper presented at the Neonatal Horizons Conference of the Northern California Region of Kaiser Permanente, San Francisco, California.

Machin, G., Keith, L. G., & Bamforth, F. (1998) *An Atlas of Multiple Pregnancy: Biology and Pathology* (Encyclopedia of Visual Medicine Series). Pearl River, New York: Parthenon Publishing Group, Inc.

Malmstrom, P. M. (Ed.). (1997). *Twin care handout collection*, rev. ed. Berkeley, California: Twin Services, Inc.

Papiernik, E. (1995). Reducing the risk of preterm delivery. In L. Keith, E. Papiernik, D. Keith, & B. Luke (Eds.), *Multiple Pregnancy*, 437–451. Pearl River, New York: Parthenon Publishing Group, Inc.

Pergament, E. (1995). Postnatal zygosity determination. In

L. Keith, E. Papiernik, D. Keith, & B. Luke (Eds.), *Multiple Pregnancy*, 625–632. Pearl River, New York: Parthenon Publishing Group, Inc.

CHAPTER 5

Harrison, H. (1983). *The premature baby book*. New York: St. Martin's Press.

Henig, R. H. (1983). *Your premature baby: The complete guide to premie care during that crucial first year*. New York: Rawson Associates.

Luke, B. (1994). The changing pattern of multiple births in the characteristics, 1973 and 1990. *Maternal-Fetal Medicine* 84, 1, 101–106.

Lutes, L. (1996, spring/summer). Co-bedding of multiples in NICU. *The Twin Services Reporter 12*, 2, 1, 4.

Lynch, L., & Berkowitz, R. L. (1995). The natural history of grand multifetal pregnancies and the effect of pregnancy reduction. In L. Keith, E. Papiernik, D. Keith, & B. Luke (Eds.), *Multiple Pregnancy*, 351–357. Pearl River, New York: Parthenon Publishing Group, Inc.

Manginello, F., (1998). *Your Premature Baby*, (rev. ed). John Wiley & Sons.

Powers, W. F., Kiely, J. L., & Fowler, M. G. (1995). The role of birth weight, gestational age, race and other infant characteristics in twin intrauterine growth and infant mortality. In L. Keith, E. Papiernik, D. Keith, & B. Luke (Eds.), *Multiple Pregnancy*, 163–174. Pearl River, New York: Parthenon Publishing Group, Inc.

Report of Final Nativity Statistics, 1996. Vol. 46, No. 11 supplement. Hyattsville, Maryland: National Center for Health Statistics, 1998.

Rothbart, B. (1994). *Multiple Blessings*. New York: William Morrow and Company, Inc.

CHAPTER 6

California reports reduction in SIDS deaths. (1997, fall/winter). *Horizons: A semi-annual publication for the California SIDS Community 2, 2.*

Grether, J. K., & Schulman, J. (1989). Sudden infant death syndrome and birth weight. *The Journal of Pediatrics 114,* 4, 561–567.

Gromada, K. K. (1985). *Mothering multiples: Breastfeeding and caring for twins.* Franklin Park, Illinois: La Leche League International.

Malmstrom, P. M. (Ed.). (1997). *Twin care handout collection,* rev. ed. Berkeley, California: Twin Services, Inc.

CHAPTER 7

Faber, A., & Mazlish, E. (1987). *Siblings without rivalry.* New York: Avon Books.

Hay, D. A. (1990). What information should the multiple birth family receive before, during and after the birth? *Acta. Genet. Med. Gemmellol. 39.* 259–269.

Letendre, P. (1988). Factors contributing to stress in families with twins. Unpublished manuscript, University of California at Berkeley.

Malmstrom, P. M. (Ed.). (1997). *Twin care handout collection,* rev. ed. Berkeley, California: Twin Services, Inc.

Malmstrom, P. M., & Biale, R. (1989, August). Measuring the psychosocial impact of twin birth. Paper presented at the Sixth International Congress on Twin Studies, Rome, Italy.

Thorpe, K., Godling, J., MacGillivray, I., & Greenwood, R. (1991, April). Comparison of prevalence of depression in mothers of twins and mothers of singletons. *British Medical Journal 302,* 875–878.

Turnball, P. (1998, February–April). Long ago. *New Zealand Multiple Birth Association Newsletter*, 21–23.

Vollmar, A. (1996, March–April). Understanding the world of postpartum depression. *Twins Magazine 14*, 16.

CHAPTER 8

Adler, T. (1991, January). Seeing Double? *APA Monitor 22*, 1, 8.

Ainslie, R. (1997). *The Psychology of Twinship*, rev. ed. Northvale, New Jersey: Jason Aronson Inc.

Arabin, B., Gembruch, U., & van Eyck, J. (1995). *Intrauterine behavior*. In L. Keith, E. Papiernik, D. Keith, & B. Luke (Eds.), *Multiple Pregnancy*, 331–347. Pearl River, New York: Parthenon Publishing Group.

Azar, B. (1997, May). Nature, nurture: Not mutually exclusive. *APA Monitor 28*, 1, 28.

Bouchard, T. J., Jr., Lykken, D. T., McGue, M., Segal, N. L., & Tellegen, A. (1990). Sources of human psychological difference: The Minnesota study of twins reared apart. *Science, 250*, 223–228.

Bryan E. (1997, spring). Individuality in twins—a painful quest? *Multiple Births Foundation Newsletter 34*, 1–2.

Falkner, F., & Matheny, A. (1995). The long-term development of twins: Anthropometric factors and cognition. In L. Keith, E. Papiernik, D. Keith, & B. Luke (Eds.), *Multiple Pregnancy*, 613–624. Pearl River, New York: Parthenon Publishing Group, Inc.

Goldsmith, H. (1991). A zygosity questionnaire for young twins: A research note. *Behavior Genetics 21*, 257–259.

Kagen, J. (1994). *Galen's prophecy: Temperament in human nature*. New York: Basic Books.

Koch, H.L. (1966). *Twins and twin relations*. Chicago: University of Chicago Press.

Lykken, D., & Tellegen, A. (1996). Happiness is a stochastic phenomenon. *Psychological Science 7*, 186–189.

REFERENCES

Machin, G. (1997, March). Some selected clinical topics in twins and twinning. Paper presented at the Neonatal Horizons Conference of the Northern California Region of Kaiser Permanente, San Francisco, California.

Malmstrom, P. M. (Ed.). (1997). *Twin care handout collection*, rev. ed. Berkeley, California: Twin Services, Inc.

Matheny, A. P. (1979). Appraisal of parental bias in twin studies, ascribed zygosity and IQ differences in twins. *Acta. Genet. Med. Gemellol., 28*, 155–160.

Matheny, A. P. (1990). Developmental behavior genetics: Contributions from the Louisville Twin Study. In M. E., Hahn, J. K., Hewitt, N. D., Henderson, & R. H. Benno, (Eds.), *Developmental behavior genetics: neural, biometrical, and evolutionary approaches*. New York: Oxford University Press.

Matheny, A. P. (1984). Twin similarity in the developmental transformations of infant temperament as measured in a multi-method, longitudinal study. *Acta. Genet. Med. Gemellol. 33*, 181–189.

Piaget, E., Gruber, H. & Voneche, J. (Eds.). (1977). *The essential Piaget*. New York: Basic Books, Inc.

Pointelli, A. (1997). Twins before and after birth. *Multiple Births Foundation Newsletter 35*, 3–4.

Poland, J. R. (1995). *Surviving your two-year-old*. New York: St. Martin's Press.

Poland, J. R. (1995). *Making friends with your three-year-old*. New York: St. Martin's Press.

Riese, M. L. (1990). Neonatal temperament in monozygotic and dizygotic twin pairs. *Child Development 61*, 1230–1237.

Robin, M., Kheroua, H., & Casati, I. (1992). Effects of early mother-twin relationships from birth to age 3 on twin bonding. *Acta. Genet. Med. Gemellol. 41*, 143–148.

Thomas, A., & Chess, S. (1977). *Temperament and development*. New York: Brunner/Mazel.

Wilson, R. (1976). Concordance in physical growth for monozygotic and dizygotic twins. *Annals of Human Biology 3*, 1, 1–10.

Wilson, R. (1983). The Louisville Twin Study: Developmental synchronies in behavior. *Child Development 54*, 298–316.

CHAPTER 9

Caplan, F., & Caplan, T. (1977). *The second twelve months of life.* New York: Grosset & Dunlap.

Falkner, F., & Matheny, A. (1995). The long-term development of twins: Anthropometric factors and cognition. In L. Keith, E. Papiernik, D. Keith, & B. Luke (Eds.), *Multiple Pregnancy*, 613–624. New York: Parthenon Publishing Group, Inc.

Kopp, C. B., & Freeman, W. H. (1994). *Baby steps: The why's of your child's behavior in the first two years.* New York: Freeman and Co.

Malmstrom, P. M. (Ed.). (1997). *Twin care handout collection*, rev. ed. Berkeley, California: Twin Services, Inc.

Piaget, E., Gruber, H., & Voneche, J. (Eds.). (1977). *The essential Piaget.* New York: Basic Books, Inc.

Riese, M. L. (1992). Temperament prediction for neonate twins. *Acta. Genet. Med. Gemellol., 41*, 123–135.

Stern, D. (1985). *The interpersonal world of the infant.* New York: Basic Books.

CHAPTER 10

Bakker, P. (1987). Autonomous language of twins. *Acta. Genet. Med. Gemellol., 36*, 233–238.

Biale, R. (1989, June). Twins have unique developmental aspects. *The Brown University Child Behavior and Development Letter, 5, 6*, 1–3.

Malmstrom, P. M. (Ed.). (1997). *Twin care handout collection*, rev. ed. Berkeley, California: Twin Services, Inc.

Matheny, A. (1996, September/October). Time for attachment. *Twins Magazine*, 44–45, 49.

McMahon, S. (1997, September). Communication skills of multiple birth children. [Precis of the Speech Pathology Association of Australia's video teleconference.] *Twin Talk—Northern Territory Multiple Birth Club, 156*, 8–9.

Mittler, P. (1971). *The study of twins*. Baltimore, Maryland: Penguin Books Inc.

Mittler, P. (1976). Language development in young twins: Biological, genetic and social aspects. *Acta. Genet. Med. Gemellol. 25*, 359–365.

Piaget, E., Gruber, H. & Voneche, J. (Eds.). (1977). *The essential Piaget*. New York: Basic Books, Inc.

Poland, J. R. (1995). *Surviving your two-year-old*. New York: St. Martin's Press.

Poland, J. R. (1995). *Making friends with your three-year-old*. New York: St. Martin's Press.

Wilson, R. (1974). Twins: mental development in the preschool years. *Developmental Psychology 10*, 580–588.

CHAPTER 11

Biale, R. (1989, June). Twins have unique developmental aspects. *The Brown University Child Behavior and Development Letter, 5, 6*, 1–3.

Hay, D. A., O'Brien, P. J., Johnston, C. J., & Prior, M. (1984). The high incidence of reading disability in twin boys and its implications for genetic analysis. *Acta. Genet. Med. Gemellol. 33*, 223–236.

Hay, D. A., Prior, M., Collett, S., & Williams, M. (1987). Speech and language development in preschool twins. *Acta. Genet. Med. Gemellol. 36*, 213–223.

Lytton, H. (1980). *Parent-child interaction—the socialization process observed in twin and singleton families*. New York & London: Plenum Press.

Malmstrom, P. M. (1997). *Twins in school: apart or together?* rev. ed. Berkeley, California: Twin Services, Inc.

Malmstrom, P. M. (Ed.). (1997). *Twin care handout collection*, rev. ed. Berkeley, California: Twin Services, Inc.

Malmstrom, P. M., & Silva, M. N. (1986). Twin talk: Manifestations of twinship in the speech of toddlers. *Journal of Child Language 13, 293–304.*

McMahon, S. (1997, September). Communication skills of multiple birth children. [Precis of the Speech Pathology Association of Australia's video teleconference.] *Twin Talk—Northern Territory Multiple Birth Club 156, 8–9.*

Piaget, E., Gruber, H., & Voneche, J. (Eds.). (1977). *The essential Piaget.* New York: Basic Books, Inc.

Poland, J. R. (1995). *Making friends with your three-year old.* New York: St. Martin's Press.

Savic, S. (1980). *How twins learn to talk.* New York: Academic Press, Inc.

Segal, N. L. (1984). Cooperation, competition and altruism within twin sets: A reappraisal. *Ethology and Sociobiology 5, 163–177.*

Wilson, R. (1974). Twins: Mental development in the preschool years. *Developmental Psychology 10, 580–588.*

CHAPTER 12

Biale, R. (1988, summer). When teachers recommend holding one twin back in school. *The Twin Services Reporter, 3, 11.*

Gleeson, C., Hay, D. A., Johnston, C. J., & Theobald, T. M. (1990). "Twins in School," an Australian-wide program. *Acta. Genet. Med. Gemellol. 39, 231–244.*

Hay, D. A., Levy, F., McStephen, M., & Rooney, R. (1998, June). Predictors of change in ADHD symptomatology in twins and their siblings: Perspectives from the Australian Twin ADHD Project. Paper presented at the Ninth International Congress on Twin Studies, Helsinki, Finland.

Hay, D. A., & Taylor, K. (1998). A family-focused approach to language intervention with multiples: Who benefits and why?. Paper presented at the Ninth International Congress on Twin Studies, Helsinki, Finland.

Malmstrom, P. M. (Ed.). (1997). *Twin care handout collection*, rev. ed. Berkeley, California: Twin Services, Inc.

Matheny, A. P., Dolan, A. B., & Wilson, R. (1976). Twins with academic learning problems: Antecedent characteristics. *Amer. J. Orthopsychiat. 46*, 3, 464–469.

Piaget, E., Gruber, H., & Voneche, J. (Eds.). (1977). *The essential Piaget*. New York: Basic Books, Inc.

Preedy, P., & Tymms, P. (1998, June). Do multiples start school at a lower point than singletons? Do they make less progress? Paper presented at the Ninth International Congress on Twin Studies, Helsinki, Finland.

Renzulli, J. S., & McGreevy, A. M. (1986). Twins included and not included in special programs for the gifted. *Roeper Review 9*, 2, 120–127.

Twins in school. (1991). La Trobe Twin Study, Department of Psychology, La Trobe University, Melbourne & Australian Multiple Birth Association Inc.

CHAPTER 13

Amau, Y. Takuma, T., & Sato, T. (1992, June). *A study on human relations among adolescent twins*. Paper presented at the Seventh International Congress on Twin Studies, Tokyo, Japan.

Ames, L. B. (1988). *Your ten-to-fourteen-year-old*. New York: Dell.

Hay, D. A. (1988). Adolescence and twins—comfort or conflict? Reprint from *Australian NH & MRC Twin Registry Newsletter*, 1–4.

Hiruta, K., & Hirano, K. (1992). Survey on human relationship seen in a twin pair during and after adolescence. *Abstracts: Seventh International Congress on Twin Studies*, 145. Tokyo:

Japan Society for Twin Studies and Japan Intractable Diseases Research Foundation.

Hopper, J., White, V., Macaskill, G., Hill, D., & Clifford, C. (1992). Alcohol use, smoking habits and the Junior Eysenck Personality Questionnaire in adolescent Australian twins. *Acta. Genet. Med. Gemellol. 41*, 311–324.

Malmstrom, P. M. (1996, March/April). Preparing to make life choices. *Twins Magazine*, 64, 67.

Malmstrom, P. M. (1996, May/June). Outrageous questions, wonderful replies. *Twins Magazine*, 48–49.

Malmstrom, P. M. (Ed.). (1997). *Twin care handout collection*, rev. ed. Berkeley, California: Twin Services, Inc.

Moilanen, I., (1996). Twins in adolescence. *Multiple Births Foundation Newsletter 31*, 1, 4.

Moilanen, I., Rantakallio, P. (1990). Living habits and personality development in adolescent twins. *Acta. Genet. Med. Gemellol.*, 39, 215–220.

Neilson, L. (1987). *Adolescent psychology: A contemporary view*. New York: Holt, Rinehart & Winston.

Piaget, E., Gruber, H., & Voneche, J. (Eds.). (1977). *The essential Piaget*. New York: Basic Books, Inc.

CHAPTER 14

Cassill, K. (1982). *Twins: Nature's amazing mystery*. New York: Atheneum.

Hiruta, K., & Hirano, K. (1992). Survey on human relationship seen in a twin pair during and after adolescence. *Abstracts: Seventh International Congress on Twin Studies*, 145. Tokyo: Japan Society for Twin Studies and Japan Intractable Diseases Research Foundation.

Kozlak, J. (1978, summer). Identical twins: Perceptions of the effects of twinship. *Humboldt Journal of Social Relations 5*, 105–130.

Pearlman, E. M. (1990). Separation-individuation, self-concept, and object relations in fraternal twins, identical twins, and singletons. *The Journal of Psychology 124*, 2, 619–628.

Scheinfeld, A. (1967). *Twins and supertwins*. Baltimore, Maryland: Penguin Books, Inc.

CHAPTER 15

Biale, R. (1989, November). Counseling families of disabled twins. *Social Work 34*, 531–535.

Brotherton, J. (1997, January). Five years "down the road." *Our newsletter: A Multiple Birth Loss Support Network XI*, 23.

Bryan, E. (1983). *Twins in the family*. London: Constable.

Davis, D. (1996). Empty cradle, broken heart. Cited in pamphlet distributed by Center for Loss In Multiple Birth (CLIMB), Palmer, AK.

Malmstrom, P. M. (Ed.). (1997). *Twin care handout collection*, rev. ed. Berkeley, CA: Twin Services, Inc.

Malmstrom, P. M., Wedge, M. W., Davis, E. F., Knudsen, J. M., & Wagner, P. (1986, September). Respite care, a lifeline for low-income multiple birth families. Paper presented at the Fifth International Congress on Twin Studies, Amsterdam, Netherlands.

McCourt, F. (1996). *Angela's Ashes*. New York: Scribner.

Segal, N. L. & Bouchard, T. J., Jr. (1993). Grief intensity following the loss of a twin and other relatives: Test of kinship genetic hypotheses. *Human Biology 65*, 87–105.

Sim, C. (1997, spring). The "healthy" twin. *Multiple Births Foundation Newsletter 34*, 3.

Teenage twins make it on their own. (1988, June 26). *San Francisco Examiner*, B1, B8.

INDEX

ABOUT THE AUTHORS

Patricia Maxwell Malmstrom is founder and president of Twin Services, Inc.® (aka TWINLINE®), a national resource helping parents cope with their "twinshock." She holds a graduate degree in early childhood and special education and is one of the foremost authorities on multiples. She serves as past chair of the international Council of Multiple Birth Organizations, and is the mother of four, including monozygotic (identical) twins.

Janet Poland is the author of five other books for parents. For many years she worked as a newspaper reporter and editor, and her writings on families and children have appeared in newspapers and national magazines. She lives in Pennsylvania with her husband and their two sons.